BEYOND THE BREAK

A YEAR OF REBUILDING YOUR HEART AND LIFE AFTER HEARTBREAK

A JOURNAL GUIDE

BY KATINA LEE

Copyright © 2025 by Katina Lee

All rights reserved.

No part of this publication may be reproduced, stored in a retrieval system, or transmitted in any form or by any means—electronic, mechanical, photocopying, recording, or otherwise—without the prior written permission of the author, except for brief quotations used in reviews or scholarly works.

This journal guide is intended for informational and personal growth purposes only. It is not a substitute for professional therapy, counseling, or medical advice.

For questions or permissions, please visit: KatinaLee.com

ISBN: 979-8-9987938-0-6

Printed in the United States of America.

Cover design by Shawn Vijayrathne

Interior layout by Xee_designs1

CONTENT

Dedication vii
A Note from Katina viii
How to Get the Most Out of This Journal ix
How to Use This Journal xi
Introduction xii
Opening Activity xiii
Letters to Him and to Yourself xiii

Month 01 1
    Week 1 4
    Week 2 10
    Week 3 16
    Week 4 22
    Closing Out Month 1 30

Month 02 31
    Week 1 34
    Week 2 41
    Week 3 48
    Week 4 55
    Closing Out Month 2 62

Month 03 63
Week 1 66
Week 2 72
Week 3 79
Week 4 85
From My Heart to Yours: Closing Out Month 3 92

Month 04 93
Week 1 96
Week 2 102
Week 3 108
Week 4 114
From My Heart to Yours: Closing Out Month 4 121

Month 05 122
Week 1 125
Week 2 132
Week 3 140
Week 4 147
Closing Out Month 5 155

Month 06 156
Week 1 159
Week 2 166
Week 3 173
Week 4 181
From My Heart to Yours: Closing Out Month 6 190

Month 07 191
Week 1 194

Week 2 200

Week 3 206

Week 4 212

Closing Out Month 7 219

Month 08 220

Week 1 223

Week 2 229

Week 3 235

Week 4 241

From My Heart to Yours: Closing Out Month 8 249

Month 09 250

Week 1 253

Week 2 260

Week 3 266

Week 4 273

Closing Out Month 9 281

Month 10 282

Week 1 285

Week 2 291

Week 3 297

Week 4 303

Closing Out Month 10 310

Month 11 311

Week 1 314

Week 2 321

Week 3 327

    Week 4 333

    From My Heart to Yours: Closing Out Month 11 342

Month 12 343

    Week 1 346

    Week 2 352

    Week 3 358

    Week 4 365

    Closing Out Month 12 373

Month 13 375

    Week 1 377

    Week 2 383

    Week 3 390

    Week 4 398

    Closing Out Month 13 407

Final Activity 409

Your Closing Ritual 411

About the Author 412

More from Katina Lee 413

DEDICATION

For the one who thought they'd never feel whole again.

For the one still crying behind closed doors.

For the one who gave too much, lost themselves, and wondered if they'd ever feel safe in their own heart again.

For anyone who thought they wouldn't survive the break.

This is for you.

You are not broken.

You are becoming.

—Katina

A NOTE FROM KATINA

——— ..•.. ———

This book is your guide. But the journal—the healing—that happens in the notebook you choose.

Make it beautiful. Make it messy. Make it yours. Scribble in the margins. Tape in photos. Draw. Cry. Rant. Laugh. Reflect.

You don't need fancy tools to heal—you just need a little space and a lot of grace.

The healing doesn't live in these pages. It lives in you.

I'm honored to walk beside you.

—Katina

P.S. Throughout this journal, I speak from my own experience—a woman healing from a relationship with a man. That's the perspective I lived, so that's the language you'll see. But your story may look different—and that's more than okay. If the pronouns don't match your truth, feel free to change them as you read or write. Your healing is just as real. This space is for you, too.

HOW TO GET THE MOST OUT OF THIS JOURNAL

— · · • · · —

- There is no right way to heal. Go at your own pace.
- You don't have to journal every day. Just keep showing up.
- Be honest—not poetic. This is your truth, not a performance.
- If you need to skip ahead or revisit an earlier chapter, do it.
- Come back after hard days. The pages will still be here.
- Celebrate your progress—even the tiniest steps count.
- Use a pen that feels good in your hand and write like no one's watching.

This journal isn't about fixing you.

It's about meeting yourself where you are—and choosing to keep going.

Make the Week Work for You:

Each week includes seven days of prompts—Day 1 through Day 7—but you don't have to follow a Monday-to-Sunday calendar. Some people find it helpful to begin their week on a Sunday, especially if they have more space on weekends for deeper reflection. This allows Day 1 (which often includes a visualization or grounding practice) and Day 7 (which includes a weekly reflection and somatic exercise) to land on days with more time or quiet.

Do what works best for your life and your energy. If you need to skip a day, pause for a few, or stay on one prompt longer, that's okay. There's no "behind" here. You're exactly where you need to be. You may want to return to certain pages as you grow. Do it. Healing is layered, and your words will meet you differently each time.

A Note About White Space:

Some pages in this journal include extra space. That space is intentional.

Even though this isn't designed as a traditional write-in workbook, you're encouraged to use those blank areas however you need:

- Jot down a passing thought
- Doodle a feeling you can't put into words
- Write a name, a prayer, or a reminder
- Pause for breath or stillness

This is your space. Your pace. Your healing. Let the white space become part of your process—quietly holding whatever you need to set down.

Welcome to Beyond the Break Healing Roadmap

This is your healing roadmap. Take it one month, one week, one breath at a time. You'll journey through:

Month	Focus	Keywords
1	Acknowledging the Pain	Naming, Feeling, Honoring
2	Letting the Feelings Flow	Emotions, Grief, Expression
3	Releasing and Forgiving	Self-blame, Comparison, Peace
4	Rebuilding Self-Worth	Identity, Boundaries, Belief
5	Reclaiming Your Voice	Expression, Power, Truth
6	Redefining Love	Self-love, Intention, Openness
7	Embracing Solitude	Stillness, Wholeness, Clarity
8	Reconnecting with Joy	Pleasure, Lightness, Laughter
9	Restoring Hope	Trust, Possibility, Forwardness
10	Rewriting the Future	Vision, Dreaming, Planning
11	Stepping Into Confidence	Boldness, Self-trust, Action
12	Living from the Heart	Alignment, Presence, Gratitude
13	Integration & Celebration	Reflection, Wholeness, Becoming

(Note: Monthly titles are simplified versions of the chapters in the book for ease of reference.)

HOW TO USE THIS JOURNAL

Beyond the Break is more than a journal—it's a guided, 52-Week journey through healing, rediscovery, and emotional growth after heartbreak. Whether your pain is recent or long ago, this journal meets you exactly where you are, offering support as you reclaim your strength, rebuild your self-worth, and step into the life waiting for you.

What You'll Find Inside

This journal spans 13 transformative months, each inspired by a chapter in the book Beyond the Break: Rebuilding Your Heart and Life. The final month is a powerful integration chapter—designed to help you reflect on how far you've come and step forward with intention.

Each month includes:

- A summary of the book chapter that aligns with that month's theme
- A monthly introduction and affirmation to ground your focus
- Four weekly themes for deeper exploration
- Daily journal prompts and gentle healing activities
- A weekly reflection check-in
- A monthly milestone letter from Katina Lee

Use With the Book (Optional)

This journal is a companion to Beyond the Break: Rebuilding Your Heart and Life, but it's fully complete on its own. You can:

1. Read one chapter per month alongside the journal
2. Read the book first, then use the journal as a deeper journey
3. Use the journal alone—the prompts and guidance are enough to carry you through

There is no wrong way to do this. Trust your timing and your instincts.

Choose Your Pace

This is designed as a 52-Week experience, but healing is never linear. You may:

1. Move quickly through some months
2. Linger longer in others
3. Take breaks and return when you're ready

Allow yourself the freedom to go at your own rhythm. This is your journey.

INTRODUCTION

Heartbreak reshapes everything—your days, your dreams, even the way you see yourself. Whether it came suddenly or crept in slowly, losing love leaves an ache that echoes through every part of you.

If you're holding this journal guide, it means you've chosen something brave: to face your pain instead of running from it. You've chosen healing.

This isn't about "getting over it." It's about moving through it—one day at a time—with honesty, compassion, and courage. It's about shedding what no longer serves you, reconnecting with who you are, and rediscovering the strength that has been inside you all along.

Over the next 13 months, this journal will walk beside you. Some days it will hold space for grief. Other days, it will remind you of your resilience. You'll explore, reflect, cry, grow, and slowly begin to write a new story—one that centers you.

You are not expected to be perfect. You are not expected to have all the answers. You only need to keep showing up—for yourself.

Let this be your soft place to land. Your mirror. Your momentum.

And most of all, your reminder that:

You are not broken. You are becoming.

Let's begin.

With love,

Katina Lee

OPENING ACTIVITY
LETTERS TO HIM AND TO YOURSELF

Before you begin month 1, take time to write two letters—one to him (or the person you're healing from), and one to yourself.

These letters are not meant to be sent. They're for you. Let them be honest. Let them be messy. Let them be healing.

Letter 1 to Him

This is the space to say everything left unsaid—the love, the hurt, the questions, the anger. This is your release.

If you need a place to start:

1. What do you wish he knew about how you feel right now?
2. What do you miss? What *don't* you miss?
3. What questions still haunt you?
4. If you could say one final thing and know he'd hear it, what would it be?
5. Do you wish things had been different?

Write it all down. This is for your healing, not his understanding.

Letter 2 to Yourself

Now shift your focus inward. Write to the version of yourself who is hurting right now.

Consider:

1. What does she need to hear today?
2. What promises can you make to her for the journey ahead?
3. What strengths does she hold—even if buried under pain?
4. If you could speak to the future version of you who will one day read this, what would you want her to know?

This letter is your first act of self-love. Let it hold you.

These letters are your starting point. A way to clear space. A way to honor where you've been—so you can step fully into what comes next.

Seal It for Later

Once you've written your letters, tuck them away. Save them to revisit during the final month—not to dwell on the past, but to witness your transformation. Because by then, you'll be someone who has walked through fire and found light again.

MONTH 01

ACKNOWLEDGING THE PAIN
BOOK SUMMARY

Heartbreak is more than just the loss of a relationship—it's the loss of familiarity, shared dreams, and even parts of yourself that felt intertwined with that person. When someone has been woven into your life for years, their absence leaves a painful void, making it difficult to know who you are without them.

The pain of heartbreak isn't just about love lost—it's about losing control over a future you thought was certain. You didn't choose this ending, but now you must face it. In the early days, it's natural to resist, to want things to go back to the way they were. But healing requires a shift from longing for the past to acknowledging the present.

The Power of Acknowledgment

Ignoring or suppressing your emotions only prolongs the pain. True healing starts with giving yourself permission to grieve. Acknowledging the pain means naming your emotions, recognizing their impact, and allowing yourself to fully feel them—without judgment. It's not about staying in the hurt; it's about honoring it as part of your journey forward.

Letting Go of Illusions

One of the hardest parts of heartbreak is confronting the illusions we hold onto—the idealized version of the relationship, the belief that it was perfect, or the idea that you'll never find love again. Often, we mourn not just the person, but the story we told ourselves about what we had and what could have been. Rewriting that story is an essential step toward healing.

Reframing the Meaning of Pain

Heartbreak feels like an ending, but it can also be a beginning—an invitation to rediscover yourself. The pain isn't proof of failure; it's proof of your ability to love deeply. And now, that same love can be turned inward. You are not just losing someone—you are gaining a deeper understanding of yourself and your capacity for resilience.

This chapter is about making space for grief while also making room for transformation. You don't have to have all the answers yet. You only need to take the first step—acknowledge the pain, sit with it, and trust that healing will come.

Reflection Question: What is one small way you can honor your pain this month while taking a step toward healing?

ACKNOWLEDGING THE PAIN MONTH JOURNAL INTRODUCTION

"Healing begins when we allow ourselves to feel."

Welcome to the first month of your healing journey. This month is about giving yourself permission to acknowledge the pain—without judgment, without rushing, and without trying to push it away. Heartbreak can feel overwhelming, but naming and understanding your emotions is the first step toward healing.

You may experience a mix of sadness, anger, confusion, or even relief. Whatever emotions arise, they are valid. This is not about fixing the pain overnight but about learning to sit with it, recognize it, and eventually move through it.

What to Expect This Month:

✓ Week 1: Recognizing your pain and exploring what hurts most

✓ Week 2: Facing the illusions and seeing the relationship more clearly

✓ Week 3: Understanding the purpose of pain and finding meaning in it

✓ Week 4: Rewriting the narrative and shifting the story you tell yourself

Each day, you'll engage in guided journaling prompts and activities designed to help you process your emotions, reflect on your experiences, and take small but meaningful steps forward. By the end of this month, you will have begun the process of reclaiming your story.

Affirmation for the Month:

"I allow myself to feel, to grieve, and to heal at my own pace. My pain does not define me—I am moving through it and growing stronger every day."

WEEK 1

INTRODUCTION RECOGNIZING YOUR PAIN

———·••●••———·

Heartbreak is brutal. There's no sugarcoating that. One day, everything feels fine—or at least manageable—and the next, it feels like the air has been stolen from your lungs. It's not just the loss of a person; it's the loss of shared moments, future plans, and even parts of yourself that felt tied to them. And that kind of loss? It hurts.

But here's what no one tells you: The pain itself isn't the enemy. The real struggle comes when we try to ignore it, avoid it, or pretend we're okay when we're not. Society tells us to "move on" quickly, to distract ourselves, to "stay busy." But healing doesn't come from numbing the pain—it comes from acknowledging it.

This week, we're making space for that.

You don't have to rush to be okay. You don't have to force yourself to feel strong when you don't. Your only job this week is to recognize what you're feeling—to name it, to sit with it, and to allow it to exist without judgment.

Some days, the grief will feel unbearable. Other days, you might feel fine—only to be hit by a memory out of nowhere. That's normal. The emotions will come in waves, sometimes small, sometimes tidal. Let them. The only way out is through.

So, this week, give yourself permission to grieve, to cry, to feel angry, to feel exhausted. Let yourself be human. Let yourself be exactly where you are without needing to fix or change it.

Because this? This is the beginning of healing. And even though it may not feel like it right now, you are already on your way.

Let's take this first step together.

Affirmation for the Month:

"I allow myself to feel, to grieve, and to heal at my own pace. My pain does not define me—I am moving through it and growing stronger every day."

Affirmation for the Week:

"My pain is real, but so is my strength."

WEEK 1

RECOGNIZING YOUR PAIN JOURNAL ACTIVITIES

---·•·---

Focus: Naming the emotions, identifying the deepest wounds, allowing yourself to grieve without judgment.

Visualization:

Close your eyes. Picture your heart as a cracked vessel. Now, imagine soft, golden light pouring into the cracks—warm, quiet, healing. It doesn't erase the pain. It honors it. Let the light stay with you as you begin this week.

Daily Practice Reminder:

At the start of each day this week, take a moment to write down and speak aloud:

Your monthly affirmation: *"I allow myself to feel, to grieve, and to heal at my own pace. My pain does not define me—I am moving through it and growing stronger every day."*

Your weekly affirmation: *"My pain is real, but so is my strength."*

Let these words guide your healing. Repeating them daily helps shift your thoughts, build emotional resilience, and rewire your self-talk.

Remember, there is no right way to journal. Write as much or as little as you need. You can follow the prompts exactly or let them take you somewhere else. Let the prompts be a guide—not a rule. If your heart leads you elsewhere, follow it. These pages are yours. Let them carry what you're holding—no expectations, no perfection required.

DAY 1

ACKNOWLEDGING THE HEARTACHE

— · · • · · —

Quote: *"The only way out is through."* – Robert Frost

Journal Prompt: What emotions are you experiencing right now? Write freely about how you feel without filtering or trying to be "okay."

Activity: Close your eyes, take a deep breath, and say out loud: "I give myself permission to feel." Write down how that feels.

Let This be Enough: You showed up for your truth today. Breathe that in. Now exhale it out. That is enough for today.

DAY 2

THE PHYSICAL WEIGHT OF HEARTBREAK

— · · • · · —

Quote: *"Your body keeps score of your pain."* – Bessel van der Kolk

Journal Prompt: Where do you feel heartbreak in your body? (Tightness in the chest? Knots in the stomach? A heavy feeling?) Describe what it feels like physically.

Activity: Spend 5 minutes practicing deep breathing or stretching to release tension.

Let This be Enough: Let your breath be your anchor. Your body hears your care.

DAY 3
GRIEVING THE LOSS OF A FUTURE

—•••●••———•

Quote: *"Grief is just love with nowhere to go."* – Jamie Anderson

Journal Prompt: What future plans, dreams, or moments are you grieving the most?

Activity: Write a short letter to "the future you thought you'd have," expressing what you miss.

Let This be Enough: Even the future you imagined was worthy of grieving. Rest gently with that.

DAY 4
TRIGGERS AND WAVES OF PAIN

—•••●••———•

Quote: *"Emotions are like waves. You can't stop them from coming, but you can choose which ones to surf."*

Journal Prompt: What are some things that trigger your sadness or longing? How do you usually react to them?

Activity: Brainstorm 3 self-soothing strategies for when a trigger hits.

Let This be Enough: When the waves come, you don't have to fight them. Just float.

DAY 5
GIVING YOURSELF GRACE

—··•··—

Quote: *"Be kind to yourself. You are doing the best you can."*

Journal Prompt: If your best friend were going through this, what would you say to them? Now, write that to yourself.

Activity: Stand in front of a mirror and say one kind thing to yourself.

Let This be Enough: You are worthy of the same kindness you offer others. Let it reach you today.

DAY 6
LETTING YOURSELF CRY (OR NOT CRY)

—··•··—

Quote: *"Tears are words the heart can't say."*

Journal Prompt: Do you let yourself cry, or do you hold it in? How do you feel about crying?

Activity: If you need to cry, give yourself time to do so. If not, write down the emotions you're holding inside.

Let This be Enough: Tears or no tears—your healing is still happening. Breathe in healing now. Exhale all that hurts. You showed up today, and that is enough.

DAY 7
WEEKLY REFLECTION – NAMING THE PAIN

Reflection Questions:
1. What emotions have surfaced the most this week?
2. What have you learned about how you process grief?
3. What is one way you showed yourself compassion this week?

Activity: Write a simple statement of acknowledgment:

"I am hurting, and that's okay." Say it out loud to yourself.

Somatic Exercise

"The body always leads us home... if we can simply learn to trust its language." – Dr. Bessel van der Kolk

"Cradling the Ache" – Somatic Integration Practice

Let your body hold the healing.

This practice invites you to hold space for your own tenderness—with breath, presence, and care.

Instructions
1. Sit or lie down somewhere comfortable.
2. Wrap your arms around yourself like a hug.
3. Breathe deeply into your chest.
4. As you inhale, think: *"I am with you."*
5. As you exhale, think: *"You are safe."*
6. Continue for about 3 minutes.

You may gently rock side to side or place a hand over your heart if that feels soothing.

Optional Reflection Prompt

What does your body need more of right now?

Let This Be Enough

You showed your body compassion today. That is a powerful kind of progress.

WEEK 2

INTRODUCTION
FACING THE ILLUSIONS

——·· •· ·——

One of the hardest things about heartbreak isn't just missing the person—it's missing the version of the relationship you thought you had.

If you're anything like me, you've probably caught yourself thinking, "But we were so good together" or "We had so much potential" or "I'll never find another connection like that." But this week, I want you to step back and ask yourself: Is that the full truth? Or is it the version I wish had been true?

When a relationship ends, it's easy to romanticize the good parts and ignore the ones that hurt. But if the relationship had been as perfect as we sometimes remember it, it wouldn't have ended. And if we truly look at it for what it was—not just what we wanted it to be—we might realize that it wasn't as whole, as healthy, or as right for us as we believed.

This week is about seeing clearly. Not just seeing the relationship for what it was, but also recognizing what we may have been holding onto—the illusions, the wishful thinking, the belief that we needed this person to be happy.

And that's hard because letting go of those illusions means facing reality. It means realizing that some of the things we thought we needed... we really don't. It means accepting that the past cannot be changed, no matter how many times we replay it.

But here's the good news: Clarity is freedom.

When you start seeing the relationship for what it really was, you loosen its grip on you. You take a step toward healing, not because the pain disappears overnight, but because you begin to trust yourself again—to trust that you don't need to hold onto something that wasn't truly meant for you.

This week, we're facing the truth with open eyes and an open heart. Because the clearer we see the past, the freer we are to create a better future.

Affirmation for the Month:

"I allow myself to feel, to grieve, and to heal at my own pace. My pain does not define me—I am moving through it and growing stronger every day."

Affirmation for the Week:

"I release the illusions that keep me tied to the past. I choose truth, clarity, and freedom."

WEEK 2
FACING THE ILLUSIONS JOURNAL ACTIVITIES

Focus: Seeing the relationship clearly, acknowledging what was real vs. what you hoped for.

Visualization:

Picture the relationship as a movie on a screen. Take a step back. See it playing out. Breathe. Now imagine gently reaching out and dimming the screen. Watch it fade. Let the space it leaves be filled with stillness.

Daily Practice Reminder:

At the start of each day this day, take a moment to write down and speak aloud:

Your **monthly affirmation:** *"I allow myself to feel, to grieve, and to heal at my own pace. My pain does not define me—I am moving through it and growing stronger every day."*

Your **weekly affirmation:** *"I release the illusions that keep me tied to the past. I choose truth, clarity, and freedom."*

Let these words guide your healing. Repeating them daily helps shift your thoughts, build emotional resilience, and rewire your self-talk.

Remember, there is no right way to journal. Write as much or as little as you need. You can follow the prompts exactly or let them take you somewhere else. Let the prompts be a guide—not a rule. If your heart leads you elsewhere, follow it. These pages are yours. Let them carry what you're holding—no expectations, no perfection required.

DAY 1

THE ILLUSION OF PERFECTION

Quote: *"We don't miss them. We miss the idea of them."*

Journal Prompt: What aspects of the relationship were you holding onto that may not have been as perfect as they seemed?

Activity: Make two columns: "What I miss" and "What I don't miss."

Let This be Enough: You looked beyond the fantasy. You named what was real. You told yourself the truth. That is enough. That is healing.

DAY 2

WHEN LOVE AND PAIN COEXIST

Quote: *"Just because it hurt doesn't mean it wasn't love. Just because it was love doesn't mean it was right."*

Journal Prompt: Write about a time in your relationship when love and pain coexisted.

Activity: Highlight any patterns you notice.

Let This be Enough: You honored the complexity. You allowed both love and pain to speak. You stopped pretending it was only one or the other. That is enough. That is healing.

DAY 3
ROMANTICIZING THE PAST

Quote: *"Nostalgia is a liar. Don't let it rewrite the truth of what you survived."* – Katina Lee

Journal Prompt: Are you remembering the relationship as it was or as you wanted it to be?

Activity: Write down the raw truth about one memory you've been idealizing.

Let This be Enough: You saw it clearly. You told the truth. You chose honesty over illusion. That is enough. That is healing.

DAY 4
BREAKING THE FANTASY

Quote: *"We must let go of the life we have planned, so as to accept the one that is waiting for us."* – Joseph Campbell

Journal Prompt: What part of the relationship do you still wish could have been different?

Activity: Write a reality-check statement: "It wasn't what I thought it was, and that's okay."

Let This be Enough: You saw it clearly. You told the truth. You chose honesty over illusion. That is enough. That is healing.

DAY 5
ACCEPTING THE ENDING

——— · •●• · ———

Quote: *"Some things break so we can build something stronger. It's not destruction—it's transformation."*

Journal Prompt: Are you still hoping they'll come back? How does holding onto that hope impact your healing?

Activity: Write down one small way you can shift your focus forward.

Let This be Enough: You faced the truth of the ending. You loosened your grip on what was. You turned even slightly toward what's next. That is enough. That is healing.

DAY 6
CHOOSING REALITY OVER FANTASY

——— · •●• · ———

Quote: *"When we know better, we do better."* - Maya Angelou

Journal Prompt: What truths about your ex or your relationship do you now see more clearly?

Activity: Say out loud: "I am choosing reality over fantasy."

Let This be Enough: You chose truth over illusion. You opened your eyes and your heart at the same time. You said it out loud. That is enough. That is healing.

DAY 7
WEEKLY REFLECTION – SEEING CLEARLY

Reflection Questions:

1. What illusion was the hardest to let go of?
2. How do you feel after writing about the relationship honestly?
3. What's one mindset shift you want to take into next week?

Activity: Tear up one false belief you wrote about this week.

Somatic Exercise

"The truth will set you free, but first it will humble you." – Iyanla Vanzant

"Eyes Wide Open" – Somatic Integration Practice

This week, you've honored your truth and clarity. Let your body hold that knowing.

Instructions

1. Stand with your feet hip-width apart.
2. Bring your awareness to your feet and gently press them into the ground.
3. Close your eyes.
4. Take a slow, steady inhale.
5. As you exhale, gently open your eyes.
6. Repeat this breath and movement cycle **5 times**.

As you move and breathe, silently repeat:

"I can see clearly. I am grounded in truth."

Optional Reflection Prompt

After the practice, write down one thing you see differently now.

Let This Be Enough:

You chose clarity today. You stood with your eyes open, and that is powerful.

WEEK 3
INTRODUCTION
FINDING MEANING IN THE PAIN

———··•··———

Nobody asks for heartbreak. If we had a choice, we'd all skip this part—the gut-wrenching sadness, the sleepless nights, the moments where we question everything. But pain, as much as we hate it, has a way of teaching us things we'd never learn otherwise.

Think about some of the strongest, most resilient people you know. Chances are, they didn't get that way because life was easy for them. They got that way because they walked through fire and came out stronger. They faced struggles that shaped them into the people they are today.

And that's what this week is about.

Right now, your pain probably feels pointless. And I won't lie to you—sometimes, it is just pain. But sometimes, it's also a teacher. It forces us to slow down, to re-evaluate, to ask ourselves the tough questions. It shows us where we've abandoned ourselves, where we need to heal, where we need to grow.

I'm not saying you have to be grateful for the pain. But I am saying that you can choose what to do with it. You can let it break you, or you can let it shape you into someone stronger, wiser, and more connected to yourself than ever before.

This week, I want you to explore what this pain is revealing to you. What is it teaching you about yourself? About love? About what you truly need?

You may not have chosen this heartbreak, but you get to choose what comes next. And when you start finding meaning in the pain, you take away its power to define you.

This is not just the breaking of something. It is the making of you. Let's step into that together.

Affirmation for the Month:

"I allow myself to feel, to grieve, and to heal at my own pace. My pain does not define me—I am moving through it and growing stronger every day."

Affirmation for the Week:

"My pain is not pointless. It is shaping me, strengthening me, and leading me toward growth."

WEEK 3
FINDING MEANING IN THE PAIN JOURNAL ACTIVITIES

Focus: Reframing heartbreak as a catalyst for growth.

Visualization:

Imagine your pain as a heavy stone you've been carrying. With each breath, picture yourself setting it down—just for now. Notice the space that opens in your body. What can grow there instead?

Daily Practice Reminder:

At the start of each day this week, take a moment to write down and speak aloud:

Your **monthly affirmation:** *"I allow myself to feel, to grieve, and to heal at my own pace. My pain does not define me—I am moving through it and growing stronger every day."*

Your **weekly affirmation**: *"My pain is not pointless. It is shaping me, strengthening me, and leading me toward growth."*

Let these words guide your healing. Repeating them daily helps shift your thoughts, build emotional resilience, and rewire your self-talk.

Remember, there is no right way to journal. Write as much or as little as you need. You can follow the prompts exactly or let them take you somewhere else. Let the prompts be a guide—not a rule. If your heart leads you elsewhere, follow it. These pages are yours. Let them carry what you're holding—no expectations, no perfection required.

DAY 1
THE PURPOSE OF PAIN

Quote: *"Pain is a teacher, not a punishment."*

Journal Prompt: What lessons might this heartbreak be trying to teach you?

Activity: Write: "One day, I'll see why this was necessary."

Let This be Enough: You listened to the ache. You asked what it had to teach you. You stayed with yourself through the discomfort. That is enough. That is healing.

DAY 2
GROWTH THROUGH SUFFERING

Quote: *"The wound is where the light enters you."* – Rumi

Journal Prompt: How has this heartbreak changed you so far?

Activity: List 3 ways you've grown already.

Let This be Enough: You let the pain shape you without hardening you. You noticed how far you've already come. That is enough. That is healing.

DAY 3
WHAT THIS BREAKUP MADE POSSIBLE

———— ··●·· ————

Quote: *"Rejection is redirection."*

Journal Prompt: What are you free to do now that you weren't before?

Activity: Make a list of opportunities this ending has created.

Let This be Enough: You looked ahead. You opened a window in the dark. You said yes to the life that's waiting. That is enough. That is healing.

DAY 4
TURNING PAIN INTO POWER

———— ··●·· ————

Quote: *"You are not what happened to you. You are what you choose to become."*

Journal Prompt: How can this experience make you stronger?

Activity: Write down one way you can reclaim your power.

Let This be Enough: You chose strength without shame. You held your pain and your power at the same time. That is enough. That is healing.

DAY 5
WHAT WOULD YOUR HEALED SELF SAY?

Quote: *"Your healed self is cheering you on."*

Journal Prompt: Imagine your healed future self. What advice would they give you today?

Activity: Write yourself a letter from the future.

Let This be Enough: You imagined healing. You listened to the wiser voice inside you. You wrote from your future strength. That is enough. That is healing.

DAY 6
RELEASING THE STORY OF VICTIMHOOD

Quote: *"You are not a victim. You are a survivor. You are not just a survivor. You are a warrior becoming whole."*

Journal Prompt: Do you see yourself as a victim of this breakup? How can you shift that perspective?

Activity: Write a new personal narrative: "I am someone who is growing through this."

Let This be Enough: You rewrote the story. You stepped into your strength. You remembered you are more than what happened. That is enough. That is healing.

DAY 7

WEEKLY REFLECTION – MEANING IN THE PAIN

Reflection Questions:

1. Can you begin thinking about what healing might look like?
2. What does that look like to you?
3. What does it feel like?

Activity: Choose one word to define this next stage of your healing.

Somatic Exercise

"The wound is the place where the Light enters you." – Rumi

"Holding the Lesson" – Somatic Integration Practice

Let your body hold what you've learned. Let the wisdom settle in your bones.

Instructions

1. Sit comfortably with a straight spine.
2. Place one hand over your heart and the other on your lower belly.
3. Breathe deeply and slowly.
4. As you inhale, think: *"I am learning."*
5. As you exhale, think: *"I am growing."*
6. Continue this rhythmic breath for 3–5 minutes, allowing the affirmation to settle into your nervous system.

Optional Reflection Prompt

Write one lesson you want your body to remember.

Let This Be Enough

You are not who you were at the beginning of this week. Let the lessons stay with you—and trust they will carry you forward.

WEEK 4

INTRODUCTION
REWRITING THE NARRATIVE

———··●··———

At some point in this healing journey, you'll realize that the story you've been telling yourself about your breakup is shaping the way you feel about it. Maybe you've told yourself that you weren't enough, that you were too much, that if only you had done things differently, it would have worked out. Maybe you've been stuck in the "what ifs," replaying conversations in your mind, trying to make sense of what happened.

This week, we're shifting that story.

Here's the truth: You are not just the person who got left, who got hurt, or who experienced heartbreak. You are the person who is still standing, still growing, still becoming. And while you may not have had control over how this relationship ended, you do have control over the story you tell yourself about it—and about what comes next.

I know how easy it is to get caught in the loop of wondering what could have been. When we care deeply, when we invest in a future with someone, it's hard to let go of the vision we had. But staying stuck in the past doesn't change it. It only robs you of the life waiting for you on the other side of this pain.

This week, I want you to challenge the thoughts that keep you tethered to the past. Ask yourself:

- Is this story I'm telling myself true, or is it just familiar?
- Is this belief helping me heal, or is it holding me back?

Healing isn't about denying the pain—it's about deciding what you do with it.

You don't need permission to move forward. You don't need an apology, an explanation, or a perfect ending to close this chapter. Closure is something you give yourself, and you can begin writing a new story right now—one where you are the main character, the hero, the one who rises.

This week, you are reclaiming your narrative. You are stepping into your power. And little by little, you are becoming the person you were always meant to be.

Affirmation for the Month:

"I allow myself to feel, to grieve, and to heal at my own pace. My pain does not define me—I am moving through it and growing stronger every day."

Affirmation for the Week:

"I am the author of my story. I choose to write a narrative of healing, strength, and renewal."

WEEK 4
REWRITING THE NARRATIVE JOURNAL ACTIVITIES

Focus: Letting go of the old story, embracing a new perspective, and reclaiming personal power.

Visualization:

Picture yourself standing at a blank page. The past story is behind you—folded, honored, but closed. Hold the pen. Begin to write. What words appear first?

Daily Practice Reminder:

At the start of each day this week, take a moment to write down and speak aloud:

Your **monthly affirmation:** *"I allow myself to feel, to grieve, and to heal at my own pace. My pain does not define me—I am moving through it and growing stronger every day."*

Your **weekly affirmation:** *"I am the author of my story. I choose to write a narrative of healing, strength, and renewal."*

Let these words guide your healing. Repeating them daily helps shift your thoughts, build emotional resilience, and rewire your self-talk.

Remember, there is no right way to journal. Write as much or as little as you need. You can follow the prompts exactly or let them take you somewhere else. Let the prompts be a guide—not a rule. If your heart leads you elsewhere, follow it. These pages are yours. Let them carry what you're holding—no expectations, no perfection required.

DAY 1

THE STORIES WE TELL OURSELVES

---•••---

Quote: *"You can't start the next chapter if you keep re-reading the last one."*

Journal Prompt: What story have you been telling yourself about this breakup? (e.g., "I wasn't enough," "I'll never love again," "I failed.")

Activity: Challenge that story—write a more compassionate version.

Let This be Enough: You questioned the script. You offered yourself a kinder version of the truth. You turned the page. That is enough. That is healing.

DAY 1

BREAKING FREE FROM "WHAT IF" THINKING

---•••---

Quote: *"What's meant for you will never need chasing."*

Journal Prompt: Are you still questioning if things could have been different? What "what ifs" do you replay the most?

Activity: Rewrite your "what if" into a truth: "Even if things had gone differently, I still deserve happiness."

Let This be Enough: You let go of the loops. You chose the truth over the fantasy. You gave yourself permission to move forward. That is enough. That is healing.

DAY 3
TAKING BACK YOUR POWER

— ··●·· —

Quote: *"No one can take your power unless you hand it to them."*

Journal Prompt: In what ways have you been giving power to your ex or the breakup? How can you take that power back?

Activity: Write a declaration: "I am reclaiming my power by _____."

Let This be Enough: You saw where you gave your energy away. You reached for it again. You remembered what was always yours. That is enough. That is healing.

DAY 4
RELEASING THE NEED FOR CLOSURE

— ··●·· —

Quote: *"Closure is something you give yourself."*

Journal Prompt: Are you waiting for something—an apology, an explanation, a final conversation? How would you feel if you never got it?

Activity: Write the words: "I release the need for closure from them. I give closure to myself."

Let This be Enough: You stopped waiting. You closed the door with your own hand. You gave yourself peace. That is enough. That is healing.

DAY 5
WRITING A NEW STORY

Quote: *"The best revenge is a life well-lived."*

Journal Prompt: Imagine your future five years from now—what does it look like when you've fully healed and moved on?

Activity: Write a letter to your future self, describing how proud you are of them.

Let This be Enough: You envisioned your future. You spoke to yourself with pride. You wrote a story you'd want to live. That is enough. That is healing.

DAY 6
WHO ARE YOU WITHOUT THEM?

Quote: *"You are whole on your own."*

Journal Prompt: Without this relationship, what are you rediscovering about yourself? What do you want to explore?

Activity: Make a list of things you want to do for you in the next six months.

Let This be Enough: You asked who you are beyond the heartbreak. You made space to rediscover joy. You chose yourself. That is enough. That is healing.

DAY 7

WEEKLY REFLECTION – REWRITING YOUR NARRATIVE

Reflection Questions:

1. How has your perspective on the breakup shifted over the past four weeks?
2. What story are you choosing to tell yourself now?
3. How will you carry this new perspective into next month?

Activity: Write one final statement: *"I am stepping into a new chapter, and I am in control of my story."*

Somatic Exercise

"There is no greater agony than bearing an untold story inside you." – Maya Angelou

"Author of My Story" – Somatic Integration Practice

End this month by standing in your truth—in your body and in your voice.

Instructions:

1. Stand tall with your feet planted firmly on the ground.
2. Inhale deeply as you raise your arms overhead, stretching toward your vision.
3. Exhale slowly as you bring your hands to rest gently over your heart space.
4. Say aloud, with presence and conviction:
5. *"This is my story. I get to choose how it continues."*
6. Let these words settle into your body. Feel the strength of your stance and the power of your voice.
7. Repeat 3 times, slowly and clearly.

Optional Prompt:

Write one thing you now believe about yourself that you didn't at the start of this month.

Let This Be Enough:

You reclaimed the pen. You chose your voice. That alone is a powerful ending—and beginning.

Monthly Reflection: Month 1 – Anchoring After the Break

What emotions were most present for me this month?

_____

What felt most disorienting after the break?

_____

What helped me feel anchored or steady again?

_____

A moment I'm proud of:

_____

A quote, mantra, or affirmation I want to carry forward:

_____

On a scale of 1–10, how connected do I feel to myself right now?

1 ☐ 2 ☐ 3 ☐ 4 ☐ 5 ☐ 6 ☐ 7 ☐ 8 ☐ 9 ☐ 10

What do I need more of next month?

☐ Rest

☐ Joy

☐ Connection

☐ Confidence

☐ Creativity

☐ Other: _____

One word to guide me next month:

_____

FROM MY HEART TO YOURS: CLOSING OUT MONTH 1

———··●··———

You've reached the end of month 1—and that is no small thing.

Whether you felt every emotion, struggled to stay consistent, skipped days, or simply showed up in your own quiet way... it all counts. This journey isn't about doing it perfectly. It's about being honest with where you are—and choosing to keep going.

This month, you allowed yourself to feel. You named the pain. You challenged the stories you were telling yourself. You looked closely at the truths and illusions that shaped your heartbreak. That takes incredible courage.

Before moving forward, take a moment to acknowledge that:

You are doing the work. You are already healing—even if it doesn't always feel like it.

You've done something extraordinary: *you stayed.*

There's no timeline for healing. There's only forward.

Set aside a little space in your notebook to write freely. There's no prompt for this one. Reflect, release, vent, celebrate, grieve—whatever still needs to be heard. Let it flow.

Maybe light a candle. Reread a favorite page. Let this moment sink in.

You've made it through the beginning. And that beginning was brave.

With love,

Katina Lee

PS: If you find yourself drawn back to a prompt, a memory, or a moment—you're allowed to return. The pages will meet you where you are, not where you were.

Sometimes, the second time you write it... you hear yourself more clearly. That is healing too.

Coming Up: Letting the Feelings Flow

In month 2, we go deeper.

Now that you've acknowledged the pain, we begin the process of letting it move through you—without judgment, without rushing, and without fear. This stage of healing is about feeling what needs to be felt... so you can finally begin to let it go.

You've already proven you're willing to face the hard stuff.

Now let's learn to move with it—one day, one breath, one page at a time.

When you're ready, turn the page.

I'll be right here with you.

MONTH
02

LETTING THE FEELINGS FLOW – BOOK SUMMARY

———   ··•·· ———

Healing isn't just about understanding your pain—it's about allowing yourself to feel it fully. Suppressing emotions only prolongs suffering, while acknowledging and expressing them creates space for healing. Grief, anger, sadness, and even moments of relief are all natural parts of the process. Rather than resisting these emotions, let them flow, knowing they are temporary and necessary steps toward growth.

Moving Through the Grief Cycle

Heartbreak mirrors grief, and healing isn't linear. Some days will feel lighter, while others will pull you back into sadness. Writing a farewell letter to your ex or the relationship can help you process and release what's been lost. Similarly, letting go of fantasies about what could have been allows you to stop dwelling on an imagined future and focus on your present reality.

Channeling Emotions into Growth

Anger, when used constructively, highlights boundaries that were crossed and helps you reclaim your self-worth. Rather than suppressing it, channel it into setting new standards for yourself. Be mindful of numbing behaviors—drinking, overworking, or dating too soon—which only delay healing. Instead, embrace healthier coping strategies like journaling, movement, or creative expression.

Embracing Solitude and No Contact

Distractions can temporarily ease loneliness, but true healing comes from embracing solitude. Learning to be comfortable in your own company is empowering. Implementing no contact gives you the space needed to grieve and heal without reopening wounds. While difficult, this step allows emotions to surface without interference, making way for closure.

By the end of this chapter, you'll have begun the process of feeling and releasing emotions instead of holding them in. Healing isn't about avoiding pain—it's about moving through it with courage. Each tear shed and each moment of self-reflection brings you closer to freedom.

Reflection Question: How can I honor my emotions this month without letting them control my healing?

LETTING THE FEELINGS FLOW – MONTH JOURNAL INTRODUCTION

This month, we shift from acknowledging the pain to allowing it to flow freely. Heartbreak brings a flood of emotions—grief, anger, sadness, relief, confusion, and even hope. Often, our instinct is to suppress or avoid these emotions because they feel too overwhelming. But healing doesn't come from avoiding the pain; it comes from moving through it.

In these next four weeks, you'll explore what it means to truly feel your emotions. You'll learn to recognize and process them without judgment, allowing them to guide you toward deeper healing. Some days, the emotions may feel too big to handle. Other days, you may feel numb. Both are natural parts of the process. This month is about learning how to sit with your feelings, express them in healthy ways, and trust that they are here to teach you something valuable.

What to Expect This Month:

✓ Week 1: Embracing the Storm of Emotions – Allowing yourself to feel, understanding emotional waves, and learning to sit with discomfort.

✓ Week 2: Embracing the Grief Cycle – Recognizing grief as a process, writing a farewell letter, and releasing unrealistic hopes.

✓ Week 3: Channeling Your Emotions into Growth – Exploring anger, transforming pain into wisdom, and embracing solitude.

✓ Week 4: Embracing Emotional Release – Understanding emotional triggers, releasing emotional baggage, and finding peace within the chaos.

Each day, you will engage in guided journaling prompts and activities designed to help you process and release your emotions. By the end of this month, you will have a deeper connection to yourself, a greater sense of clarity, and the ability to honor your emotions without fear or resistance.

Affirmation for the Month:

"I give myself permission to feel deeply and fully. Every emotion I experience is a step toward healing, and I trust that I will emerge stronger on the other side."

WEEK 1
INTRODUCTION EMBRACING THE STORM OF EMOTIONS

Heartbreak is messy. It doesn't arrive in neat, organized stages—it crashes over you in waves, unexpected and overwhelming. One moment, you think you're doing okay, and the next, a memory, a song, or a scent sends you spiraling. And that's okay.

Pain demands to be felt. It doesn't go away just because we ignore it or push it down. If we try to suppress it, it finds another way out—through exhaustion, anxiety, or even anger directed at ourselves. This week is about giving yourself permission to let the emotions come. To stop fighting the tide and, instead, let yourself be carried by it.

Grief isn't a sign of weakness—it's a sign that something mattered. You loved, you dreamed, you invested part of your heart into something that didn't last the way you hoped it would. And now, your heart is reacting to that loss. This isn't about "getting over it" or trying to speed up the process. It's about acknowledging that you are human and that your feelings—every single one of them—are valid.

There will be days when you don't want to feel. When you'd rather distract yourself, numb the pain, or pretend you're fine. But true healing doesn't come from avoidance—it comes from moving through.

This week, I want you to let yourself *feel*. Cry if you need to. Scream into a pillow. Write angry letters you never send. Do whatever you need to do to allow the pain to move through you, rather than burying it inside. You are not broken because you hurt. You are healing because you allow yourself to feel.

And one day, these waves won't knock you down. One day, they will simply pass through you, leaving you standing taller than before.

Let's begin.

Affirmation for the Month:

"I give myself permission to feel deeply and fully. Every emotion I experience is a step toward healing, and I trust that I will emerge stronger on the other side."

Affirmation for the Week:

"I welcome my emotions as messengers, not threats. Each feeling has something to teach me, and by allowing them space, I create room for peace to return."

WEEK 1
EMBRACING THE STORM OF EMOTIONS JOURNAL ACTIVITIES

Focus:

Allowing yourself to feel, understanding emotional waves, and learning to sit with discomfort.

Visualization:

Close your eyes. Picture yourself standing on a shore as waves crash and retreat. Each wave represents an emotion—grief, anger, sadness, relief. You don't need to fight them. Let them roll in. Let them roll out. You are still standing.

Daily Practice Reminder:

At the start of each day this week, take a moment to write down and speak aloud:

Your **monthly affirmation:** *"I give myself permission to feel deeply and fully. Every emotion I experience is a step toward healing, and I trust that I will emerge stronger on the other side."*

Your **weekly affirmation:** *"I welcome my emotions as messengers, not threats. Each feeling has something to teach me, and by allowing them space, I create room for peace to return."*

Let these words guide your healing. Repeating them daily helps shift your thoughts, build emotional resilience, and rewire your self-talk.

Remember, there is no right way to journal. Write as much or as little as you need. You can follow the prompts exactly or let them take you somewhere else. Let the prompts be a guide—not a rule. If your heart leads you elsewhere, follow it. These pages are yours. Let them carry what you're holding—no expectations, no perfection required.

DAY 1

THE WEIGHT OF GRIEF

Quote: *"Grief is just love with nowhere to go."* – Jamie Anderson

Prompt: What emotions feel the heaviest right now? How are they showing up in your body?

Activity: Take five deep breaths, place a hand over your heart, and say: "It's okay to feel this." Write what comes up.

Let This be Enough: You allowed yourself to feel what's heavy. You stayed with your heart. You didn't look away. That is enough. That is healing.

DAY 2

WHEN THE TEARS WON'T STOP
(OR WON'T COME AT ALL)

Quote: *"Sometimes crying is the only way your eyes can speak..."*

Prompt: Do you let yourself cry, or do you hold it in? Why?

Activity: If you need to cry, create space to do so. If not, write down what emotions are staying inside.

Let This be Enough: You made space for your feelings, even the ones that hide. You let your body lead. That is enough. That is healing.

DAY 3
THE ROLLERCOASTER OF HEARTBREAK

Quote: *"Healing doesn't happen in a straight line."*

Prompt: Describe a time when you thought you were okay—only to be hit by grief again.

Activity: Write: "This is temporary. I am healing."

Let This be Enough: You didn't judge your ups and downs. You let the waves rise and fall. You kept breathing through it. That is enough. That is healing.

DAY 4
NAMING THE EMOTIONS

Quote: *"You can't heal what you don't allow yourself to feel."*

Prompt: What emotions are most frequent—sadness, anger, guilt, relief? Describe them.

Activity: Write a letter to your emotions.

Let This be Enough: You called your emotions by name. You welcomed what showed up. You gave yourself permission to feel. That is enough. That is healing.

DAY 5
SITTING WITH DISCOMFORT

Quote: *"The only way out is through."* – Robert Frost

Prompt: What emotions have you tried to avoid? Why?

Activity: Set a timer for 5 minutes. Sit quietly and locate that emotion in your body.

Let This be Enough: You sat with what you usually run from. You stayed five minutes longer. You made space instead of shrinking. That is enough. That is healing.

DAY 6
THE UNEXPECTED MOMENTS OF PEACE

Quote: *"One day, you will wake up and realize the ache has softened."* – Katina Lee

Prompt: Have you noticed any moments of peace? What were you doing?

Activity: Write a note of encouragement to your future self.

Let This be Enough: You noticed a quiet moment. You didn't question the calm. You let peace visit. That is enough. That is healing.

DAY 7

WEEKLY REFLECTION – RIDING THE EMOTIONAL WAVES

Reflection Questions:

1. What emotions surfaced most this week?
2. What helped you move through them?
3. How did it feel to sit with your emotions instead of avoiding them?

Activity: Write: *"I am feeling my emotions, and that means I am healing."*

Somatic Exercise

"You can't stop the waves, but you can learn to surf." – Jon Kabat-Zinn

"Breath Like the Ocean" – Somatic Integration Practice

You've ridden emotional waves. Now let your breath move like the tide—steady and calm.

Instructions

1. Sit comfortably with your spine tall.
2. Inhale slowly through your nose for a count of **4**.
3. Hold for **2** counts.
4. Exhale gently through your mouth for a count of **6**.
5. As you breathe, imagine your inhale pulling in fresh energy like a rising wave, and your exhale releasing tension like a receding tide.
6. Repeat this breath cycle for **5 minutes**, letting each wave of breath soothe and steady you.

Optional Reflection Prompt

How did your emotional waves shift after the breathwork? What does your body feel like now?

Let This Be Enough:

You met your emotions without running. That is resilience. That is healing.

WEEK 2

INTRODUCTION
EMBRACING THE GRIEF CYCLE

Grief is exhausting. It drains you physically, emotionally, and mentally. Some days, it feels like a heavy weight pressing down on your chest, making it impossible to breathe. Other days, it sneaks up on you when you least expect it—when you see their favorite snack at the grocery store, hear a song that reminds you of them, or catch yourself reaching for your phone to send a message you'll never send.

What makes grief even more difficult is that it doesn't follow a clear path. One moment, you feel like you're moving forward, and the next, you're right back where you started. You might feel sadness one day, anger the next, followed by a strange sense of peace—only for longing to come crashing back again. That's the thing about grief—it moves in waves, and no two waves look the same.

If you've ever thought, *"I should be over this by now"* or *"Why does this still hurt so much?"*—you're not alone. The truth is, grief isn't about getting over something—it's about learning to live with what happened, to make peace with it, and to release what no longer serves you.

This week is about allowing yourself to move through the grief without judgment.

✓ You'll explore how grief shows up in your daily life and recognize its patterns.

✓ You'll write a farewell letter—not just to your ex, but to the version of yourself that existed in that relationship.

✓ You'll begin letting go of the "what ifs" and the hopes that keep you tied to the past.

You might feel resistant to these exercises—and that's okay. Part of you might still be holding on because letting go feels like losing something all over again. But letting go isn't about forgetting. It's about freeing yourself. It's about making space for something new, even if you don't know what that "new" looks like yet.

This week, we are taking a crucial step—not in forgetting, but in choosing to move forward. Grief is not a sign of weakness; it is a sign that something mattered. And now, you are learning to release what was, so you can begin to embrace what will be.

Let's begin.

Affirmation for the Month:

"I give myself permission to feel deeply and fully. Every emotion I experience is a step toward healing, and I trust that I will emerge stronger on the other side."

Affirmation for the Week:

"I trust that grief is part of my healing. Each wave I face brings me closer to peace."

WEEK 2
EMBRACING THE GRIEF CYCLE JOURNAL ACTIVITIES

Focus: Understanding grief as a process and beginning to release the past.

Visualization:

Close your eyes. Picture your grief as ocean waves—some soft, some crashing. Instead of resisting, you let yourself float. You're not drowning. You're learning to ride the waves.

Daily Practice Reminder:

At the start of each day this week, take a moment to write down and speak aloud:

Your **monthly affirmation:** *"I give myself permission to feel deeply and fully. Every emotion I experience is a step toward healing, and I trust that I will emerge stronger on the other side."*

Your **weekly affirmation:** *"I trust that grief is part of my healing. Each wave I face brings me closer to peace."*

Let these words guide your healing. Repeating them daily helps shift your thoughts, build emotional resilience, and rewire your self-talk.

Remember, there is no right way to journal. Write as much or as little as you need. You can follow the prompts exactly or let them take you somewhere else. Let the prompts be a guide—not a rule. If your heart leads you elsewhere, follow it. These pages are yours. Let them carry what you're holding—no expectations, no perfection required.

DAY 1

UNDERSTANDING THE STAGES OF GRIEF

Quote: *"Grief is not a straight line but feels a lot like a maze."* – Katina Lee

Journal Prompt: Which stage of grief do you feel most in right now—denial, anger, bargaining, sadness, acceptance? How does it show up in your thoughts or actions?

Activity: Write down one thing you are ready to accept, even if just a little.

Let This be Enough: You recognized where you are. You acknowledged what hurts. You allowed the stage to shift. That is enough. That is healing.

DAY 2

WRITING A FAREWELL LETTER

Quote: *"Goodbyes are not the end. They are the beginning of healing."*

Journal Prompt: If you could say anything to your ex (or the relationship itself), what would it be?

Activity: Write a farewell letter—express gratitude, anger, sadness, and finally, release.

Let This be Enough: You put it into words. You gave shape to the goodbye. You made space to release. That is enough. That is healing.

DAY 3
RELEASING THE "WHAT IFS"

Quote: *"You can't rewrite the past, but you can choose how you carry it."*

Journal Prompt: What "what if" thoughts run through your mind? What emotions do they stir up?

Activity: Rewrite each "what if" into a statement of closure.

Example: *"What if I had tried harder?"* → *"I did my best, and that is enough."*

Let This be Enough: You rewrote the haunting questions. You chose self-compassion. You stepped toward closure. That is enough. That is healing.

DAY 4
MOURNING THE FUTURE THAT WON'T HAPPEN

Quote: *"Grief is just love with nowhere to go."* – Jamie Anderson

Journal Prompt: What future dreams or plans are hardest to let go of?

Activity: Write down one future event you envisioned together. Now, write a new vision—one that belongs only to you.

Let This be Enough: You grieved what never came to be. You honored the dream. You gave yourself a new one. That is enough. That is healing.

DAY 5
ACCEPTING UNANSWERED QUESTIONS

Quote: *"Some closures are silent."*

Journal Prompt: What unanswered questions still linger? What do you wish you knew?

Activity: Write this truth: *"Even if I never get the answers, I can still heal."* Say it aloud.

Let This be Enough: You lived with the silence. You made peace with not knowing. You chose freedom anyway. That is enough. That is healing.

DAY 6
LETTING GO OF THEIR PRESENCE IN YOUR LIFE

Quote: *"You don't need them to heal. You need you."*

Journal Prompt: Are you still checking their social media, rereading texts, or keeping tabs? How does it impact you?

Activity: Choose one step today—unfollow, delete, archive, or commit to 30 days of no contact.

Let This be Enough: You took a bold step back. You made space for your peace. You chose yourself. That is enough. That is healing.

DAY 7

WEEKLY REFLECTION – ACKNOWLEDGING GRIEF'S PURPOSE

Reflection Questions:

1. What emotions came up most this week?
2. How did writing your farewell letter make you feel?
3. What's one "what if" you feel lighter about now?

Activity: Write: *"I am letting go, not because it's easy, but because I deserve peace."*

Somatic Exercise

"You don't have to carry it all."

"Release Through the Hands" – Somatic Integration Practice

Grief often settles quietly in the body. Let it move through your hands and out into the world.

Instructions

1. Sit quietly and place your hands on your lap, palms facing up.
2. Take a slow, deep breath in and exhale fully.
3. Begin to gently open and close your fists.
4. With each release, imagine letting go of something you've been carrying—grief, tension, fear.
5. Repeat this motion for 2–3 minutes. Let the rhythm soften your body and quiet your mind.

Optional Reflection Prompt

What did your body feel like it released today?

Let This Be Enough:

You opened your hands. You released what you didn't need to carry. That's healing in motion.

WEEK 3
INTRODUCTION CHANNELING YOUR EMOTIONS INTO GROWTH

———· ·•· ·———

There's something exhausting about carrying pain. It sits in your chest like a heavy weight, dragging down your energy, your thoughts, and sometimes even your hope for the future. In the beginning, it feels impossible to imagine ever feeling different. But at some point, you realize the pain isn't just something happening to you—it's something you're holding onto.

And if you're holding onto it, that means you also have the power to begin letting it go.

This week is about shifting your relationship with pain. Up until now, it may have felt like pain was running the show—determining how you feel, what you think about, and how much space heartbreak takes up in your mind. But what if pain wasn't just something that controlled you? What if it was something that could teach you? Something that, instead of breaking you, could be shaping you?

Pain is one of life's greatest teachers. We don't want it, we don't ask for it, but once it arrives, it brings lessons we can't ignore. It forces us to stop and examine things we might have ignored in the past. It highlights where we've abandoned ourselves, where we've ignored red flags, and where we've settled for less than we deserve. It shows us where we need to set better boundaries, where we need to love ourselves more, and where we need to grow.

That's the focus this week: shifting from *Why is this happening to me?* to *What can I learn from this?*

- ✓ You'll start looking at your pain as a source of wisdom rather than just suffering.
- ✓ You'll reflect on how this experience has already begun to change you.
- ✓ You'll begin to reclaim your personal power—choosing to grow instead of staying stuck.

This doesn't mean the pain disappears overnight. It doesn't mean that just because you're finding meaning in this, you'll stop hurting right away. But it does mean that, little by little, you are transforming.

You didn't choose this heartbreak, but you can choose what happens next. You can choose to grow, to rebuild, to learn. Pain is not your enemy—it is the fire that will forge you into something stronger than you ever imagined.

Let's begin.

Affirmation for the Month:

"I give myself permission to feel deeply and fully. Every emotion I experience is a step toward healing, and I trust that I will emerge stronger on the other side."

Affirmation for the Week:

"I honor my pain as part of my transformation. With every step forward, I reclaim my strength."

WEEK 3
CHANNELING YOUR EMOTIONS INTO GROWTH JOURNAL ACTIVITIES

Focus: Using emotions as tools for healing rather than allowing them to control you.

Visualization:

Picture yourself standing at the edge of a forest. In your hands is a heavy pack filled with pain, regret, and unanswered questions. One by one, begin placing those items on the ground. With each release, your body feels lighter. You are not discarding your story—you're choosing to carry it differently.

Daily Practice Reminder:

At the start of each day this week, take a moment to write down and speak aloud:

Your monthly affirmation: *"I give myself permission to feel deeply and fully. Every emotion I experience is a step toward healing, and I trust that I will emerge stronger on the other side."*

Your weekly affirmation: *"I honor my pain as part of my transformation. With every step forward, I reclaim my strength."*

Let these words guide your healing. Repeating them daily helps shift your thoughts, build emotional resilience, and rewire your self-talk.

Remember, there is no right way to journal. Write as much or as little as you need. You can follow the prompts exactly or let them take you somewhere else. Let the prompts be a guide—not a rule. If your heart leads you elsewhere, follow it. These pages are yours. Let them carry what you're holding—no expectations, no perfection required.

DAY 1
THE PURPOSE OF PAIN

——— ··●·· ———

Quote: *"Pain is a teacher, not a punishment."*

Journal Prompt: What lessons might this heartbreak be trying to teach you?

Activity: Write: "One day, I'll see why this was necessary."

Let This be Enough: You leaned in. You asked what the pain was teaching. You trusted it would shape you. That is enough. That is healing.

DAY 2
GROWTH THROUGH SUFFERING

——— ··●·· ———

Quote: *"The wound is where the light enters you."* – Rumi

Journal Prompt: How has this heartbreak changed you so far?

Activity: List 3 ways you've grown already.

Let This be Enough: You traced your growth through the hard parts. You named how you've changed. That is enough. That is healing.

DAY 3

WHAT THIS BREAKUP MADE POSSIBLE

——— ··●·· ———

Quote: *"Rejection is redirection."*

Journal Prompt: What are you free to do now that you weren't before?

Activity: Make a list of opportunities this ending has created.

Let This be Enough: You opened to the life ahead. You honored the doors that heartbreak unlocked. That is enough. That is healing.

DAY 4

TURNING PAIN INTO POWER

——— ··●·· ———

Quote: *"You are not what happened to you. You are what you choose to become."* – Carl Jung

Journal Prompt: How can this experience make you stronger?

Activity: Write down one way you can reclaim your power.

Let This be Enough: You took something hard and made it sacred. You reached for strength. You reclaimed your voice. That is enough. That is healing.

DAY 5
WHAT WOULD YOUR HEALED SELF SAY?

Quote: *"Your healed self is cheering you on."*

Journal Prompt: Imagine your healed future self. What advice would they give you today?

Activity: Write yourself a letter from the future.

Let This be Enough: You called in your future wisdom. You let her speak. You listened. That is enough. That is healing.

DAY 6
RELEASING THE STORY OF VICTIMHOOD

Quote: *"You are not a victim. You are a survivor."*

Journal Prompt: Do you see yourself as a victim of this breakup? How can you shift that perspective?

Activity: Write a new personal narrative: "I am someone who is growing through this."

Let This be Enough: You shifted the narrative. You remembered your strength. You became the author again. That is enough. That is healing.

DAY 7

WEEKLY REFLECTION – MEANING IN THE PAIN

Reflection Questions:

1. What emotions surfaced most this week?
2. How did looking at pain as a teacher change your perspective?
3. What is one lesson you want to carry into the next phase of your healing?

Activity: Choose *one word* that represents this next stage of your healing.

Write it on a sticky note or place it somewhere visible as a daily reminder.

Let it be your anchor as you move forward.

Somatic Exercise

"I survived this. I'm still here."

"Compassion Breath" with Heart + Belly Hold

This gentle, touch-based breathwork supports emotional integration and self-soothing.

Instructions

1. Sit or lie down in a quiet space.
2. Place one hand over your heart and the other over your belly.
3. Begin breathing deeply and slowly—in through your nose, out through your mouth.
4. With each inhale, imagine drawing in compassion.
5. With each exhale, picture letting go of pain or tension.
6. Whisper gently to yourself: *"I survived this. I'm still here."*
7. Continue for 2–3 minutes, letting the warmth of your hands soothe and ground you.

Optional Reflection Prompt

What does compassion feel like in your body today?

Let This Be Enough:

You breathed. You softened. You stayed.

That is enough. That is healing.

WEEK 4
INTRODUCTION
EMBRACING EMOTIONAL RELEASE

———··•··———

Letting go is hard. Even when you know it's necessary—even when you've made peace with the ending—there's something about releasing the past that feels final. And sometimes, that finality is what makes it so difficult.

For weeks now, you've been allowing yourself to feel. You've named your emotions, faced the truth of your grief, and started shifting your perspective. But now comes the next step—the step where your actions begin to reflect your internal growth. Because healing isn't just about insight—it's about making space for the new by releasing what no longer serves you.

This week is about physical and emotional release. That might mean boxing up old memories, unfollowing someone online, or changing the energy of your space to match the person you're becoming. Letting go isn't about pretending the past didn't happen—it's about honoring what was, while creating space for what could be.

✓ You'll identify the things in your environment that still carry emotional weight.

✓ You'll choose how you want to symbolically and physically release them.

✓ You'll take ownership of your space, your energy, and your future.

This isn't about erasing your story—it's about claiming your next chapter.

You are not the same person who began this month. You've softened, deepened, and strengthened. And now, you're ready to release what's weighing you down so you can rise into what's next.

Let's begin.

Affirmation for the Month:

"I give myself permission to feel deeply and fully. Every emotion I experience is a step toward healing, and I trust that I will emerge stronger on the other side."

Affirmation for the Week:

"I release what no longer serves me. With every step, I create space for healing, peace, and renewal."

WEEK 4
EMBRACING EMOTIONAL RELEASE JOURNAL ACTIVITIES

———·· • ··———

Focus: Letting go physically and emotionally to create space for healing and growth.

Visualization:

Close your eyes. Picture yourself standing beside a river. You're holding a bundle of memories, regrets, and pain. One by one, you begin placing them into the current—watching them float away, not in anger or denial, but in peace. As each one disappears downstream, you feel lighter, clearer, and more grounded in who you're becoming.

Daily Practice Reminder:

At the start of each day this week, take a moment to write down and speak aloud:

Your monthly affirmation: *"I give myself permission to feel deeply and fully. Every emotion I experience is a step toward healing, and I trust that I will emerge stronger on the other side."*

Your weekly affirmation: *"I release what no longer serves me. With every step, I create space for healing, peace, and renewal."*

Let these words guide your healing. Repeating them daily helps shift your thoughts, build emotional resilience, and rewire your self-talk.

Remember, there is no right way to journal. Write as much or as little as you need. You can follow the prompts exactly or let them take you somewhere else. Let the prompts be a guide—not a rule. If your heart leads you elsewhere, follow it. These pages are yours. Let them carry what you're holding—no expectations, no perfection required.

DAY 1

RECOGNIZING EMOTIONAL BAGGAGE IN YOUR SPACE

— · · • · · —

Quote: *"Your environment reflects your inner world."*

Journal Prompt: Look around your home—what items still feel tied to your ex or the past relationship? How do they make you feel?

Activity: Make a list of the things you're ready to put away, move, or remove completely.

Let This be Enough: You looked around and told the truth. You saw what you were still holding. You got ready to release. That is enough. That is healing.

DAY 2

BOXING UP THE MEMORIES

— · · • · · —

Quote: *"Letting go doesn't mean forgetting—it means making space for something new."*

Journal Prompt: How do you feel about putting away items tied to your ex? What fears or emotions come up?

Activity: Begin gathering physical reminders (photos, letters, gifts) and place them in a box. You don't have to throw them away—just put them somewhere out of sight for now.

Let This be Enough: You held the memories without getting stuck. You began putting the past in its place. That is enough. That is healing.

DAY 3

REMOVING THEIR PRESENCE FROM YOUR DIGITAL WORLD

Quote: *"Healing begins when you stop checking if the wound is still there."*

Journal Prompt: Are there photos, messages, or social media connections that keep you emotionally stuck? How does it feel when you see their name pop up?

Activity: Take one step toward digital detox—whether that's unfollowing, archiving photos, or moving messages to a folder you won't check.

Let This be Enough: You made a clean break. You silenced what triggered the ache. You chose peace. That is enough. That is healing.

DAY 4

RECLAIMING YOUR SPACE

Quote: *"This is your space. It should reflect you, not your past."*

Journal Prompt: If you could create a space that feels fully yours, what would it look like?

Activity: Move furniture, add something new, or change something in your space that reminds you of them. Even a small shift can shift your energy.

Let This be Enough: You reshaped the energy around you. You made your space reflect who you are now. That is enough. That is healing.

DAY 5
A RITUAL OF RELEASE

Quote: *"Sometimes, closure isn't something you get. It's something you create."*

Journal Prompt: What is one thing you are officially saying goodbye to today?

Activity: Choose a ritual to symbolize this release—burn a letter, throw away an item, light a candle, or say a personal goodbye in your own way.

Let This be Enough: You created a ceremony for your soul. You honored the goodbye. You made it real. That is enough. That is healing.

DAY 6
EMBRACING THE EMPTY SPACE

Quote: *"Where there was once sadness, there will be room for joy."*

Journal Prompt: How does it feel now that you've cleared some of the reminders? What emotions are surfacing?

Activity: Write a list of things you want to bring into your life now that you've made space for something new.

Let This be Enough: You let the quiet in. You made room for the new. You saw emptiness as sacred. That is enough. That is healing.

DAY 7

WEEKLY REFLECTION – MAKING ROOM FOR HEALING

Reflection Questions:

1. How did letting go physically impact your emotions?
2. What was the hardest part of this process?
3. What's one thing you are now ready to welcome into your life?

Activity: Take a moment to reflect on how your space feels now. What's one more thing you could do to make it feel more like *you*? Maybe it's painting a wall a new color, buying fresh sheets, or even investing in a new bed. Let it be something that says: *This is my space now*. Write: "I am creating space for healing, peace, and new beginnings."

Somatic Exercise

"I welcome healing. I return to myself."

Open to Healing – Breath + Heart Expansion

This breath-led movement encourages openness and grounds your healing energy in the heart.

Instructions

1. Stand or sit tall with your spine aligned and shoulders relaxed.
2. As you inhale, gently lift your arms outward and up, allowing your chest to open.
3. As you exhale, slowly lower your arms and bring your hands to your heart space.
4. Repeat this flowing movement for 1–2 minutes, syncing your breath with the motion.
5. With each inhale, silently say: "I welcome healing."
6. With each exhale, whisper: "I return to myself."

Optional Reflection Prompt

What did it feel like to create physical space for healing today?

Let This Be Enough:

You opened. You received. You returned.

That is enough. That is healing.

Monthly Reflection: Month 2

What emotions were most present for me this month?

What was hardest to let go of?

What shifted once I released it?

A moment I'm proud of:

A quote, mantra, or affirmation I want to carry forward:

On a scale of 1–10, how connected do I feel to myself right now?

1 ☐ 2 ☐ 3 ☐ 4 ☐ 5 ☐ 6 ☐ 7 ☐ 8 ☐ 9 ☐ 10

What do I need more of next month?

☐ Rest

☐ Joy

☐ Connection

☐ Confidence

☐ Creativity

☐ Other: _____

One word to guide me next month:

FROM MY HEART TO YOURS: CLOSING OUT MONTH 2

You've done something incredibly brave this month—you've allowed yourself to feel. You've sat with emotions that were uncomfortable, painful, and even overwhelming at times. You've made space for grief, for anger, for sadness, and maybe even for moments of relief. And that? That is healing.

Healing isn't about erasing what happened. It's not about waking up one day and suddenly feeling nothing at all. It's about learning to live alongside your emotions without letting them control you. It's about moving through them rather than running from them. And that's exactly what you've done this month.

You've faced memories that still sting. You've acknowledged the weight of what you've lost. You've given yourself permission to cry, to write, to be angry, to sit in the discomfort of it all. And then, you took action. You began the process of releasing—putting away the physical reminders, shifting the space around you, and making room for something new.

That isn't just processing heartbreak—that's transforming through it.

I know this hasn't been easy. I know there were probably days when you wanted to give up, to put the journal aside and stop thinking about the pain. And if you did step away for a little while, that's okay. What matters is that you came back. That you continued. That you chose to keep showing up for yourself, even when it was hard.

And that is the very thing that will carry you through the rest of this journey.

So, before we move forward, take a moment to honor yourself. You are not the same person who started this journal two months ago. You are someone who is choosing to heal. Someone who is learning to let go, piece by piece. Someone who is showing up for themselves in a way they may never have before.

I am so incredibly proud of you.

Just like before, there's no prompt today—just space. Space to breathe, to reflect, to let it all be exactly what it is.

Next month, we'll shift into **Releasing and Forgiving**. This is where we begin loosening the emotional ties that still bind you to the past—not by forcing forgiveness or rushing the process, but by freeing yourself from the weight of it all.

But for now, just breathe. Let yourself take in everything you've accomplished this month. Because you are moving forward.

And that is everything.

With love and belief in your strength,

Katina Lee

MONTH 03

RELEASING AND FORGIVING – BOOK SUMMARY

Holding onto pain, blame, and resentment may feel like protection, but in reality, it keeps you tethered to the past. True healing happens when you let go—not for them, but for yourself.

Letting Go of Self-Blame and Comparison

It's natural to replay moments and wonder if you could have done something differently, but their choices were never a reflection of your worth. Comparing yourself to who came after you only drains your energy. Your value stands on its own.

Releasing Resentment and Choosing Peace

Anger and resentment can feel like strength, but they only keep you tied to the person who hurt you. Acknowledge your emotions, feel them fully, then release them—not because they deserve it, but because you do.

The Power of Forgiveness

Forgiveness isn't about excusing their actions or letting them back in—it's about freeing yourself from their hold. It also means forgiving yourself for staying too long, ignoring red flags, or losing yourself in the relationship. Every step toward release is a step toward freedom.

Creating Space for Growth

Letting go happens in every aspect—emotionally, mentally, and physically. Whether it's removing old mementos, rewriting the stories you tell yourself, or setting new boundaries, release creates space for healing.

Reframing Pain as a Path to Growth

You cannot change what happened, but you can change how you carry it. When you see pain as a teacher instead of an anchor, you shift from being a victim of heartbreak to an active participant in your healing.

By the end of this chapter, you'll have begun the process of letting go—not just of the relationship, but of the emotions and patterns holding you back. This is your time to step forward into a life where your past no longer controls your present.

Reflection Question: What emotions, beliefs, or attachments am I ready to release so I can move forward with greater peace?

RELEASING AND FORGIVING – MONTH JOURNAL INTRODUCTION

"Forgiveness is not for them; it's for you."

As you continue your healing journey, this month is about releasing what no longer serves you and embracing the power of forgiveness—not for the sake of the person who hurt you, but for your own peace and freedom. Forgiveness is not about excusing past pain or forcing yourself to move on before you're ready; it's about letting go of blame, comparison, resentment, and guilt so you can reclaim your emotional energy and begin moving forward.

You may still feel moments of anger, sadness, or regret. That's normal. This month, you'll learn how to recognize these emotions without letting them define you. Through guided reflection, you'll begin to shift your focus from the past to the present—releasing the weight of self-blame, comparison, and resentment while making space for healing and growth.

What to Expect This Month:

- ✓ Week 1: Letting go of self-blame and embracing self-compassion
- ✓ Week 2: Releasing comparison and finding confidence in your own path
- ✓ Week 3: Recognizing and releasing resentment and anger
- ✓ Week 4: Understanding the power of forgiveness and reframing your pain

Each day, you'll work through journaling prompts and activities that will guide you toward releasing emotional burdens and reclaiming your sense of self. By the end of this month, you will have taken meaningful steps toward freeing yourself from the past, opening the door to greater peace, healing, and self-acceptance.

Starting this month, you'll also begin a daily gratitude practice. Each day includes a gratitude prompt focused on the day's theme—but in addition to that, you are invited to pause and name 1 to 3 additional things you're grateful for. These could be as small as a warm cup of coffee, a breeze on your face, or a kind message from a friend. Gratitude grounds you in the present and gently shifts your awareness from what you've lost to what still supports you. It's not about ignoring the pain—it's about remembering there's still light to be found.

Affirmation for the Month:

"I choose to release the weight of the past and free myself from resentment. Forgiveness is not for them—it's for me, and I am ready to move forward with peace."

WEEK 1
INTRODUCTION
LETTING GO OF SELF-BLAME

—··●··—

Heartbreak often leaves us asking, *what did I do wrong?* We analyze every moment, replay every argument, and convince ourselves that if we had just been different—more patient, more loving, less emotional—things would have turned out differently. But the truth is, their choice to leave was never about your worth.

Blaming yourself might feel like control—like if you can find the "mistake," you can prevent future pain. But self-blame doesn't protect you. It only keeps you stuck. The reality is relationships don't end because of one wrong step. They end because they weren't meant to last. And no amount of self-punishment will change that.

This week, we begin the process of letting go of self-blame and embracing self-compassion. You are not responsible for someone else's inability to show up for you the way you deserved. Their choices are not a reflection of your value. You were enough then. You are enough now.

But letting go isn't just about releasing pain—it's also about creating space for gratitude. Starting this week, each journal entry will include a moment of daily gratitude. This isn't to bypass the pain, but to remind you that even in heartbreak, there is something to hold onto—something good, even if it's just a small moment of relief, kindness, or hope.

Healing begins when we stop blaming ourselves and start believing in our resilience.

This week let's begin that shift together.

Affirmation for the Month:

"I choose to release the weight of the past and free myself from resentment. Forgiveness is not for them—it's for me, and I am ready to move forward with peace."

Affirmation for the Week:

"I release myself from blame. I was enough, and I am enough."

WEEK 1
LETTING GO OF SELF-BLAME JOURNAL ACTIVITIES

Focus: Releasing self-blame, embracing self-compassion, and shifting the internal narrative.

Visualization:

Close your eyes. Picture yourself standing beside a quiet river at sunrise. In your hands, you hold small stones—each one representing a moment you've blamed yourself, a memory filled with "if only" and "I should have." One by one, you gently release each stone into the water.

As they sink, watch the ripples expand, carrying your self-blame away from you. With every stone you let go, feel the weight on your chest lighten. The current doesn't resist—it welcomes what you're ready to release.

When the last stone is gone, place your hand on your heart and breathe deeply. You are still standing. You are still whole. You are worthy of grace, especially your own.

Daily Practice Reminder:

At the start of each day this week, take a moment to write down and speak aloud:

Your **monthly affirmation:** *"I choose to release the weight of the past and free myself from resentment. Forgiveness is not for them—it's for me, and I am ready to move forward with peace."*

Your **weekly affirmation:** *"I release myself from blame. I was enough, and I am enough."*

Let these words guide your healing. Repeating them daily helps shift your thoughts, build emotional resilience, and rewire your self-talk.

Daily Gratitude Reminder:

After completing your journal prompt each day, take a moment to write down 1 to 3 additional things you are grateful for. These could be people, moments, comforts, or anything that brought you peace or warmth today—no matter how small. Gratitude is a gentle yet powerful way to return to the present and remind yourself of what still supports you.

Remember, there is no right way to journal. Write as much or as little as you need. You can follow the prompts exactly or let them take you somewhere else. Let the prompts be a guide—not a rule. If your heart leads you elsewhere, follow it. These pages are yours. Let them carry what you're holding—no expectations, no perfection required.

DAY 1

THE WEIGHT OF SELF-BLAME

Quote: *"You can't go back and change the beginning, but you can start where you are and change the ending."* – C.S. Lewis

Journal Prompt: In what ways have you blamed yourself for the end of the relationship? Write honestly about the thoughts that come up.

Activity: Write down one self-blaming thought, then cross it out. Beneath it, write a statement of self-compassion, such as, *"I did the best I could with what I knew at the time."*

Daily Gratitude: What is one small thing you are grateful for today?

Let This be Enough: You stopped carrying what was never yours. You let go of the need to be perfect. That is enough. That is healing.

DAY 2

WERE YOU REALLY IN CONTROL?

Quote: *"Not everything that weighs you down is yours to carry."*

Journal Prompt: Were there things in the relationship that were out of your control? Write about the choices or actions that belonged to them, not you.

Activity: Make two lists—one titled *"What I controlled"* and the other *"What I could never control."* Reflect on the second list and remind yourself that you don't have to carry those burdens anymore.

Daily Gratitude: What is something about yourself that you appreciate today?

Let This be Enough: You released the illusion of control. You chose to forgive what you couldn't change. That is enough. That is healing.

DAY 3
THE TRUTH ABOUT "IF ONLY"

——— ··●·· ———

Quote: *"You did what you could with what you had, and that is enough."*

Journal Prompt: Do you ever catch yourself saying, *"If only I had..."*? Write about a moment when you've second-guessed yourself. What would you say to a friend who was blaming themselves the same way?

Activity: Stand in front of a mirror and say, *"I am human. I made choices, and so did they. I will not punish myself for things I could not change."* Write down how this makes you feel.

Daily Gratitude: What is one act of kindness you received today?

Let This be Enough: You untangled yourself from regret. You gave your past compassion. That is enough. That is healing.

DAY 4
WHO YOU WERE VS. WHO YOU ARE BECOMING

——— ··●·· ———

Quote: *"You are not who you were when you made those choices. Growth is your proof."*

Journal Prompt: Think about who you were in the relationship. How have you changed since then? What wisdom do you have now that you didn't before?

Activity: Write a letter from your present self to your past self. What do you want to tell them about what they deserve?

Daily Gratitude: What is something about your healing process that you are grateful for?

Let This be Enough: You honored your growth. You let yourself evolve. That is enough. That is healing.

DAY 5
LEARNING TO SHOW YOURSELF GRACE

Quote: *"Be as kind to yourself as you would to a child learning to walk."*

Journal Prompt: If your best friend were blaming themselves the way you do, what would you tell them? Now, write those words as if they were meant for you.

Activity: Write a list of things you are proud of yourself for—whether big or small. Keep adding to this list throughout your healing journey.

Daily Gratitude: What moment today made you feel a little lighter?

Let This be Enough: You offered yourself softness instead of shame. You practiced forgiveness inward. That is enough. That is healing.

DAY 6
RELEASING THE NEED TO BE PERFECT

Quote: *"You are allowed to be both a masterpiece and a work in progress."* – Sophia Bush

Journal Prompt: Have you been holding yourself to impossible standards? Where can you give yourself permission to be human?

Activity: Write down this mantra: *"I don't have to be perfect to be worthy of love."* Say it out loud to yourself and write about how it feels.

Daily Gratitude: What simple pleasure brought you comfort today?

Let This be Enough: You allowed yourself to be human. You let yourself breathe without striving. That is enough. That is healing.

DAY 7

WEEKLY REFLECTION – LETTING GO OF SELF-BLAME

Reflection Questions:

1. What self-blaming thoughts did you challenge this week?
2. How does it feel to release the weight of responsibility that was never yours?
3. What is one way you can continue showing yourself self-compassion next week?

Activity: Write yourself a note of encouragement as if you were writing to a friend. Keep it somewhere you can see it.

Daily Gratitude: What are you most grateful for in yourself right now?

Somatic Exercise

"I am worthy of grace. I offer it to myself now."

Self-Compassion Sway – Hug + Forgiveness Breath

This exercise invites emotional release and self-kindness through nurturing touch and movement.

Instructions

1. Place your right hand on your left shoulder and your left hand on your right shoulder—giving yourself a gentle hug.
2. Close your eyes and begin to slowly sway side to side. Let the movement be soothing and natural.
3. With each breath, imagine releasing judgment and offering yourself forgiveness:
4. Inhale: "I am learning."
5. Exhale: "I forgive myself."
6. Continue swaying and breathing for 1–2 minutes.
7. Finish by holding yourself still for a moment and whispering: "I am worthy of grace. I offer it to myself now."

Optional Reflection Prompt

How did it feel to offer yourself forgiveness through touch and movement?

Let This Be Enough:

You offered grace. You embraced yourself. You released judgment.

That is enough. That is healing.

WEEK 2
INTRODUCTION
RELEASING COMPARISON AND FINDING CONFIDENCE

Comparison is one of the greatest thieves of peace during heartbreak. It creeps in quietly but carries a heavy weight. It shows up when you wonder if your ex is happier without you, if the person they moved on with is better than you, or when you question why they chose someone else.

And in my story, that "someone else" wasn't just anyone—it was the same person who had always lingered in the background. The same person I had spent far too long comparing myself to. I asked myself all the questions we ask in the dark: *Was she more lovable? Easier to be with? What did she have that I didn't?* And every time I asked, I felt myself shrink.

But here's what I learned: comparison doesn't bring clarity. It only brings pain. She wasn't the reason the relationship ended. He was. His choices, his limitations, his inability to be the partner I needed him to be—that's what ended it. And the more I stopped making it about her, the more I could make it about me again—about my healing, my growth, and my future.

Comparison isn't just about other people. Sometimes, it's about where we think we *should* be. You might look at others and think, *they're already dating again. They've moved on.* Or even worse, *I should be over this by now.* But healing isn't linear, and it's certainly not a competition. Your pace is perfect. Your journey is yours.

This week is about reclaiming your confidence. Not because you've been chosen by someone else, but because you're choosing *yourself*. It's about shifting the focus from what someone else has to what you already hold—your strength, your softness, your story.

You are not comparable. Your healing is not behind. You are exactly where you're meant to be.

Let's spend this week letting go of the need to measure your worth against anyone or anything else.

You're not behind. You're not too much. You are already enough.

Let's begin.

Affirmation for the Month:

"I choose to release the weight of the past and free myself from resentment. Forgiveness is not for them—it's for me, and I am ready to move forward with peace."

Affirmation for the Week:

"I am incomparable. My journey is mine, and my worth stands on its own."

WEEK 2

RELEASING COMPARISON AND FINDING CONFIDENCE JOURNAL ACTIVITIES

Focus: Releasing comparison and reclaiming your worth by shifting your attention inward.

Visualization:

Close your eyes. Imagine yourself standing in front of a mirror, but instead of your own reflection, you see flashes of other people—their highlight reels, their relationships, their achievements. With each image, you feel yourself shrinking, like your light is being dimmed.

Now, slowly reach for the mirror and wipe it clean. The other faces begin to fade, and your own reflection comes into focus—soft, strong, radiant. You place your hand on the glass, connecting with the version of you that is grounded, whole, and more than enough.

Breathe in deeply. Say to yourself: *"I return my focus to me. I am enough."*

Let the mirror reflect your truth: that no one else can take your place in this world.

Daily Practice Reminder:

At the start of each day this week, take a moment to write down and speak aloud:

Your monthly affirmation: *"I choose to release the weight of the past and free myself from resentment. Forgiveness is not for them—it's for me, and I am ready to move forward with peace."*

Your weekly affirmation: *"I am incomparable. My journey is mine, and my worth stands on its own."*

Let these words guide your healing. Repeating them daily helps shift your thoughts, build emotional resilience, and rewire your self-talk.

Daily Gratitude Reminder:

After completing your journal prompt each day, take a moment to write down 1 to 3 additional things you are grateful for. These could be people, moments, comforts, or anything that brought you peace or warmth today—no matter how small. Gratitude is a gentle yet powerful way to return to the present and remind yourself of what still supports you.

Remember, there is no right way to journal. Write as much or as little as you need. You can follow the prompts exactly or let them take you somewhere else. Let the prompts be a guide—not a rule. If your heart leads you elsewhere, follow it. These pages are yours. Let them carry what you're holding—no expectations, no perfection required.

DAY 1

THE ILLUSION OF PERFECTION

Quote: *"We don't miss them. We miss the idea of them."*

Journal Prompt: What aspects of the relationship were you holding onto that may not have been as perfect as they seemed?

Activity: Make two columns:

1. *What I Miss*
2. *What I Don't Miss*
3. *Reflect on the second column—how does it feel to see these things written out?*

Daily Gratitude: What is something about your life that you wouldn't trade with anyone?

Let This be Enough: You challenged the fantasy. You made room for the real story. That is enough. That is healing.

DAY 2

WHEN LOVE AND PAIN COEXIST

Quote: *"Just because it hurt doesn't mean it wasn't love. Just because it was love doesn't mean it was right."*

Journal Prompt: Write about a time in your relationship when love and pain coexisted.

Activity: Highlight any patterns you notice in how you accepted pain as part of love.

Daily Gratitude: What is something in your life that is unfolding at its own perfect pace?

Let This be Enough You held both at once. You made space for contradiction. That is enough. That is healing.

DAY 3
ROMANTICIZING THE PAST

Quote: *"Nostalgia is a liar."*

Journal Prompt: Are you remembering the relationship as it was or as you wanted it to be?

Activity: "Then vs. Now" List

1. *Draw a line down the middle of a page.*
2. *On the left side, write what you used to believe about the relationship when you were in it.*
3. *On the right side, write what you see more clearly now.*

This is not about judgment—it's about clarity

Daily Gratitude: Are you able to identify at least one reason you are grateful the relationship is over?

Let This be Enough: You told the truth about what really was. You chose clarity over illusion. That is enough. That is healing.

DAY 4
BREAKING THE FANTASY

Quote: *"We must let go of the life we have planned, so as to accept the one that is waiting for us."* – Joseph Campbell

Journal Prompt: What part of the relationship do you still wish could have been different?

Activity: Write a reality-check statement: *"It wasn't what I thought it was, and that's okay."*

Daily Gratitude: What is one thing in your life that is real, unfiltered, and beautiful just as it is?

Let This be Enough: You showed up. You told the truth. You kept going. That is enough. That is healing.

DAY 5
ACCEPTING THE ENDING

Quote: *"Some things break so we can build something stronger."*

Journal Prompt: Are you still hoping they'll come back? How does holding onto that hope impact your healing?

Activity: Write down one small way you can shift your focus forward.

Daily Gratitude: What moment of progress, no matter how small, are you grateful for today?

Let This be Enough: You acknowledged that it ended. You began turning toward what comes next. That is enough. That is healing.

DAY 6
CHOOSING REALITY OVER FANTASY

Quote: *"When we know better, we do better."* – Maya Angelou

Journal Prompt: What truths about your ex or your relationship do you now see more clearly?

Activity: Say out loud: *"I am choosing reality over fantasy."*

Daily Gratitude: What is something in your future that you're looking forward to?

Let This be Enough: You stopped pretending. You opened your eyes to what was. That is enough. That is healing.

DAY 7
WEEKLY REFLECTION – SEEING CLEARLY

Reflection Questions:

1. What illusion was the hardest to let go of?
2. How do you feel after writing about the relationship honestly?
3. What's one mindset shift you want to take into next week?

Activity: Tear up one false belief you wrote about this week.

Daily Gratitude: What do you love about yourself that has nothing to do with anyone else?

Somatic Exercise

"My truth is mine to own. I am safe in it."

Truth Scan – Heart-Opening + Visualization

This practice encourages emotional clarity, presence, and ownership through gentle movement and visualization.

Instructions

1. Sit in stillness and gently roll your shoulders back, lifting your heart.
2. With your eyes closed, slowly turn your head side to side, as if scanning the horizon.
3. With each turn, breathe deeply and say silently or aloud:
4. "I see clearly."
5. "I honor my truth."
6. "I release shame."
7. Visualize yourself seeing your truth without distortion—just clarity and compassion.
8. End by placing one hand on your heart and the other on your belly. Breathe in deeply and affirm: "My truth is mine to own. I am safe in it."

Optional Reflection Prompt

What truth became clearer to you today?

Let This Be Enough:

You looked within. You honored your truth. You released shame.

That is enough. That is healing.

WEEK 3

INTRODUCTION
RELEASING RESENTMENT AND ANGER

———··•··———

Anger is an emotion that demands to be felt. It burns hot, rising in your chest when you think about the lies, the betrayal, the way they walked away without looking back. Maybe you're angry at them, for what they did or didn't do. Maybe you're angry at yourself, for not seeing the signs, for staying too long, for giving them so much of you. And maybe, some days, the anger makes you feel powerful—like holding onto it keeps you from feeling the deeper pain beneath it.

But here's what I've learned: anger, when left unchecked, is like carrying a hot coal with the intent to throw it at someone else. In the end, the only person who gets burned is you.

That doesn't mean you shouldn't feel it. Quite the opposite—anger can be a guide. It can reveal the places where boundaries were crossed, where you lost yourself, where you deserved better. But staying stuck in anger, feeding it day after day, only ties you tighter to the person you are trying to let go of.

This week is about *releasing* that anger—not by ignoring it, but by acknowledging it and choosing to no longer let it own you. It's about setting down the weight of resentment, not for them, but for you. Because they don't feel your anger—you do. And you deserve to walk forward unburdened.

You don't have to let go of everything overnight. But you can start loosening your grip, one small step at a time. And with every step, you are choosing peace over bitterness, freedom over pain, and yourself over the past.

Affirmation for the Month:

"I choose to release the weight of the past and free myself from resentment. Forgiveness is not for them—it's for me, and I am ready to move forward with peace."

Affirmation for the Week:

"I release the weight of resentment and choose peace. My healing matters more than my anger."

WEEK 3
RELEASING RESENTMENT AND ANGER JOURNAL ACTIVITIES

Focus: Acknowledging anger, understanding its purpose, and choosing to release resentment for your own healing.

Visualization:

Close your eyes. Picture yourself standing in a quiet field at sunset, holding a heavy backpack filled with stones. Each stone represents a resentment, a betrayal, a moment that still stings. One by one, you remove the stones, naming each as you place it gently on the ground. With every stone released, your body feels lighter. The sun begins to set behind you, casting golden light over the field. You take a deep breath, standing taller, freer. You are walking away—not with bitterness, but with peace.

Daily Practice Reminder:

At the start of each day this week, take a moment to write down and speak aloud:

Your **monthly affirmation:** *"I choose to release the weight of the past and free myself from resentment. Forgiveness is not for them—it's for me, and I am ready to move forward with peace."*

Your **weekly affirmation:** *"I release the weight of resentment and choose peace. My healing matters more than my anger."*

Let these words guide your healing. Repeating them daily helps shift your thoughts, build emotional resilience, and rewire your self-talk.

Daily Gratitude Reminder:

After completing your journal prompt each day, take a moment to write down 1 to 3 additional things you are grateful for. These could be people, moments, comforts, or anything that brought you peace or warmth today—no matter how small. Gratitude is a gentle yet powerful way to return to the present and remind yourself of what still supports you.

Remember, there is no right way to journal. Write as much or as little as you need. You can follow the prompts exactly or let them take you somewhere else. Let the prompts be a guide—not a rule. If your heart leads you elsewhere, follow it. These pages are yours. Let them carry what you're holding—no expectations, no perfection required.

DAY 1

THE WEIGHT OF RESENTMENT

Quote: *"Holding onto anger is like drinking poison and expecting the other person to die."*

Journal Prompt: What specific things are you still angry about? Write them all out, unfiltered.

Activity: Write down your anger on paper, then crumple or tear it up as a symbolic act of release.

Daily Gratitude: What is something in your life right now that brings you peace, no matter how small?

Let This be Enough: You showed up. You told the truth. You kept going. That is enough. That is healing.

DAY 2

ANGER AS A MESSENGER

Quote: *"Your anger is the part of you that knows you deserve better."*

Journal Prompt: What is your anger trying to tell you? What boundaries were crossed? What did you need that you didn't get?

Activity: Highlight one lesson your anger has taught you that you can take forward.

Daily Gratitude: What is something you have learned from this experience that makes you stronger?

Let This be Enough: You showed up. You told the truth. You kept going. That is enough. That is healing.

DAY 3

THE BURN OF HOLDING ON

•————— ··●·· —————•

Quote: *"Resentment is like setting yourself on fire to keep someone else warm."*

Journal Prompt: How has holding onto anger affected your daily life, emotions, or healing?

Activity: Close your eyes, take three deep breaths, and say aloud: *"I choose to let this go."*

Daily Gratitude: Name a moment this week when you felt even the smallest relief from your pain.

Let This be Enough: You showed up. You told the truth. You kept going. That is enough. That is healing.

DAY 4

THE FANTASY OF CLOSURE

•————— ··●·· —————•

Quote: *"Closure isn't something they give you. It's something you give yourself."*

Journal Prompt: Are you waiting for an apology, explanation, or moment of validation from them? How is that holding you back?

Activity: Write a letter to them about everything you wish they would acknowledge. Then decide: Do you want to keep waiting, or do you want to release it for yourself?

Daily Gratitude: What is one thing about yourself that you love, no matter what has happened?

Let This be Enough: You showed up. You told the truth. You kept going. That is enough. That is healing.

DAY 6
RELEASING THE NEED FOR REVENGE

---•••●••---

Quote: *"The best revenge is no revenge. Move on. Be happy."*

Journal Prompt: Have you had thoughts of wanting them to suffer, regret, or see you thriving? How does that energy serve or drain you?

Activity: Write a declaration: "My healing is not dependent on their suffering. I set myself free."

Daily Gratitude: Who or what in your life right now reminds you that you are loved and supported?

Let This be Enough: You showed up. You told the truth. You kept going. That is enough. That is healing.

DAY 6
CHOOSING PEACE OVER BITTERNESS

---•••●••---

Quote: *"Bitterness keeps you trapped in the past. Peace lets you move forward."*

Journal Prompt: Imagine a life where you are no longer consumed by resentment. What does it look like? How do you feel?

Activity: List three things you can do this week to shift your focus away from them and back to yourself.

Daily Gratitude: What is one act of self-care you can do for yourself today?

Let This be Enough: You showed up. You told the truth. You kept going. That is enough. That is healing.

DAY 7

WEEKLY REFLECTION – SETTING DOWN THE WEIGHT

Reflection Questions:

1. How has your relationship with anger changed this week?
2. What did you learn about yourself by acknowledging your resentment?
3. How does it feel to consider releasing it?

Activity: Write a closing statement: *"I am choosing my peace over my pain."*

Daily Gratitude: Reflect on something beautiful that happened this week, no matter how small.

Somatic Exercise

"I don't have to carry what no longer belongs to me."

Shoulder Drop Release

This simple release clears physical tension and signals emotional lightness.

Instructions

1. Stand with your arms relaxed at your sides.
2. Inhale and lift your shoulders up toward your ears.
3. Exhale and drop them heavily, letting gravity help you release.
4. Repeat this movement 5–7 times, each time imagining that you are letting go of invisible burdens—expectations, worries, old pain.
5. Let each drop be an embodied reminder: "I don't have to carry what no longer belongs to me."

Optional Reflection Prompt

What burden are you ready to set down today?

Let This Be Enough:

You released the weight. You made space for peace.

That is enough. That is healing.

WEEK 4

INTRODUCTION
THE POWER OF FORGIVENESS

———··•··———

Forgiveness. Just the word itself might make you tense up. Maybe you're thinking, *there's no way I can forgive them. Not after everything they did.* And honestly? I get it. Forgiveness feels impossible when the pain is still fresh, when the wounds haven't fully healed, and when the person who hurt you hasn't even acknowledged the damage they caused.

But here's what forgiveness *isn't*: It's not about excusing what they did. It's not about forgetting the hurt or pretending it didn't matter. And it's definitely not about letting them back in.

Forgiveness is about *you*. It's about choosing to no longer let their actions control your emotions. It's about reclaiming your energy, your peace, and your freedom. Because the truth is, when you hold onto resentment, you're the one carrying the weight. They're out there living their life, while you're the one reliving the pain over and over again.

Forgiveness doesn't mean you have to feel warm, loving feelings toward them. It doesn't mean you ever have to see them again. It simply means loosening your grip on the anger, the sadness, the bitterness— *for your own sake.*

And just as important as forgiving them? *Forgiving yourself.* Maybe you regret staying too long, ignoring red flags, or giving too many chances. Maybe you blame yourself for not seeing the truth sooner. But you were doing the best you could with what you knew at the time. You don't have to carry guilt for the choices you made when you were just trying to love someone.

This week, we're taking small steps toward releasing the hold the past has on us. We're not rushing forgiveness or forcing it before we're ready. We're simply making space for the possibility of it—because in the end, forgiveness isn't something you give to them. It's something you give to yourself.

Affirmation for the Month:

"I choose to release the weight of the past and free myself from resentment. Forgiveness is not for them—it's for me, and I am ready to move forward with peace."

Affirmation for the Week:

"I release the past so I can step fully into my future. Forgiveness is my path to freedom."

WEEK 4

THE POWER OF FORGIVENESS JOURNAL ACTIVITIES

Focus: Exploring forgiveness, releasing resentment, and reclaiming emotional freedom.

Visualization:

Close your eyes. Picture yourself holding a heavy rope tied tightly around your waist. On the other end is the weight of the past—memories, regrets, pain, and people who hurt you. Feel how it tugs, how it limits your steps forward. Now imagine yourself slowly untying the knot, loosening the rope, and letting it drop. As it falls away, you feel your body lighten, your chest expand, and your path open up in front of you. You're no longer tethered. You are free to move forward—stronger, lighter, and no longer defined by what once held you back.

Daily Practice Reminder:

At the start of each day this week, take a moment to write down and speak aloud:

Your **monthly affirmation:** *"I choose to release the weight of the past and free myself from resentment. Forgiveness is not for them—it's for me, and I am ready to move forward with peace."*

Your **weekly affirmation:** *"I release the past so I can step fully into my future. Forgiveness is my path to freedom."*

Let these words guide your healing. Repeating them daily helps shift your thoughts, build emotional resilience, and rewire your self-talk.

Daily Gratitude Reminder:

After completing your journal prompt each day, take a moment to write down 1 to 3 additional things you are grateful for. These could be people, moments, comforts, or anything that brought you peace or warmth today—no matter how small. Gratitude is a gentle yet powerful way to return to the present and remind yourself of what still supports you.

Remember, there is no right way to journal. Write as much or as little as you need. You can follow the prompts exactly or let them take you somewhere else. Let the prompts be a guide—not a rule. If your heart leads you elsewhere, follow it. These pages are yours. Let them carry what you're holding—no expectations, no perfection required.

DAY 1
THE TRUTH ABOUT FORGIVENESS

——— ··●·· ———

Quote: *"Forgiveness is not about them. It's about setting yourself free."*

Journal Prompt: When you hear the word "forgiveness," what emotions come up for you? What beliefs do you have about what it means to forgive?

Activity: Write down one thing you're open to releasing—even if you're not ready to forgive yet.

Daily Gratitude: What is something in your life right now that brings you a sense of peace?

Let This be Enough: You showed up. You told the truth. You kept going. That is enough. That is healing.

DAY 2
THE FIRST STEP TOWARD LETTING GO

——— ··●·· ———

Quote: *"Forgiveness doesn't excuse their behavior; it prevents their behavior from destroying your heart."* – Hemant Smarty

Journal Prompt: If you *could* forgive them one day, what would that look like? How would it feel to no longer carry this pain?

Activity: Write a forgiveness letter you don't intend to send. Pour out everything you feel, then close it with, *"I release this pain, so it no longer controls me."*

Daily Gratitude: What is one personal strength this experience has revealed in you?

Let This be Enough: You showed up. You told the truth. You kept going. That is enough. That is healing.

DAY 3
FORGIVING YOURSELF

Quote: *"You did what you knew how to do at the time. Now you know better, and you will do better."* – Maya Angelou

Journal Prompt: What regrets do you hold about your role in the relationship? How can you extend the same compassion to yourself that you would to a friend?

Activity: Stand in front of a mirror and say: *"I forgive myself for _____. I release the guilt and choose to move forward."*

Daily Gratitude: What is one thing you admire about yourself?

Let This be Enough: You showed up. You told the truth. You kept going. That is enough. That is healing.

DAY 4
RELEASING THE NEED FOR AN APOLOGY

Quote: *"You may never get the apology you deserve. But you can still give yourself the closure you need."*

Journal Prompt: Are you waiting for them to admit they were wrong? How does holding onto that expectation affect you?

Activity: Write a statement of closure to yourself: *"Even if they never apologize, I choose to move forward."*

Daily Gratitude: What is one way you are creating a better future for yourself?

Let This be Enough: You showed up. You told the truth. You kept going. That is enough. That is healing.

DAY 5

LETTING GO OF WHAT NO LONGER SERVES YOU

——————· ·•· · ——————

Quote: *"You can't reach for the future if your hands are full of the past."* Louise Smith

Journal Prompt: What are you still holding onto that no longer serves you? (Old messages, gifts, memories, or even thought patterns?)

Activity: Choose one thing to physically remove from your space today—whether it's deleting a message, putting away an item, or cleaning out a space that feels heavy with memories.

Daily Gratitude: What is one new thing you are making space for in your life?

Let This be Enough: You showed up. You told the truth. You kept going. That is enough. That is healing.

DAY 6

YOUR FUTURE WITHOUT THE WEIGHT OF THE PAST

——————· ·•· · ——————

Quote: *"One day, you will wake up and realize you feel light again."* Paulo Coelho

Journal Prompt: Imagine your future one year from now, completely free from resentment and pain. What does that life look like? How do you feel?

Activity: Write a letter from your future healed self, offering encouragement to the version of you who is struggling today.

Daily Gratitude: What is something about your future that excites you?

Let This be Enough: You showed up. You told the truth. You kept going. That is enough. That is healing.

DAY 7

WEEKLY REFLECTION – A LIGHTER HEART

——— ··●·· ———

Reflection Questions:

1. What has been the hardest part of this journey toward forgiveness?
2. What progress have you made in letting go?
3. How do you feel after exploring forgiveness this week?

Activity: Write a final statement for this month: *"I am releasing the past, one step at a time. I am choosing peace over pain."*

Daily Gratitude: What is one thing you can appreciate about yourself right now?

Somatic Exercise

"I am releasing the past, one step at a time. I am choosing peace over pain."

Lightness Breath + Soft Smile

This practice gently signals safety and ease to your nervous system, inviting peace from the inside out.

Instructions

1. Sit comfortably with your spine upright. Bring a soft, gentle smile to your face—no need to force it.
2. Rest your hands palm-up on your knees in a relaxed position.
3. With each inhale, imagine lightness entering your chest—a sense of openness and calm.
4. With each exhale, visualize any heaviness floating away—doubt, tension, or sadness releasing with your breath.
5. Stay with this practice for 3 minutes, allowing your smile and breath to soften your whole body.

Optional Reflection Prompt

What does lightness feel like in your body today?

Let This Be Enough:

You smiled. You softened. You let go.

That is enough. That is healing.

Monthly Reflection: Month 3

What emotions were most present for me this month?

What small act made me feel stronger?

Where did I surprise myself with my own courage?

A moment I'm proud of:

A quote, mantra, or affirmation I want to carry forward:

On a scale of 1–10, how connected do I feel to myself right now?

1 ☐ 2 ☐ 3 ☐ 4 ☐ 5 ☐ 6 ☐ 7 ☐ 8 ☐ 9 ☐ 10

What do I need more of next month?

☐ Rest

☐ Joy

☐ Connection

☐ Confidence

☐ Creativity

☐ Other: _____

One word to guide me next month:

FROM MY HEART TO YOURS: CLOSING OUT MONTH 3

Dear You,

You've just completed one of the most emotionally complex parts of this healing journey—the work of releasing. This month, you sat with anger. You looked closely at resentment. You confronted the weight of comparison and began to understand the emotional toll of holding on. That takes *incredible courage*.

Forgiveness isn't a straight path. It's a spiral. Some days you may feel free, only to find yourself tangled in old emotions again. That's okay. That's normal. Healing doesn't ask for perfection—it simply asks for presence. And you showed up.

You chose to look at your pain with honesty. You questioned the stories you've carried, released what no longer serves you, and maybe—just maybe—extended grace toward the one person who needed it most: yourself.

Maybe you're not fully there yet. Maybe you still feel the sting of old wounds. But I want you to know—you've already done something powerful. You've created space for peace. Space for softness. Space for joy to begin finding its way back in.

Just like before, there's no prompt today—just space. Space to breathe. Space to feel. Space to notice how much lighter it feels to carry less.

Next month, we shift into *Rediscovering You*—a chapter dedicated to reconnecting with your identity, your joy, and the beautiful parts of yourself that may have gotten lost along the way. But before we do that, take a moment. Be still. Reflect on all you've worked through this month.

You are no longer carrying what isn't yours. You are walking in freedom.

And that is no small thing.

With so much love and admiration for your strength,

Katina Lee

PS: If you find yourself drawn back to a prompt, a memory, or a moment—you're allowed to return. The pages will meet you where you are, not where you were.

Sometimes, the second time you write it… you hear yourself more clearly. That is healing too.

MONTH
04

REDISCOVERING YOU – BOOK SUMMARY

After a breakup, it's common to feel like a part of you is missing. The life you built with someone else may have shaped your identity in ways you didn't even realize. Now, without that relationship, you may be left wondering: Who am I without them? This chapter is about answering that question—not by trying to return to the person you were before, but by embracing who you are now and who you have the power to become.

Reclaiming Your Identity

Relationships can blur the line between "me" and "us," often leading us to set aside parts of ourselves for the sake of togetherness. Now is the time to reclaim those pieces—your voice, your independence, your sense of self. This process isn't about mourning what was lost, but about rediscovering the strength and individuality that were always within you.

Reconnecting with Passion and Joy

Healing isn't just about moving on; it's about creating a life that excites you again. The things that once brought you joy may have been pushed aside during the relationship. Now is your chance to explore what truly lights you up—whether that's picking up an old hobby, discovering a new passion, or simply allowing yourself to have fun without guilt.

Embracing Your Complexity and Strength

You are not defined by your past, nor do you have to fit into anyone's expectations of who you should be. This chapter encourages you to embrace your multitudes—the parts of you that make you unique, complex, and beautifully whole. Instead of shrinking yourself to fit into someone else's life, you'll learn to expand into the fullest version of yourself.

Redefining Your Future

As you rediscover who you are, you also have the opportunity to redefine what you want for your future. Healing is not just about letting go; it's about stepping forward with clarity and confidence. What do you value? What dreams have you put on hold? By realigning with your purpose, you'll set the foundation for a future that is built on your desires, not the remnants of the past.

By the end of this chapter, you'll have reconnected with the parts of yourself that were lost or neglected. Rediscovery is not about going backward—it's about moving forward with a deeper understanding of who you are and what you deserve.

Reflection Question: What parts of myself have I neglected, and how can I begin to nurture them again?

REDISCOVERING YOU – MONTH JOURNAL INTRODUCTION

―――― ·· ● ·· ――――

"You are not lost. You are simply becoming." – Katina Lee

This month is about reconnecting with yourself—beyond heartbreak, beyond the roles you played in your past relationship, and beyond the version of you that may have been shaped by someone else. After a breakup, it's common to feel disconnected from who you are. This is your opportunity to rediscover the passions, dreams, and strengths that make you uniquely you.

Healing isn't just about letting go of the past; it's about stepping into the person you are becoming. You'll explore what excites you, what fulfills you, and what truly aligns with your values. This journey of self-discovery isn't about rushing to define yourself—it's about giving yourself the space to grow into your next chapter with clarity and confidence.

What to Expect This Month:

✓ Week 1: Reclaiming Your Identity – Recognizing who you were before, who you are now, and who you want to become

✓ Week 2: Exploring Your Passions – Reconnecting with interests, hobbies, and dreams that bring you joy

✓ Week 3: Embracing Change – Accepting growth, releasing old versions of yourself, and stepping into possibility

✓ Week 4: Creating a New Vision – Defining your values, setting personal goals, and designing a life that excites you

Each day, you'll engage in guided journaling and activities designed to help you uncover the parts of yourself that may have been neglected, suppressed, or forgotten. By the end of this month, you will have taken meaningful steps toward rediscovering who you are—on your own terms, with a newfound sense of self-worth and direction.

Affirmation for the Month:

"I am more than who I was in my past relationship. I embrace the journey of rediscovering myself, my passions, and my purpose."

WEEK 1
INTRODUCTION
RECLAIMING YOUR IDENTITY

Breakups don't just take away a relationship; they often take pieces of who you thought you were. You may find yourself questioning, *who am I without them?* If you poured so much of yourself into the relationship—your time, your energy, your love—you may feel like you've been left with an empty space where your identity once was. But here's the truth: you haven't lost yourself. You are still here. You are simply in the process of rediscovery.

It's easy to fall into the habit of defining yourself based on the past—who you were in the relationship, the version of you that existed alongside them. But that was never the full picture. You are not just the person who loved them, nor are you the person they left behind. You are someone who is still evolving, still growing, still discovering new facets of who you are.

This week is about reclaiming your identity—not by returning to the person you were before, but by embracing the person you are becoming. It's about looking at yourself with fresh eyes, recognizing the strength you've gained, and giving yourself permission to step into a future that is entirely your own.

Maybe you sacrificed parts of yourself to fit into the relationship. Maybe you forgot what it felt like to make choices purely for you. Maybe you were waiting for permission to fully be yourself. But now, you are free to choose—free to define yourself on your own terms.

This isn't about getting "back" to who you were before the relationship. It's about moving forward, stepping into your wholeness, and embracing all the things that make you, *you*.

You don't have to have all the answers right now. This week is simply about reconnecting with yourself—one small step at a time.

Affirmation for the Month:

"I am more than who I was in my past relationship. I embrace the journey of rediscovering myself, my passions, and my purpose."

Affirmation for the Week:

"I am whole on my own. I am reclaiming my identity and stepping into my full power."

WEEK 1
RECLAIMING YOUR IDENTITY JOURNAL ACTIVITIES

Focus: Recognizing who you were before, who you are now, and who you want to become.

Visualization:

Close your eyes. Imagine standing in front of a mirror, but instead of seeing only your reflection, you see different versions of yourself standing behind you—the child who dreamed big, the teenager full of curiosity, the woman who once felt unstoppable. Slowly, they step forward, one by one, placing their hands on your shoulders. They remind you that you are still her—every version of you still exists within. You smile, not because you've found your old self, but because you're beginning to see the full, beautiful picture of who you are becoming.

Daily Practice Reminder:

At the start of each day this week, take a moment to write down and speak aloud:

Your **monthly affirmation:** *"I am more than who I was in my past relationship. I embrace the journey of rediscovering myself, my passions, and my purpose."*

Your **weekly affirmation:** *"I am whole on my own. I am reclaiming my identity and stepping into my full power."*

Let these words guide your healing. Repeating them daily helps shift your thoughts, build emotional resilience, and rewire your self-talk.

Daily Gratitude Reminder:

After completing your journal prompt each day, take a moment to write down 1 to 3 additional things you are grateful for. These could be people, moments, comforts, or anything that brought you peace or warmth today—no matter how small. Gratitude is a gentle yet powerful way to return to the present and remind yourself of what still supports you.

Remember, there is no right way to journal. Write as much or as little as you need. You can follow the prompts exactly or let them take you somewhere else. Let the prompts be a guide—not a rule. If your heart leads you elsewhere, follow it. These pages are yours. Let them carry what you're holding—no expectations, no perfection required.

DAY 1

WHO WAS I BEFORE THE RELATIONSHIP?

— · · ● · · —

Quote: *"You existed before them, and you will exist after them."*

Journal Prompt*:* What were you passionate about before this relationship? What dreams, goals, or interests did you have that may have been set aside?

Activity: Write a letter to your past self, reminding them of their worth outside of this relationship.

Daily Gratitude: What is one thing about yourself that you're grateful for today?

Let This be Enough: You remembered who you were before the world told you to forget. That's not just reflection — that's resurrection.

DAY 2

WHO AM I NOW?

— · · ● · · —

Quote: *"You are not who you were a year ago, a month ago, or even yesterday. You are always growing."*

Journal Prompt: How has this breakup changed you? What have you learned about yourself in this process?

Activity: Write down three strengths you've developed through this experience.

Daily Gratitude: What is something about your present self that you appreciate?

Let This be Enough: You looked at yourself with honest eyes and chose compassion over critique. That's growth. That's grace.

DAY 3
WHAT PARTS OF MYSELF DID I LOSE?

— ··•·· —

Quote: *"You do not need to shrink to be loved."*

Journal Prompt: Were there parts of yourself you felt you had to suppress in your relationship? Were there things you stopped doing because of them?

Activity: Make a list of things you want to reclaim—hobbies, personality traits, interests, or dreams.

Daily Gratitude: What is one thing you're grateful to have learned from this experience?

Let This be Enough: You reached for the parts of yourself you once abandoned. You called them back home. That is enough. That is healing.

DAY 4
EMBRACING THE EVOLUTION

— ··•·· —

Quote: *"You are not lost. You are simply becoming."* – Katina Lee

Journal Prompt: What parts of yourself are you excited to explore or develop moving forward?

Activity: Write down one small step you can take this week to reconnect with yourself.

Daily Gratitude: What is one new habit or mindset you've gained that you're grateful for?

Let This be Enough: You made space for the version of you that's still unfolding. You didn't rush her — you welcomed her. That is enough.

DAY 5

LETTING GO OF WHO YOU THOUGHT YOU'D BE

Quote: *"Sometimes we need to let go of who we thought we were supposed to be in order to embrace who we are meant to become."*

Journal Prompt: How did you imagine your life would look in this relationship? How does it feel to release that vision and make space for something new?

Activity: Write a statement of release: "I let go of the life I thought I would have, and I trust in the future I am creating."

Daily Gratitude: What is one thing you're looking forward to in this next chapter of your life?

Let This be Enough: You released the life you outgrew to make room for the one that fits. That courage deserves to be honored.

DAY 6

MAKING PEACE WITH CHANGE

Quote: *"Growth requires change, and change requires letting go."*

Journal Prompt: What fears do you have about rediscovering yourself? What excites you?

Activity: Write a list of things you are willing to embrace as part of this new chapter.

Daily Gratitude: What is one change in your life that you are grateful for?

Let This be Enough: You stopped fearing change and started befriending it. You softened into the unknown. That is enough. That is becoming.

DAY 7

WEEKLY REFLECTION – RECLAIMING MY IDENTITY

---·· • ·· ---

Reflection Questions:

1. What was the biggest realization you had this week about yourself?
2. What qualities or passions are you excited to reclaim?
3. What's one thing you can do next week to continue rediscovering yourself?
4. **Activity:** Write an affirmation for yourself that starts with "I am…"

(Example: *I am strong, I am growing, I am rediscovering myself.*

Daily Gratitude: What is one thing about yourself that you've grown to appreciate this week?

Somatic Exercise

"I am me."

Identity Expansion + Embodied Expression

This exercise uses physical openness and voice to embody authenticity, presence, and pride in who you are.

Instructions

1. Stand with your feet planted firmly on the ground. Feel your connection to the earth.
2. Spread your arms wide—open, unapologetic. Say aloud with strength and clarity: "I am me."
3. Begin to move your body however it wants to move. Sway. Stretch. Reach upward. Twist.
4. Let your body express what it feels like to fully own your identity.

Optional Reflection Prompt

What did it feel like to physically claim your space and your truth?

Let This Be Enough:

You stood tall. You spoke your truth. You took up space.

That is enough. That is healing.

WEEK 2

INTRODUCTION EXPLORING YOUR PASSIONS

Somewhere along the way, you may have stopped prioritizing the things that once brought you joy. Maybe you set aside your passions to focus on the relationship. Maybe you convinced yourself that your interests weren't as important. Or maybe, over time, you just forgot how much fulfillment they used to bring you.

This week is about rediscovering those things—the hobbies, dreams, and activities that make you feel alive. It's not about forcing yourself to return to everything you used to love; it's about giving yourself permission to explore. You are allowed to evolve. What brought you joy in the past may still resonate with you, or you may find new interests that align with who you are becoming.

In my own journey, I remember feeling like I didn't even know what I enjoyed anymore. So much of my time, my thoughts, and my energy had been wrapped up in the relationship that when it ended, I felt empty. I had to start from scratch, trying new things just to see what sparked something inside me. Some activities felt forced, some just weren't for me—but then, there were moments when I felt a small flicker of excitement, a reminder of what it felt like to truly enjoy something for myself.

This week, I want you to approach life with curiosity. Allow yourself to try new things, revisit old passions, and embrace the process of exploration. You don't have to have all the answers. You just have to be open to discovering what lights you up again.

You are more than the love you lost. You are a person with depth, dreams, and endless potential.

Let's start exploring.

Affirmation for the Month:

"I am more than who I was in my past relationship. I embrace the journey of rediscovering myself, my passions, and my purpose."

Affirmation for the Week:

"I am reconnecting with the things that bring me joy. I deserve to live a life that excites me."

WEEK 2

EXPLORING YOUR PASSIONS JOURNAL ACTIVITIES

Focus: Reconnecting with hobbies, dreams, and activities that bring joy and fulfillment.

Visualization:

Close your eyes. Imagine walking through a vibrant, open-air market filled with colors, music, and creativity. Each booth represents a part of you—your interests, dreams, and forgotten joys. Some are familiar, others feel new and curious. You wander freely, stopping where you feel drawn. Maybe it's a canvas and paints, a notebook and pen, a pair of hiking boots, a dance floor, or an instrument. As you explore, notice the spark of excitement returning to your chest. You're not lost—you're in the process of rediscovery. Let this space remind you that joy is not behind you. It's still within reach, waiting to be picked back up.

Daily Practice Reminder:

At the start of each day this week, take a moment to write down and speak aloud:

Your **monthly affirmation:** *"I am more than who I was in my past relationship. I embrace the journey of rediscovering myself, my passions, and my purpose."*

Your **weekly affirmation:** *"I am reconnecting with the things that bring me joy. I deserve to live a life that excites me."*

Let these words guide your healing. Repeating them daily helps shift your thoughts, build emotional resilience, and rewire your self-talk.

Daily Gratitude Reminder:

After completing your journal prompt each day, take a moment to write down 1 to 3 additional things you are grateful for. These could be people, moments, comforts, or anything that brought you peace or warmth today—no matter how small. Gratitude is a gentle yet powerful way to return to the present and remind yourself of what still supports you.

Remember, there is no right way to journal. Write as much or as little as you need. You can follow the prompts exactly or let them take you somewhere else. Let the prompts be a guide—not a rule. If your heart leads you elsewhere, follow it. These pages are yours. Let them carry what you're holding—no expectations, no perfection required.

DAY 1
WHAT USED TO BRING ME JOY?

Quote: *"Sometimes you have to go back to where you started to find where you belong."*

Journal Prompt: Think back to a time when you felt happiest. What were you doing? What activities, hobbies, or interests used to bring you excitement?

Activity: Make a list of past passions or hobbies you'd like to revisit. Choose one to explore this week.

Daily Gratitude: What is one small thing that brought you joy today?

Let This be Enough: You reached back to remember what once lit you up. That spark still lives in you. That remembering is enough.

DAY 2
WHAT HAVE I ALWAYS WANTED TO TRY?

Quote: *"Your curiosity is your compass."*

Journal Prompt: Is there something you've always wanted to try but never did? What's held you back?

Activity: Research or plan how you can take the first step toward trying this activity.

Daily Gratitude: What is something new you learned today?

Let This be Enough: You listened to your curiosity. You said yes to possibility. That is enough. That is how new joy begins.

DAY 3
MAKING SPACE FOR WHAT FULFILLS ME

Quote: *"We make time for the things that matter."*

Journal Prompt: Do you prioritize the things that bring you joy? If not, what tends to get in the way?

Activity: Identify one thing in your schedule you can adjust to make time for something that brings you joy.

Daily Gratitude: What is one moment today where you felt at peace?

Let This be Enough: You made room for what matters. You honored your joy like it was sacred—because it is. That is enough.

DAY 4
TRYING SOMETHING NEW

Quote: *"Growth happens outside your comfort zone."*

Journal Prompt: How do you feel when you step outside your comfort zone? What's something new you can try this week?

Activity: Choose one small new thing to try today—even if it's just a different route on your walk, a new recipe, or a new playlist.

Daily Gratitude: What is something good that happened today?

Let This be Enough: You stepped into unfamiliar territory with an open heart. That bravery, however small, is a powerful beginning.

DAY 5

THE DIFFERENCE BETWEEN DISTRACTION AND FULFILLMENT

Quote: *"Not everything that keeps you busy brings you joy."*

Journal Prompt: Have you ever used distractions to avoid facing your emotions? How can you tell the difference between healthy passion and mindless distraction?

Activity: Write down one way you can be more intentional about how you spend your time.

Daily Gratitude: What is something you're proud of yourself for today?

Let This be Enough: You asked yourself what really feeds your soul. You chose presence over avoidance. That is enough.

DAY 6

RECONNECTING WITH PLAYFULNESS

Quote: *"You are never too old to set another goal or dream a new dream."* – C.S. Lewis

Journal Prompt: When was the last time you did something just for fun? What made it enjoyable?

Activity: Do something lighthearted today—dance, play, laugh, or engage in something that sparks joy.

Daily Gratitude: What made you smile today?

Let This be Enough: You let yourself play. You let joy back in without needing a reason. That is enough. That is freedom.

DAY 7

WEEKLY REFLECTION – FINDING JOY AGAIN

Reflection Questions:

1. What was the most enjoyable or surprising thing you discovered about yourself this week?
2. Did anything feel forced or not align with who you are now?
3. How can you continue making space for joy in your life?

Activity: Write yourself a permission slip to explore, play, and find what excites you. Example: *I give myself permission to try new things without pressure or expectation. I am allowed to rediscover what makes me happy.*

Daily Gratitude: What is one thing about yourself that you appreciate?

Somatic Exercise

"I give myself permission to try new things without pressure or expectation. I am allowed to rediscover what makes me happy."

Free Movement + Joy Activation

This practice helps reconnect you to aliveness and emotional release through intuitive, embodied joy.

Instructions

1. Turn on one of your favorite songs—something that lifts your spirit or brings back a sense of freedom.
2. Begin to move your body in any way that feels good. You might sway gently, stretch your arms overhead, or dance with wild abandon.
3. There's no right or wrong—just presence.
4. Let your body remember what joy feels like. Let movement rise from within, not from performance.
5. Even two minutes is enough.

Optional Reflection Prompt

What did your body remember about joy today?

Let This Be Enough:

You moved. You smiled. You felt free.

That is enough. That is healing.

WEEK 3

INTRODUCTION EMBRACING CHANGE

———··•··———

Change is uncomfortable. It forces you out of what's familiar and into the unknown. And after heartbreak, change can feel overwhelming—like everything you once knew has been stripped away, leaving you standing in unfamiliar territory. But here's something I've learned: as unsettling as change is, it's also where transformation begins.

For a long time, I resisted change. I clung to the past, hoping that if I held on tightly enough, things might return to how they once were. But the harder I fought against change, the more stuck I felt. It wasn't until I loosened my grip, until I allowed myself to embrace the shifts happening in my life, that I realized change wasn't my enemy. It was my doorway to something new.

This week is about shifting your perspective on change. Instead of seeing it as something to fear, I want you to start seeing it as something to embrace. Growth doesn't happen in comfort zones. The person you are becoming—the stronger, wiser, more confident version of you—can only emerge when you stop resisting and start allowing.

You are not meant to stay the same. You are meant to evolve. And though change may feel daunting, I promise you, it is leading you to something better.

This week, we're stepping into that truth together.

Affirmation for the Month:

"I am more than who I was in my past relationship. I embrace the journey of rediscovering myself, my passions, and my purpose."

Affirmation for the Week:

"I embrace change as an opportunity for growth. I trust that every shift in my life is guiding me toward something greater."

WEEK 3

EMBRACING CHANGE JOURNAL ACTIVITIES

—··•··—

Focus: Accepting growth, releasing old versions of yourself, and stepping into possibility.

Focus: Naming the emotions, identifying the deepest wounds, allowing yourself to grieve without judgment.

Visualization:

Close your eyes. Imagine standing at the edge of a forest path. Behind you is familiar ground—the version of you that once was. Ahead is a winding path, partially hidden, filled with unfamiliar but beautiful terrain. You feel nervous, maybe even afraid, but something inside you nudges you forward. With each step you take, you notice light breaking through the trees, revealing glimpses of new strength, confidence, and peace. You don't need to see the entire path to trust where it's leading. All you need is the courage to take the next step. You are not walking away from yourself—you are walking toward who you're becoming.

Daily Practice Reminder:

At the start of each day this week, take a moment to write down and speak aloud:

Your **monthly affirmation:** *"I am more than who I was in my past relationship. I embrace the journey of rediscovering myself, my passions, and my purpose."*

Your **weekly affirmation:** *"I embrace change as an opportunity for growth. I trust that every shift in my life is guiding me toward something greater."*

Let these words guide your healing. Repeating them daily helps shift your thoughts, build emotional resilience, and rewire your self-talk.

Daily Gratitude Reminder:

After completing your journal prompt each day, take a moment to write down 1 to 3 additional things you are grateful for. These could be people, moments, comforts, or anything that brought you peace or warmth today—no matter how small. Gratitude is a gentle yet powerful way to return to the present and remind yourself of what still supports you.

Remember, there is no right way to journal. Write as much or as little as you need. You can follow the prompts exactly or let them take you somewhere else. Let the prompts be a guide—not a rule. If your heart leads you elsewhere, follow it. These pages are yours. Let them carry what you're holding—no expectations, no perfection required.

DAY 1
RESISTANCE TO CHANGE

Quote: *"When we resist change, we resist growth."*

Journal Prompt: In what ways have you resisted change since your breakup? What fears or doubts have kept you holding on to the past?

Activity: Write down one change you've already navigated since the breakup and how it has helped you grow.

Daily Gratitude: What is one small thing about your life right now that you appreciate?

Let This be Enough: You acknowledged your fear and still showed up for growth. That is courage. That is enough.

DAY 2
OUTGROWING OLD VERSIONS OF YOURSELF

Quote: *"You can't become who you're meant to be while holding on to who you were."*

Journal Prompt: How have you changed since your relationship ended? What parts of yourself are you outgrowing?

Activity: Write a short letter to the old version of yourself, acknowledging their struggles and thanking them for getting you here.

Daily Gratitude: What is something about yourself that has improved or grown stronger?

Let This be Enough: You honored who you were and chose to keep evolving. That honoring is healing. That is enough.

DAY 3
BREAKING FREE FROM THE PAST

Quote: *"Your new life will cost you your old one."* – Brooke Hampton

Journal Prompt: Are there any habits, routines, or mindsets from your relationship that no longer serve you? How can you begin releasing them?

Activity: Make a list of things from your past that you are ready to let go of.

Daily Gratitude: What is one change you are learning to accept?

Let This be Enough: You loosened your grip on what no longer serves you. That release was an act of self-respect. That is enough.

DAY 4
EMBRACING THE UNKNOWN

Quote: *"Uncertainty is where all possibilities exist."*

Journal Prompt: Does the unknown excite or scare you? Why? How can you begin to trust the unfolding of your journey?

Activity: Write a statement of trust, affirming that you are open to whatever comes next. Example: *"I trust that what's ahead of me is better than what I've left behind."*

Daily Gratitude: What is something unexpected that turned out to be a blessing?

Let This be Enough: You opened your heart to what's next—even without all the answers. That is faith. That is enough.

DAY 5
RELEASING EXPECTATIONS

———··●··———

Quote: *"Sometimes the best things in life happen when we least expect them."*

Journal Prompt: What expectations did you have for your life and relationship that didn't unfold as planned? How can you begin embracing what is, rather than what you thought should be?

Activity: Write about a time in your life when things didn't go as planned but turned out for the better.

Daily Gratitude: What is one possibility that excites you about the future?

Let This be Enough: You let go of what should've been and made space for what could be. That surrender is strength. That is enough.

DAY 6

TRUSTING YOURSELF THROUGH TRANSITION

———··●··———

Quote: *"You've survived every change you've ever faced. You will survive this too."*

Journal Prompt: What strengths have helped you get through past challenges? How can you remind yourself that you are capable of navigating change?

Activity: List three affirmations that remind you of your resilience.

Daily Gratitude: What is something about yourself that you trust?

Let This be Enough: You leaned on your own strength and chose to believe in yourself again. That choice is a victory. That is enough.

DAY 7

WEEKLY REFLECTION – WELCOMING CHANGE

Reflection Questions:

1. How has your perspective on change shifted this week?
2. What is one area of your life where you're learning to let go?
3. What excites you about the person you're becoming?

Activity: Write a commitment to yourself about how you will approach change moving forward. Example: *"I choose to welcome change with openness and curiosity, knowing that it is shaping me into the person I am meant to be."*

Daily Gratitude: What is something about change that you are beginning to appreciate?

Somatic Exercise

"The only way to make sense out of change is to plunge into it, move with it, and join the dance." – Alan Watts

Box Breathing + Safe to Change Mantra

This rhythmic breathwork helps regulate the nervous system and reinforces the message that change can be both safe and empowering.

Instructions

1. Find a comfortable position—either lying on your back or sitting cross-legged. Close your eyes and begin box breathing:
2. Inhale for 4 seconds
3. Hold for 4 seconds
4. Exhale for 4 seconds
5. Hold for 4 seconds
6. As you breathe, repeat silently or internally: "I am safe to change."
7. Continue this pattern for 4–6 full cycles. Let each breath soften tension and invite calm.

Optional Reflection Prompt

How does your body respond when you tell it that change is safe?

Let This Be Enough:

You breathed into change. You softened into possibility.

That is enough. That is healing.

WEEK 4

INTRODUCTION
CHOOSING YOURSELF & MOVING FORWARD

—··●··—

Heartbreak has a way of making us feel uncertain—not just about love, but about ourselves. You may have spent so much time focusing on the relationship that you lost sight of your own needs, your own dreams, and your own voice. Now, without that relationship defining your path, you get to choose where you go next.

This week is about learning to trust yourself again—to listen to your own intuition, make decisions that feel right for YOU, and build a life that aligns with your true self. Healing isn't about rushing into the future or feeling pressured to have everything figured out. It's about taking small, intentional steps forward—on your own terms.

You don't have to plan your entire future right now. You don't have to know exactly where you're headed. You just have to be willing to take the next step—to choose yourself every single day, in big and small ways.

Because you are the foundation of your own happiness.

Let's step into this week with confidence.

Affirmation for the Month:

"I am more than who I was in my past relationship. I embrace the journey of rediscovering myself, my passions, and my purpose."

Affirmation for the Week:

"I trust myself to make choices that align with who I am and who I am becoming."

WEEK 4

CHOOSING YOURSELF & MOVING FORWARD JOURNAL ACTIVITIES

———··•●·· ———

Focus: Tuning into your inner voice, trusting your intuition, and taking empowered steps toward a life that reflects your truth.

Visualization:

Close your eyes. Picture yourself standing at a crossroads, holding a map. But this map doesn't show roads or cities—it shows moments where you've doubted yourself, compromised your needs, or waited for someone else's permission. Now, imagine gently folding that old map and tucking it away. In your other hand, you hold a compass—it glows softly, pulsing with your own energy. You take a breath, feel the strength in your chest, and take a step forward—not because you know exactly where the path leads, but because you trust yourself to walk it.

Daily Practice Reminder:

At the start of each day this week, take a moment to write down and speak aloud:

Your **monthly affirmation:** *"I am more than who I was in my past relationship. I embrace the journey of rediscovering myself, my passions, and my purpose."*

Your **weekly affirmation:** *"I trust myself to make choices that align with who I am and who I am becoming."*

Let these words guide your healing. Repeating them daily helps shift your thoughts, build emotional resilience, and rewire your self-talk.

Daily Gratitude Reminder:

After completing your journal prompt each day, take a moment to write down 1 to 3 additional things you are grateful for. These could be people, moments, comforts, or anything that brought you peace or warmth today—no matter how small. Gratitude is a gentle yet powerful way to return to the present and remind yourself of what still supports you.

Remember, there is no right way to journal. Write as much or as little as you need. You can follow the prompts exactly or let them take you somewhere else. Let the prompts be a guide—not a rule. If your heart leads you elsewhere, follow it. These pages are yours. Let them carry what you're holding—no expectations, no perfection required.

DAY 1

LEARNING TO TRUST YOURSELF AGAIN

Quote: *"Your intuition knows what to do. Trust it."*

Journal Prompt: Where in your life do you struggle to trust yourself? How can you begin strengthening your confidence in your own decisions?

Activity: Write a letter to your future self, offering encouragement and support.

Daily Gratitude: What is one decision you made recently that you're proud of?

Let This be Enough: You listened to your own voice today, even if just for a moment. That is trust returning. That is enough.

DAY 2

LETTING GO OF WHAT NO LONGER FITS

Quote: *"Growth requires letting go of what no longer aligns with you."*

Journal Prompt: What parts of your old life or old identity no longer serve who you are becoming?

Activity: Make a list of things—habits, beliefs, commitments—that you are ready to release.

Daily Gratitude: What is one thing you've let go of that has made space for something better?

Let This be Enough: You gave yourself permission to release what no longer serves you. That release is power. That is enough.

DAY 3

DEFINING WHAT FULFILLMENT MEANS TO YOU

———— ··●·· ————

Quote: *"Happiness is not a destination. It's a way of life."* – Burton Hills

Journal Prompt: What makes you feel fulfilled—not just in relationships, but in life?

Activity: Write down five things that bring you fulfillment and one way to incorporate them more into your daily life.

Daily Gratitude: What is one simple joy in your life right now?

Let This be Enough: You named what matters most to you. That clarity is a homecoming. That is enough.

DAY 4

TAKING OWNERSHIP OF YOUR LIFE

———— ··●·· ————

Quote: *"You are not a supporting character in someone else's story. You are the main character of your own."*

Journal Prompt: In what areas of your life do you still feel like you are waiting for permission? How can you start taking control?

Activity: Write a personal declaration: *"I take ownership of my life by _____."*

Daily Gratitude: What is one way you've taken control of your own happiness recently?

Let This be Enough: You chose yourself as the author of your story. That decision is transformation. That is enough.

DAY 5

STEPPING INTO YOUR INDEPENDENCE

Quote: *"The more you love your decisions, the less you need others to love them."*

Journal Prompt: What does independence mean to you? What areas of your life do you want to feel more independent in?

Activity: List one action you can take this week to embrace your independence.

Daily Gratitude: What is something you've done for yourself that made you feel strong?

Let This be Enough: You stood on your own and honored your choices. That strength is freedom. That is enough.

DAY 6

BECOMING THE PERSON YOU WANT TO BE

Quote: *"You are becoming. Keep going."*

Journal Prompt: What qualities do you admire in others that you would like to strengthen in yourself?

Activity: Write down three ways you can start embodying those qualities in your daily life.

Daily Gratitude: What is something about yourself that you already love?

Let This be Enough: You moved with intention toward the person you are becoming. That becoming is beautiful. That is enough.

DAY 7

WEEKLY REFLECTION – MOVING FORWARD WITH CONFIDENCE

———·· • ··———

Reflection Questions:

1. What is one thing you've learned about yourself this month?
2. How has rediscovering yourself changed the way you view your future?
3. What's one mindset shift you want to carry into next month?

Activity: Write one final statement of confidence: *"I trust myself to build a life that feels right for me."*

Daily Gratitude: What is one thing about the future that excites you?

Somatic Exercise

"With realization of one's own potential and self-confidence in one's ability, one can build a better world." – Dalai Lama

Power Pose + Embodied Strength

This posture activates confidence physically and mentally—reminding you that you are capable, grounded, and ready to step into your next chapter.

Instructions

1. Stand tall in a power pose:
2. Feet hip-width apart
3. Shoulders back
4. Hands on your hips or raised overhead in a victory stance
5. Hold this position for 1–2 minutes.
6. Breathe deeply and feel the strength in your body.
7. With each inhale, invite courage. With each exhale, release fear.
8. As you stand, silently or aloud, affirm: "I am strong. I can move forward. My body remembers my power."

Optional Reflection Prompt

What shifts when you allow your body to embody confidence?

Let This Be Enough:

You stood strong. You owned your power. You breathed into your next step.

That is enough. That is healing.

Monthly Reflection: Month 4

What emotions were most present for me this month?

When did I feel most like myself?

What part of my identity feels clearer or stronger?

A moment I'm proud of:

A quote, mantra, or affirmation I want to carry forward:

On a scale of 1–10, how connected do I feel to myself right now?

1☐ 2☐ 3☐ 4☐ 5☐ 6☐ 7☐ 8☐ 9☐ 10

What do I need more of next month?

☐ Rest

☐ Joy

☐ Connection

☐ Confidence

☐ Creativity

☐ Other: _____

One word to guide me next month:

FROM MY HEART TO YOURS: CLOSING OUT MONTH 4

Dear You,

This month was about coming home to yourself. You've taken a brave and beautiful step—not just by looking back at who you were, but by leaning into who you are becoming.

Rediscovery isn't about returning to the past. It's about unearthing the parts of you that may have been buried—your voice, your joy, your spark. It's about giving yourself permission to grow, to evolve, to shed old roles and reclaim the fullness of your identity.

You've done that here. Through reflection, curiosity, and honesty, you've begun to uncover the version of you that was never lost—only waiting to be seen again.

You may not feel completely clear yet. You may still be figuring out what excites you or what direction to take next. That's okay. This is not about arriving. This is about awakening.

As you move forward, hold onto this truth: *You are worthy of knowing yourself deeply and loving yourself completely.* You are your own greatest source of stability, wisdom, and strength. And every step you take toward yourself is a step toward healing that lasts.

Before you turn the page, give yourself space to reflect. There's no journal prompt today—just a gentle invitation to write whatever is on your heart. Let it flow. Let it be honest. Let it be yours.

Next month, we'll begin rebuilding your confidence. But you've already started. Choosing yourself this month? That's the foundation.

I'm so proud of you. Keep going.

With love and deep admiration,

Katina Lee

PS: If you find yourself drawn back to a prompt, a memory, or a moment—you're allowed to return. The pages will meet you where you are, not where you were.

Sometimes, the second time you write it... you hear yourself more clearly. That is healing too.

MONTH 05

REBUILDING CONFIDENCE – BOOK SUMMARY

Heartbreak can shake your confidence, making you question your worth and doubt your ability to move forward. This chapter is about reclaiming your inner strength, rebuilding self-esteem, and stepping back into your power. True confidence isn't about perfection or external validation—it's about recognizing your worth, setting boundaries, and believing in yourself even when doubt creeps in.

Recognizing What Shattered Your Confidence

Breakups often leave behind feelings of rejection or inadequacy, but confidence isn't defined by someone else's actions—it's built by how you see yourself. Instead of viewing past wounds as proof of your shortcomings, reframe them as opportunities for growth.

Rewriting Negative Self-Talk

Your inner critic can be relentless, but negative thoughts are not facts. Rebuilding confidence starts with challenging self-doubt and replacing it with self-affirming truths. You are not "too much" or "not enough"—you are exactly who you're meant to be.

Building Confidence Through Action

Confidence grows with small, intentional actions—setting boundaries, speaking up, or prioritizing self-care. Every time you choose yourself, you reinforce your worth.

Reclaiming Your Voice and Setting Boundaries

Losing confidence often stems from silencing yourself to keep the peace. Reclaiming your voice means honoring your truth, even when it's uncomfortable. Clear boundaries teach both you and others that your needs and feelings matter.

The Power of Self-Care and Positive Surroundings

How you treat yourself and who you surround yourself with impact your confidence. Supportive relationships, affirmations, movement, and creativity all reinforce self-worth and remind you of your strength.

Embracing Your Unique Strengths

You were never meant to shrink for someone else's comfort. Confidence comes from fully owning your quirks, passions, and dreams. What makes you different is what makes you powerful.

By the end of this chapter, you'll have taken intentional steps to rebuild confidence—not by becoming someone new, but by rediscovering and honoring the strong, capable person you already are.

Reflection Question: How can I actively rebuild my confidence this month by celebrating my strengths and stepping outside my comfort zone?

REBUILDING CONFIDENCE – MONTH JOURNAL INTRODUCTION

"You don't have to be fearless. You just have to keep showing up." – **Unknown**

After heartbreak, self-doubt can creep in, making you question your worth, your choices, and your ability to move forward. This month is about reclaiming your confidence—not by becoming someone new, but by recognizing the strength that was within you all along.

Confidence isn't built overnight. It's developed through small, intentional actions that remind you of your power. This chapter will help you break free from self-doubt, rebuild trust in yourself, and step into a mindset of self-assurance. Through daily reflection, boundary-setting, and small acts of courage, you'll begin to see yourself through a new lens—one of strength, resilience, and self-belief.

What to Expect This Month:

✓ Week 1: Recognizing What Broke Your Confidence – Identifying patterns, past wounds, and limiti beliefs

✓ Week 2: Rewriting Your Inner Narrative – Reframing self-doubt, embracing self-affirmation, and practicing self-compassion

Week 3: Taking Bold Steps – Challenging yourself to step outside your comfort zone and reclaim your voice

✓ Week 4: Building Lasting Confidence – Strengthening boundaries, maintaining self-respect, and reinforcing personal growth

Each day, you'll engage in journaling prompts and exercises designed to help you rebuild your self-worth and self-trust. By the end of this month, you will have taken significant steps toward feeling confident, capable, and proud of who you are.

Affirmation for the Month:

"I am strong, capable, and worthy of love and success. Every step I take is a step toward the confident and empowered person I am becoming."

WEEK 1

INTRODUCTION

RECOGNIZING WHAT BROKE YOUR CONFIDENCE

Confidence isn't something you lose overnight. It erodes slowly—through small moments, careless words, and experiences that make you question yourself. Sometimes, it's obvious: a relationship where you felt unappreciated, a betrayal that left you doubting your worth, or words spoken in anger that stuck in your mind long after they were said. Other times, it's subtle: repeated disappointments, being overlooked, or staying quiet to keep the peace.

Heartbreak has a way of magnifying those doubts. The ending of a relationship can leave you questioning everything—Was I not enough? Did I do something wrong? Will I ever feel confident again? If you've had these thoughts, you're not alone. But the truth is, your worth was never tied to their ability to see it.

This week is about looking at the moments, patterns, and experiences that shook your confidence. Not to dwell in them, but to understand them—to see them clearly so you can take back the power they stole from you. By identifying what chipped away at your confidence, you can start reclaiming it, piece by piece.

You do not have to stay in this place of doubt. Confidence is something you can rebuild. And it starts right here.

Affirmation for the Month:

"I am strong, capable, and worthy of love and success. Every step I take is a step toward the confident and empowered person I am becoming."

Affirmation for the Week:

"I release the doubts that were never mine to carry. I am learning to trust and believe in myself again."

WEEK 1

RECOGNIZING WHAT BROKE YOUR CONFIDENCE

JOURNAL ACTIVITIES

———··•··———

Focus: Identifying past wounds, limiting beliefs, and patterns that contributed to self-doubt.

Visualization:

Close your eyes and take a deep breath.

Picture yourself walking down a hallway of mirrors, each one reflecting moments when your confidence wavered. You see your younger self—silent, unsure, questioning her worth.

Now imagine a warm light behind you. As it grows, the reflections shift. You begin to see strength, resilience, and quiet courage in your past self.

At the end of the hallway is a single mirror. This one shows who you are now—powerful, kind, and worthy.

Breathe her in. She is you.

Daily Practice Reminder:

At the start of each day this week, take a moment to write down and speak aloud:

Your **monthly affirmation:** *"I am strong, capable, and worthy of love and success. Every step I take is a step toward the confident and empowered person I am becoming."*

Your **weekly affirmation:** *"I release the doubts that were never mine to carry. I am learning to trust and believe in myself again."*

Let these words guide your healing. Repeating them daily helps shift your thoughts, build emotional resilience, and rewire your self-talk.

🌿 Daily Gratitude Reminder:

After completing your journal prompt each day, take a moment to write down 1 to 3 additional things you are grateful for. These could be people, moments, comforts, or anything that brought you peace or warmth today—no matter how small. Gratitude is a gentle yet powerful way to return to the present and remind yourself of what still supports you.

Remember, there is no right way to journal. Write as much or as little as you need. You can follow the prompts exactly or let them take you somewhere else. Let the prompts be a guide—not a rule. If your heart leads you elsewhere, follow it. These pages are yours. Let them carry what you're holding—no expectations, no perfection required.

DAY 1

THE CONFIDENCE SHAKERS

—··•··—

Quote: *"You've been criticizing yourself for years, and it hasn't worked. Try approving of yourself and see what happens."* – Louise Hay

Journal Prompt: What experiences or words have made you doubt yourself the most? How did they shape the way you see yourself?

Activity: Write down three negative beliefs you've carried about yourself. Cross them out and rewrite them as empowering truths.

Daily Gratitude: What is one thing about yourself that you are proud of today?

Let This be Enough: You faced the story that made you shrink, and you chose a new one. That courage is healing. That is enough.

DAY 2

THE POWER OF WORDS

—··•··—

Quote: *"The way we talk to ourselves matters."*

Journal Prompt: Have there been words spoken to you (or by you) that left a lasting impact on your confidence? How have they shaped your self-image?

Activity: Write a letter to yourself, using only kind and supportive words. Read it out loud.

Daily Gratitude: What is one inner strength you possess?

Let This be Enough: You spoke to yourself with tenderness today. That shift in tone is the beginning of change. That is enough.

DAY 3
THEIR ACTIONS, YOUR WORTH

Quote: *"Someone else's inability to love you does not mean you are unlovable."*

Journal Prompt: Have you ever tied your confidence to how someone treated you? How can you start separating your worth from their actions?

Activity: Write down five qualities about yourself that have nothing to do with your past relationships. These are yours, no matter what anyone else thinks.

Daily Gratitude: What is one thing you love about who you are becoming?

Let This be Enough: You remembered that your value doesn't depend on anyone else. That knowing is power. That is enough.

DAY 4
BREAKING FREE FROM THE PAST

Quote: *"You are not what happened to you. You are what you choose to become."* – Carl Jung

Journal Prompt: What old stories about yourself are you still carrying that no longer serve you?

Activity: Rewrite one of these stories into an empowering truth. Example: "I wasn't enough" becomes "I was always enough, even if they couldn't see it."

Daily Gratitude: What is one lesson from your past that has made you stronger?

Let This be Enough: You released a story that was never yours to carry. That release is freedom. That is enough.

DAY 5
RELEASING THE WEIGHT OF SELF-DOUBT

Quote: *"Confidence isn't about having all the answers. It's about trusting yourself even when you don't."*

Journal Prompt: What is one area of your life where you second-guess yourself the most? Why?

Activity: Make a "confidence jar." Write down small wins, compliments, or things you love about yourself on slips of paper. Add to it throughout the month.

Daily Gratitude: What is something you accomplished recently that made you feel good?

Let This be Enough: You chose self-trust over self-doubt—even just for a moment. That moment matters. That is enough.

DAY 6
LOOKING AT YOURSELF WITH LOVE

Quote: *"Talk to yourself like someone you love."* – Brené Brown

Journal Prompt: If you saw yourself through the eyes of someone who loves you, what would you see?

Activity: Stand in front of a mirror, look yourself in the eyes, and say: "I am worthy. I am enough. I am learning to believe in myself again."

Daily Gratitude: What is something about your personality that you appreciate?

Let This be Enough: You saw yourself through softer eyes. That tenderness is transformation. That is enough.

DAY 7

WEEKLY REFLECTION – LETTING GO OF DOUBT

Reflection Questions:

1. What patterns or beliefs about yourself did you recognize this week?
2. What are you ready to let go of?
3. How did it feel to challenge your self-doubt?

Activity: Write a commitment to yourself: "I choose to believe in myself. I am enough as I am." Read it out loud.

Daily Gratitude: What is one thing you are beginning to believe about yourself again?

Somatic Exercise

"Believe you can and you're halfway there." – Theodore Roosevelt

Shoulder Sweep + Confidence Breath

This somatic exercise clears stored tension from the shoulders and uses breath and movement to calm the nervous system—supporting emotional release and confidence restoration.

Instructions

1. Stand or sit comfortably. Begin by gently rolling your shoulders:
2. Roll back three times.
3. Roll forward three times.
4. Inhale deeply as you raise your shoulders up toward your ears.
5. Exhale with an audible sigh as you let them drop.
6. Repeat this movement 3–5 times to release tension.
7. Now, using both hands, gently brush down each arm—starting at your shoulders and sweeping down to your fingertips.
8. As you do, say aloud: "I release the doubts that were never mine to carry."

Optional Reflection Prompt

What did your body feel like after releasing doubt through movement?

Let This Be Enough:

You released the weight of doubt. You made space for belief.

That is enough. That is healing.

WEEK 2

INTRODUCTION
REWRITING YOUR INNER NARRATIVE

---·· •·· ---

Confidence isn't just about how the world sees you—it's about how you see yourself. The words you tell yourself daily shape the way you move through life. If your inner voice is filled with self-doubt, shame, or negativity, it becomes impossible to build confidence. But here's the good news: your inner dialogue is not fixed. It can be rewritten.

For many of us, self-doubt doesn't come from nowhere. It's built over time, shaped by the experiences we've had, the words people have spoken over us, and the relationships that made us feel small. If we aren't careful, we start to believe these false stories. "I'm not good enough." "I'm too much." "I'll never be truly loved." These thoughts settle into our subconscious, creating a script we repeat to ourselves—a script that was never ours to begin with.

But just because you've believed something for a long time doesn't mean it's true. This week, we're challenging those false narratives. We're looking at the stories you've been telling yourself and replacing them with truths that reflect who you really are.

You are not your past. You are not the words someone else used to define you. You are powerful, worthy, and capable of rewriting your story.

One of the most powerful tools I discovered during my own healing was learning to name my inner critic. I call her Nancy—short for "Negative Nancy." She pops up with all the usual doubts: "Are you sure you're good enough?" "This is going to fail." "Why even try?"

Instead of trying to silence her completely, I've learned to talk to her with compassion: "Thanks for your concern, Nancy, but we're doing things differently now." "I appreciate you trying to keep me safe, but I don't need fear to guide me anymore."

Giving that voice a name helped me separate those thoughts from my identity. They became just thoughts—not truths. You can try this too. Give your inner critic a name. Make her a character. Speak to her kindly, but firmly. You're the one in charge now.

This week, as you begin to rewrite your inner narrative, remember: you're not trying to become someone you're not. You're coming home to who you've always been—before the world taught you to doubt it.

Affirmation for the Month:

"I am strong, capable, and worthy of love and success. Every step I take is a step toward the confident and empowered person I am becoming."

Affirmation for the Week:

"I choose to rewrite my story with love and self-respect. My voice is powerful, and my worth is undeniable."

WEEK 2

REWRITING YOUR INNER NARRATIVE JOURNAL ACTIVITIES

——— ··•·· ———

Focus: Challenging self-doubt, replacing negative self-talk, and building a mindset of self-belief.

Focus: Naming the emotions, identifying the deepest wounds, allowing yourself to grieve without judgment.

Visualization:

Find a quiet space where you won't be disturbed. Sit comfortably, close your eyes, and take three deep breaths. Imagine yourself walking into a beautiful, peaceful room filled with soft golden light. In front of you stands an ornate, full-length mirror. But this isn't an ordinary mirror—this one doesn't reflect what others have said about you or the doubts you've held onto. This mirror shows only truth.

As you stand before it, you begin to see your reflection shift. The critical voice quiets. You see yourself with kindness, strength, and compassion. You see the version of you who knows her worth—who is no longer held back by old stories or self-doubt.

Now imagine the mirror whispering your new truth: *"You are worthy. You are enough. You are rewriting your story with love."*

Take a moment to absorb this truth, then slowly open your eyes and return to the present. Carry this image of your reflection with you throughout the week.

Daily Practice Reminder:

At the start of each day this week, take a moment to write down and speak aloud:

Your **monthly affirmation:** *"I am strong, capable, and worthy of love and success. Every step I take is a step toward the confident and empowered person I am becoming."*

Your **weekly affirmation:** *"I choose to rewrite my story with love and self-respect. My voice is powerful, and my worth is undeniable."*

Let these words guide your healing. Repeating them daily helps shift your thoughts, build emotional resilience, and rewire your self-talk.

Daily Gratitude Reminder:

After completing your journal prompt each day, take a moment to write down 1 to 3 additional things you are grateful for. These could be people, moments, comforts, or anything that brought you peace or warmth today—no matter how small. Gratitude is a gentle yet powerful way to return to the present and remind yourself of what still supports you.

Remember, there is no right way to journal. Write as much or as little as you need. You can follow the prompts exactly or let them take you somewhere else. Let the prompts be a guide—not a rule. If your heart leads you elsewhere, follow it. These pages are yours. Let them carry what you're holding—no expectations, no perfection required.

DAY 1

CHALLENGING THE LIES YOU'VE BELIEVED

— ··•·· —

Quote: *"Don't believe everything you think."*

Journal Prompt: What negative beliefs have you carried about yourself that you now realize may not be true?

Activity: Write down three self-doubting thoughts and challenge them with truth. Example: "I'm not lovable" → "I deserve deep and healthy love."

Daily Gratitude: What is one strength you recognize in yourself?

Let This be Enough: You showed up. You listened inward. You honored your process. That is enough. That is healing.

DAY 2

THE POWER OF WORDS

— ··•·· —

Quote: *"What you tell yourself every day will either lift you up or tear you down."*

Journal Prompt: How do you usually speak to yourself? If a friend spoke to you that way, would it feel supportive or hurtful?

Activity: Write a love letter to yourself. Fill it with encouragement, kindness, and reminders of your worth.

Daily Gratitude: What is one part of your body or mind that you are thankful for today?

Let This be Enough: You spoke to yourself with compassion today. That kindness is a seed—water it often. That is enough.

DAY 3
FLIPPING THE SCRIPT

Quote: *"You've been criticizing yourself for years, and it hasn't worked. Try approving of yourself and see what happens."* – Louise Hay

Journal Prompt: What is one recurring thought that makes you doubt yourself? How can you reframe it into something positive?

Activity: Each time a self-doubting thought appears today, consciously replace it with a positive one.

Daily Gratitude: What is something you love about your personality?

Let This be Enough: You challenged an old thought and chose a better one. That shift matters. That is enough.

DAY 4
SPEAKING TO YOURSELF WITH LOVE

Quote: *"Be careful how you talk to yourself, because you are always listening."*

Journal Prompt: What words of encouragement do you wish you had heard more often? Write them down and say them to yourself.

Activity: Stand in front of a mirror, look yourself in the eyes, and say three kind things about yourself.

Daily Gratitude: What is one small victory you had this week?

Let This be Enough: You gave yourself the words you've always needed. That self-honoring is everything. That is enough.

DAY 5
YOUR INNER CHILD STILL LISTENS

Quote: *"The way we talk to our children becomes their inner voice. The same is true for how we speak to ourselves."*

Journal Prompt: Imagine speaking to yourself as if you were a child who needed love and reassurance. What would you say?

Activity: Write a letter to your younger self, offering them love and kindness.

Daily Gratitude: What childhood dream or passion do you still carry with you?

Let This be Enough: You reached back and offered love to the younger you. That tenderness is healing. That is enough.

DAY 6
CREATING A PERSONAL MANTRA

Quote: *"Affirmations aren't magic, but they change the way you see yourself over time."*

Journal Prompt: If you had to create a mantra to remind yourself of your worth, what would it be?

Activity: Write your mantra down and place it somewhere you will see it every day.

Daily Gratitude: What is something you are looking forward to?

Let This be Enough: You gave your worth a voice—and promised to keep speaking it. That promise is powerful. That is enough.

DAY 7
WEEKLY REFLECTION – EMBRACING A NEW STORY

Reflection Questions:

1. What negative thoughts did you recognize this week?
2. How did it feel to challenge them?
3. What words will you choose to define yourself moving forward?

Activity: Write a declaration to yourself: "I am rewriting my story with love and confidence." Say it out loud.

Daily Gratitude: What is one thing you are starting to believe about yourself again?

Somatic Exercise

"The stories we tell ourselves shape the lives we live." – Brené Brown

Mirror Breath + Heart Touch

This practice uses breath, touch, and direct eye contact to shift your inner narrative—rewiring your self-talk through presence and self-recognition.

Instructions

1. Stand in front of a mirror. Place one hand gently over your heart.
2. Close your eyes and take three slow, intentional breaths:
3. Inhale through your nose.
4. Exhale through your mouth.
5. Open your eyes. While keeping your hand on your heart, speak your chosen affirmation aloud.
6. Example: "I am rewriting my story with love and confidence."
7. After speaking your affirmation, gently tap your chest three times to help anchor the words into your body.

Optional Reflection Prompt

What shifts when you look into your own eyes and speak truth with love?

Let This Be Enough:

You spoke to yourself with love. You reclaimed your voice.

That is enough. That is healing.

WEEK 3

INTRODUCTION TAKING BOLD STEPS

———•··•●•··———

Confidence isn't just something you think about—it's something you build through action. No matter how much we rewrite our inner narrative, self-belief grows strongest when we step outside our comfort zone and prove to ourselves that we are capable.

But taking bold steps doesn't mean you have to do something extreme or reckless. It's about choosing yourself in small, meaningful ways. It's about speaking up when you'd normally stay silent, setting boundaries even when it's uncomfortable, or trying something new despite the fear of failure. Each time you do something that pushes you beyond your doubts, you strengthen your belief in yourself.

For a long time, I thought confidence was something people were born with—something I lacked. But I've learned that confidence isn't a feeling that magically appears; it's a muscle that grows every time you use it. The more you act with courage, the more confident you become.

This week, I want you to take action—not just in your thoughts, but in your choices. You don't have to feel fully ready. You just have to be willing to take one small step forward. Because confidence isn't about eliminating fear—it's about doing it anyway.

Affirmation for the Month:

"I am strong, capable, and worthy of love and success. Every step I take is a step toward the confident and empowered person I am becoming."

Affirmation for the Week:

"I grow more confident with every step I take. My actions reflect my strength, courage, and self-worth."

WEEK 3

TAKING BOLD STEPS JOURNAL ACTIVITIES

—— ··•·· ——

Focus: Stepping outside your comfort zone, taking small risks, and proving to yourself that you are capable.

Visualization:

Close your eyes and take a few deep, grounding breaths. Picture yourself standing at the edge of a wide canyon. On the other side is the version of you who has stepped fully into her power—confident, radiant, and unafraid to take up space. Between you and her is a sturdy bridge.

As you take your first step, you feel unsure, maybe even scared. But each plank beneath your feet glows with light as you walk—each one built from your courage, your choices, your willingness to show up for yourself. With every step forward, you feel your posture rise and your heart open.

When you reach the other side, stand tall. Look back at how far you've come, then forward toward all that awaits. Say to yourself: *"I am brave. I am moving forward. My confidence grows with every step."*

Open your eyes and hold onto that feeling of momentum and self-trust.

Daily Practice Reminder:

At the start of each day this week, take a moment to write down and speak aloud:

Your **monthly affirmation:** *"I am strong, capable, and worthy of love and success. Every step I take is a step toward the confident and empowered person I am becoming."*

Your **weekly affirmation:** *"I grow more confident with every step I take. My actions reflect my strength, courage, and self-worth."*

Let these words guide your healing. Repeating them daily helps shift your thoughts, build emotional resilience, and rewire your self-talk.

Daily Gratitude Reminder:

After completing your journal prompt each day, take a moment to write down 1 to 3 additional things you are grateful for. These could be people, moments, comforts, or anything that brought you peace or warmth today—no matter how small. Gratitude is a gentle yet powerful way to return to the present and remind yourself of what still supports you.

Remember, there is no right way to journal. Write as much or as little as you need. You can follow the prompts exactly or let them take you somewhere else. Let the prompts be a guide—not a rule. If your

heart leads you elsewhere, follow it. These pages are yours. Let them carry what you're holding—no expectations, no perfection required.

DAY 1
CONFIDENCE COMES FROM ACTION

Quote: *"You don't have to be fearless. You just have to take the next step."*

Journal Prompt: Think of a time you did something that scared you. How did it turn out?

Activity: Do something small today that pushes you out of your comfort zone—anything from speaking up in a conversation to trying something new.

Daily Gratitude: What past experience has helped shape your resilience?

Let This be Enough: You showed up. You listened inward. You honored your process. That is enough. That is healing.

DAY 2
FACING FEAR AND DOING IT ANYWAY

Quote: *"Everything you want is on the other side of fear."* – Jack Canfield

Journal Prompt: What is one thing you've been avoiding because of fear or self-doubt?

Activity: Write a plan for how you can take one small step toward facing that fear.

Daily Gratitude: What part of your personality makes you strong?

Let This be Enough: You named your fear and made a plan. That courage, even in its smallest form, is everything. That is enough.

DAY 3

EMBRACING THE POSSIBILITY OF FAILURE

— ··•·· —

Quote: *"Failure is not the opposite of success—it's part of success."*

Journal Prompt: What is something you didn't do because you were afraid to fail? What did you miss out on by not trying?

Activity: Reframe failure as a lesson. Write down one thing you've "failed" at and the lesson it taught you.

Daily Gratitude: What challenge in your life turned out to be a blessing?

Let This be Enough: You looked at failure with new eyes today. In that shift, you reclaimed power. That is enough.

DAY 4

RECLAIMING YOUR POWER IN RELATIONSHIPS

— ··•·· —

Quote: *"Confidence is not 'They will like me.' Confidence is 'I'll be okay even if they don't.'"*

Journal Prompt: When in your past relationship did you ignore your own needs or silence your voice?

Activity: Write a statement of empowerment: "I will no longer shrink myself to make someone else comfortable." Say it out loud.

Daily Gratitude: What boundary have you set that has protected your peace?

Let This be Enough: You honored your voice and declared your worth. That boldness is healing. That is enough.

DAY 5
TAKING UP SPACE WITHOUT APOLOGY

Quote: *"You have every right to be exactly who you are."*

Journal Prompt: Have you ever felt like you needed to make yourself smaller—physically, emotionally, or intellectually—to fit in?

Activity: Do something today that makes you feel bold and unafraid—wear something you love, speak your mind, or take up space without apology.

Daily Gratitude: What is one thing that makes you unique?

Let This be Enough: You chose not to shrink. You showed up as your full self. That presence is more than enough.

DAY 6
CONFIDENCE THROUGH SELF-RESPECT

Quote: *"Confidence isn't walking into a room thinking you're better than everyone. It's walking in without needing to compare yourself at all."*

Journal Prompt: What is one way you can show yourself respect this week?

Activity: Make a promise to yourself and keep it—whether it's waking up early, staying off social media, or choosing self-care over people-pleasing.

Daily Gratitude: What choice have you made that made you proud?

Let This be Enough: You kept a promise to yourself. In that small act, you built trust. That is enough.

DAY 7
WEEKLY REFLECTION – THE POWER OF BOLD ACTION

Reflection Questions:

1. What bold steps did you take this week?
2. How did acting despite fear make you feel?
3. What is one way you will continue stepping outside your comfort zone?

Activity: Write a letter to your future self about the courage you showed this week.

Daily Gratitude: What new belief about yourself are you beginning to trust?

Somatic Exercise

"You gain strength, courage and confidence by every experience in which you really stop to look fear in the face." – Eleanor Roosevelt

Courage Walk – Visualization + Movement

This simple movement practice grounds your confidence in action, reinforcing your courage through repetition, posture, and visualization.

Instructions

1. Stand tall and begin to walk slowly in a straight line across your space.
2. As you move, visualize yourself crossing the bridge from your week 3 visualization—the one leading to your most confident, empowered self.
3. With each step, repeat aloud or silently:
4. "I am brave."
5. "I move forward."
6. "My confidence grows."
7. Walk with presence and intention for at least 1–2 minutes.
8. At the end, pause. Place your hands on your hips in a power pose, take a deep breath, and smile gently.

Optional Reflection Prompt

How did your body feel as you walked with courage?

Let This Be Enough:

You moved forward. You owned your bravery. You made fear your companion—not your cage.

That is enough. That is healing.

WEEK 4

INTRODUCTION BUILDING LASTING CONFIDENCE

Confidence isn't something you gain once and never have to think about again—it's a lifelong practice. It's a commitment to choosing yourself, even when doubt creeps in. It's about trusting your ability to handle whatever life brings and knowing that your worth is not up for debate.

But confidence isn't just about how you feel—it's about how you show up for yourself. It's about setting boundaries, prioritizing your well-being, and reinforcing your self-worth through daily choices. The way you speak to yourself, the people you surround yourself with, and the actions you take every day all shape the confidence you carry.

This week is about strengthening what you've built. You've identified what broke your confidence, rewritten the negative stories, and taken bold steps toward believing in yourself again. Now, it's time to make it last. Confidence isn't about never feeling insecure—it's about knowing how to support yourself when doubt arises.

The strongest confidence comes from trusting yourself. Trusting that you are capable. Trusting that you are worthy. Trusting that even when challenges come, you will not abandon yourself.

Let's make that confidence unshakable.

Affirmation for the Month:

"I am strong, capable, and worthy of love and success. Every step I take is a step toward the confident and empowered person I am becoming."

Affirmation for the Week:

"My confidence is unshakable because it is built on self-trust, self-respect, and self-love."

WEEK 4

BUILDING LASTING CONFIDENCE JOURNAL ACTIVITIES

———··•··———

Focus: Strengthening boundaries, reinforcing self-worth, and creating habits that support confidence.

Visualization:

Begin by sitting comfortably and closing your eyes. Breathe in deeply and slowly exhale. In your mind's eye, see a small flame glowing gently in the center of your chest. This is your inner confidence—your self-trust, your resilience, your truth.

With each breath, the flame grows stronger—not wild or uncontrollable, but steady and calm. It lights up the darkest corners of your doubt. It warms the places that felt forgotten. It glows with every time you honored a boundary, spoke kindly to yourself, or chose self-respect over self-sacrifice.

Feel the warmth radiate from this flame and know that it can never be extinguished—not by fear, not by failure, not by anyone's opinion. This is yours.

Take one more deep breath and say to yourself: *"My confidence comes from within. I trust myself to keep this flame burning."* When you're ready, open your eyes and step into your day with that warmth in your heart.

Daily Practice Reminder:

At the start of each day this week, take a moment to write down and speak aloud:

Your **monthly affirmation:** *"I am strong, capable, and worthy of love and success. Every step I take is a step toward the confident and empowered person I am becoming."*

Your **weekly affirmation:** *"My confidence is unshakable because it is built on self-trust, self-respect, and self-love."*

Let these words guide your healing. Repeating them daily helps shift your thoughts, build emotional resilience, and rewire your self-talk.

Daily Gratitude Reminder:

After completing your journal prompt each day, take a moment to write down 1 to 3 additional things you are grateful for. These could be people, moments, comforts, or anything that brought you peace or warmth today—no matter how small. Gratitude is a gentle yet powerful way to return to the present and remind yourself of what still supports you.

Remember, there is no right way to journal. Write as much or as little as you need. You can follow the prompts exactly or let them take you somewhere else. Let the prompts be a guide—not a rule. If your

heart leads you elsewhere, follow it. These pages are yours. Let them carry what you're holding—no expectations, no perfection required.

DAY 1
SELF-TRUST AS THE ROOT OF CONFIDENCE

Quote: *"The best way to build confidence is to keep the promises you make to yourself."*

Journal Prompt: What is one promise you can make to yourself this week?

Activity: Follow through on one commitment today—big or small—to prove to yourself that you can trust yourself.

Daily Gratitude: What personal strength do you appreciate most?

Let This be Enough: You showed up for yourself today. One promise kept becomes a foundation. That is enough.

DAY 2
BOUNDARIES THAT PROTECT YOUR CONFIDENCE

Quote: *"Confidence is knowing your worth and never settling for less than you deserve."*

Journal Prompt: What is one boundary you've struggled to maintain? How has that impacted your confidence?

Activity: Write a statement of commitment to enforcing that boundary moving forward.

Daily Gratitude: What boundary have you set that made you feel strong?

Let This be Enough: You honored your worth by defending your peace. That act of self-respect is more than enough.

DAY 3
SPEAKING TO YOURSELF WITH KINDNESS

Quote: *"Talk to yourself like someone you love."* – Brené Brown

Journal Prompt: What negative self-talk patterns do you catch yourself repeating?

Activity: Write three self-affirming statements to counteract those negative thoughts. Read them out loud.

Daily Gratitude: What is one thing you genuinely like about yourself?

Let This be Enough: You changed the conversation within. That shift rewrites everything. That is enough.

DAY 4
THE CONFIDENCE OF SAYING NO

Quote: *"Saying no to others is saying yes to yourself."*

Journal Prompt: Have you ever said yes to something when you really wanted to say no? How did it make you feel?

Activity: Practice saying no today, even in small ways.

Daily Gratitude: What is something you've done for yourself recently that made you feel good?

Let This be Enough: You chose yourself without apology. That "no" was a bold step toward freedom. That is enough.

DAY 5
SURROUNDING YOURSELF WITH THE RIGHT PEOPLE

Quote: *"Confidence is contagious. Surround yourself with those who lift you up."*

Journal Prompt: Who in your life makes you feel confident and supported? Who drains your confidence?

Activity: Make a conscious effort to spend time or connect with someone who uplifts you.

Daily Gratitude: Who in your life has been a positive influence on your self-worth?

Let This be Enough: You chose connection that uplifts, not depletes. That choice honors your growth. That is enough.

DAY 6
CREATING CONFIDENCE RITUALS

Quote: *"Confidence is built daily, not all at once."*

Journal Prompt: What is one daily habit you can implement to reinforce confidence?

Activity: Design a morning confidence ritual—this could be affirmations, a power song, journaling, or anything that sets a confident tone for your day.

Daily Gratitude: What daily habit has had the biggest positive impact on your healing?

Let This be Enough: You built something steady and sacred for yourself. That consistency is powerful. That is enough.

DAY 7
WEEKLY REFLECTION – A STRONGER, MORE CONFIDENT YOU

Reflection Questions:

1. What was the most powerful lesson you learned about confidence this month?
2. How have you changed from when you started this journey?
3. What are three things you can remind yourself of on days when self-doubt creeps in?

Activity: Write yourself a note of encouragement to read anytime you need a confidence boost.

Daily Gratitude: What is one thing about yourself that you will never doubt again?

Somatic Exercise

"Confidence comes not from always being right but from not fearing to be wrong." – Peter T. McIntyre

Confidence Flame Breath + Grounding Touch

This practice uses breath, imagery, and physical touch to anchor a sense of confidence deeply into your body.

Instructions

1. Sit comfortably and close your eyes. Place both hands over your solar plexus—just above your navel.
2. Visualize the golden flame from this week's visualization: a steady, glowing light at the center of your being.
3. Breathe deeply and slowly.
4. On each inhale: Imagine the flame glowing brighter.
5. On each exhale: Feel the warmth strengthen your spine, your posture, your voice.
6. Continue for 1–2 minutes, allowing the rhythm of your breath to feed this inner fire.
7. When you're ready to close, gently press your feet into the ground and say aloud: "My confidence comes from within. I am grounded in who I am."

Optional Reflection Prompt

What did your inner flame feel like today?

Let This Be Enough:

You tended your fire. You stood in your strength.

That is enough. That is healing.

Monthly Reflection: Month 5

What emotions were most present for me this month?

What made it hard to allow joy?

What reminded me that joy is still possible?

A moment I'm proud of:

A quote, mantra, or affirmation I want to carry forward:

On a scale of 1–10, how connected do I feel to myself right now?

1 ☐ 2 ☐ 3 ☐ 4 ☐ 5 ☐ 6 ☐ 7 ☐ 8 ☐ 9 ☐ 10

What do I need more of next month?

☐ Rest

☐ Joy

☐ Connection

☐ Confidence

☐ Creativity

☐ Other: _____

One word to guide me next month:

FROM MY HEART TO YOURS: CLOSING OUT MONTH 5

Dear You,

Confidence isn't something you find—it's something you build. And this month, that's exactly what you did.

Confidence is not about always having the right words or never feeling insecure again. It's about trusting yourself to show up, even when it's hard. It's standing in front of the mirror, looking yourself in the eye, and deciding—sometimes quietly, sometimes boldly—*I believe in me.*

Throughout this chapter, you've taken intentional steps to silence your inner critic, reclaim your voice, and reinforce your self-worth. You've drawn boundaries, challenged doubt, and taken action from a place of strength. And even on the days when it felt shaky, you showed up anyway. That's what confidence truly is.

There will still be days when insecurity whispers. But now, you have a deeper truth to lean on. You are capable. You are powerful. You are worthy. And no one—not even the past version of you—can take that away.

This isn't just a chapter of your healing—it's a turning point. A foundation you'll continue to stand on as you move forward with clarity, strength, and self-trust.

Before you begin month 6, take a moment to breathe and reflect. There's no journal prompt today—just space. Let your heart speak freely. Let your pen move without a plan. You've earned this moment of pause.

Keep believing in yourself. You're doing more than you think.

With confidence and love,

Katina Lee

PS: If you find yourself drawn back to a prompt, a memory, or a moment—you're allowed to return. The pages will meet you where you are, not where you were.

Sometimes, the second time you write it... you hear yourself more clearly. That is healing too.

MONTH 06

EMBRACING INDEPENDENCE – BOOK SUMMARY

Heartbreak can leave you feeling lost, as if a piece of you is missing. But independence isn't about being alone—it's about standing strong on your own, trusting yourself, and creating a fulfilling life on your terms. This chapter is about reclaiming your personal power and embracing the freedom to shape your future without relying on external validation.

Redefining Independence

Independence isn't isolation—it's learning to rely on yourself emotionally, mentally, and physically. It's about knowing that while relationships add value, they don't define your worth. By making daily choices that reinforce self-trust, you rewire your brain for confidence and self-sufficiency.

From Loneliness to Empowerment

Solitude may feel like an absence at first, but it's actually an opportunity for self-discovery. Rather than focusing on what's missing, shift your mindset to what you're gaining—clarity, peace, and the ability to make decisions that align with your true desires.

Breaking Free from Codependency

Love should complement, not complete you. True confidence comes from within, not from someone else's validation. This chapter will help you cultivate self-trust and emotional independence.

Owning Your Space and Time

Without the influence of a partner, you now have the freedom to focus on what truly brings you joy. Use this time to explore new interests and reclaim your sense of self.

Building Emotional Independence

True independence means managing your emotions without depending on someone else to fix or validate them. Self-soothing techniques, boundary-setting, and emotional regulation will help you process feelings in a way that strengthens rather than depletes you.

Finding Joy in Solitude

Independence isn't just self-sufficiency—it's learning to enjoy your own company. By embracing solitude, you'll build confidence, inner peace, and a deeper connection with yourself.

Reflection Question: How can I shift my mindset from seeing solitude as loneliness to embracing it as an opportunity for growth and self-discovery?

EMBRACING INDEPENDENCE – MONTH JOURNAL INTRODUCTION

―――― ··●·· ――――

"Your happiness does not depend on someone else. It begins with you." – **Unknown**

Independence after a breakup can feel both freeing and overwhelming. Whether you were deeply intertwined with your partner's life or simply accustomed to shared routines, stepping into your independence is a journey of self-discovery and empowerment. This month is about reclaiming your autonomy, learning to enjoy your own company, and building a life that feels whole—whether or not someone else is in it.

Independence isn't just about being alone; it's about becoming self-sufficient in your happiness, your decisions, and your sense of fulfillment. This chapter will guide you in building confidence in your independence, exploring what brings you joy on your own, and cultivating a life that feels complete within yourself.

What to Expect This Month:

✓ Week 1: Embracing Solitude – Learning to enjoy your own company and strengthening self-reliance

✓ Week 2: Taking Ownership of Your Life – Releasing reliance on external validation and making empowered choices

✓ Week 3: Exploring New Possibilities – Trying new experiences, setting personal goals, and stepping into independence

✓ Week 4: Cultivating Inner Strength – Trusting yourself, prioritizing self-care, and reinforcing your ability to thrive alone

Each day, you'll engage in activities and reflections that encourage independence, self-sufficiency, and joy in your own presence. By the end of this month, you will have built a deeper sense of confidence in your ability to stand strong on your own.

Affirmation for the Month:

"I am complete on my own. My happiness is not dependent on anyone else—I am building a life that is fulfilling, joyful, and uniquely mine."

WEEK 1
INTRODUCTION EMBRACING SOLITUDE

There's a difference between being alone and being lonely. At first, solitude might feel like an emptiness—something missing, a quiet too loud to bear. But what if, instead of an absence, you saw it as an opportunity? A space to breathe, to reflect, and to reconnect with yourself?

Being alone isn't a punishment; it's a gift. It's a chance to learn who you are outside of anyone else's influence. It's the space where you stop seeking external validation and begin trusting yourself again. In solitude, you get to make your own choices, explore what excites you, and create a life that is sincerely yours.

This week is about shifting your perspective. Instead of dreading the quiet, what if you leaned into it? Instead of fearing loneliness, what if you discovered the peace and power that solitude can bring?

There's a beautiful kind of freedom in knowing that your happiness doesn't depend on anyone else. Let's embrace that freedom together.

Affirmation for the Month:

"I am complete on my own. My happiness is not dependent on anyone else—I am building a life that is fulfilling, joyful, and uniquely mine."

Affirmation for the Week:

"I am comfortable in my own company. Solitude is not loneliness—it is my opportunity to grow, heal, and rediscover myself."

WEEK 1

EMBRACING SOLITUDE JOURNAL ACTIVITIES

———••●••———

Focus: Learning to enjoy your own company and strengthening self-reliance.

Visualization:

Find a quiet space, close your eyes, and take a deep breath.

Imagine you're standing on a quiet, sunlit path winding through a forest. There's no one around—just the sound of birds, the rustling of leaves, and the steady rhythm of your breath. You feel safe here. Every step you take is yours alone—deliberate, free, peaceful.

As you walk, notice the space around you expand—not as emptiness, but as possibility. This solitude is not isolation—it's spaciousness for your growth, your voice, your desires.

Pause. Place your hand on your heart and whisper, "I am enough. I am whole. I am safe in my own company."

Breathe that in. And when you're ready, open your eyes—carrying this inner calm with you today.

Daily Practice Reminder:

At the start of each day this week, take a moment to write down and speak aloud:

Your **monthly affirmation:** *"I am complete on my own. My happiness is not dependent on anyone else—I am building a life that is fulfilling, joyful, and uniquely mine."*

Your **weekly affirmation:** *"I am comfortable in my own company. Solitude is not loneliness—it is my opportunity to grow, heal, and rediscover myself."*

Let these words guide your healing. Repeating them daily helps shift your thoughts, build emotional resilience, and rewire your self-talk.

Daily Gratitude Reminder:

After completing your journal prompt each day, take a moment to write down 1 to 3 additional things you are grateful for. These could be people, moments, comforts, or anything that brought you peace or warmth today—no matter how small. Gratitude is a gentle yet powerful way to return to the present and remind yourself of what still supports you.

Remember, there is no right way to journal. Write as much or as little as you need. You can follow the prompts exactly or let them take you somewhere else. Let the prompts be a guide—not a rule. If your heart leads you elsewhere, follow it. These pages are yours. Let them carry what you're holding—no expectations, no perfection required.

DAY 1

THE FEAR OF BEING ALONE

Quote: *"You cannot be lonely if you like the person you're alone with."* – Wayne Dyer

Journal Prompt: What are your biggest fears about being alone? Are they based on reality or old beliefs?

Activity: Write down three benefits of spending time alone and how they could help you grow.

Daily Gratitude: What is one thing you appreciate about your own company?

Let This be Enough: You faced the quiet instead of running from it. That courage is more than enough.

DAY 2
SITTING WITH SILENCE

Quote: *"Silence isn't empty. It's full of answers."*

Journal Prompt: How do you feel when everything is quiet? What thoughts come up?

Activity: Spend 10 minutes in complete silence today—no distractions, no phone, just stillness. Write about the experience.

Daily Gratitude: What did you notice or enjoy in the silence today?

Let This be Enough: You made space for stillness. In doing so, you listened to your soul. That is enough.

DAY 3
THE FREEDOM TO CHOOSE

— ··●·· —

Quote: *"Independence is happiness."* – Susan B. Anthony

Journal Prompt: What choices do you now have that you didn't in your last relationship?

Activity: Plan a solo activity—something you'd normally do with someone else, but just for you.

Daily Gratitude: What is one decision you made recently that made you feel empowered?

Let This be Enough: You honored your independence with intention. That freedom is a gift. That is enough.

DAY 4
DISCOVERING WHAT YOU ENJOY

— ··●·· —

Quote: *"The best way to find yourself is to lose yourself in what you love."* - Mahatma Gandhi

Journal Prompt: What activities, hobbies, or interests make you feel most like yourself? Have you been neglecting any of them?

Activity: Choose one of those hobbies and do it today, just for you.

Daily Gratitude: What's something small you did today that brought you joy?

Let This be Enough: You reconnected with joy, even in small ways. That spark matters. That is enough.

DAY 5
BECOMING YOUR OWN BEST FRIEND

———— ··●·· ————

Quote: *"Talk to yourself like someone you love."* – Brené Brown

Journal Prompt: If your best friend was going through what you are now, what advice would you give them? Now, write that same advice to yourself.

Activity: Stand in front of a mirror and say one kind, encouraging thing to yourself.

Daily Gratitude: What's one thing you love about who you're becoming?

Let This be Enough: You offered yourself the kindness you once waited for. That tenderness is everything. That is enough.

DAY 6
ROMANTICIZING YOUR OWN LIFE

———— ··●·· ————

Quote: *"You are the love of your own life."*

Journal Prompt: What are some ways you can make your everyday life feel more special?

Activity: Create a small self-care ritual that makes you feel loved—light candles, cook yourself dinner, take a long walk—something just for you.

Daily Gratitude: What is one little thing you did today that made you feel cared for?

Let This be Enough: You made your life feel like love today. That beauty, that choice, is more than enough.

DAY 7
WATCHING "WHY WALKING ALONE WILL TAKE YOU FARTHER THAN ANY RELATIONSHIP"

Quote: *"The strongest people are the ones who spend time alone, not as a punishment, but as a conscious decision to build themselves from the inside out."*

Activity: Watch Joe Dispenza's YouTube video, *"Why Walking Alone Will Take You Farther Than Any Relationship."*

After watching, answer the following questions in your journal:

1. What emotions surfaced while watching the video?
2. How does walking alone create a deeper connection with yourself?
3. What is one action you can take this week to strengthen your independence?

Journal Prompt: After watching Joe Dispenza's video, what was your biggest takeaway? Did anything challenge the way you think about solitude?

Reflection Questions:

1. How has your perception of solitude changed this week?
2. What was the most enjoyable moment you spent alone?
3. What did you learn about yourself this week?

Activity: Write a statement of gratitude for your independence:

"I am grateful for..."

Daily Gratitude: What are you most thankful for in this season of solitude?

Somatic Exercise

"In stillness, I find strength. In solitude, I come home." – Unknown

Rooted in Solitude – Grounding Practice

This grounding movement helps anchor you in your own presence, building emotional steadiness through embodied awareness.

Instructions

1. Stand tall with both feet planted firmly on the ground, hip-width apart.
2. Let your arms hang loosely by your sides. Close your eyes if it feels safe.
3. Begin to gently sway from side to side, slowly, like a tree moving in the breeze.
4. Feel the strength in your legs, your spine, your center.
5. With each sway, say aloud or internally:
6. "I am grounded."
7. "I am steady."
8. "I belong to myself."
9. After 1–2 minutes, pause.

10. Place one hand on your heart, the other on your belly. Take a deep breath in... and out.
11. To close, whisper: "In stillness, I find strength. In solitude, I come home."

Optional Reflection Prompt

What did your body teach you about being alone today?

Let This Be Enough:

You stood rooted. You swayed with trust. You came home to yourself.

That is enough. That is healing.

WEEK 2

INTRODUCTION
TAKING OWNERSHIP OF YOUR LIFE

For so long, you may have looked to someone else for reassurance, validation, or direction—perhaps without even realizing it. In relationships, it's easy to default to shared decisions, collective routines, and external feedback before making choices. But this week is about taking full ownership of your life—not just in the big ways, but in the small, everyday decisions that reinforce your ability to trust yourself.

Taking ownership means recognizing that your happiness, your choices, and your growth are in your hands. No one else gets to decide your worth. No one else has the power to dictate your future. You do.

When I first stepped into my independence, I had to confront the habits I had unknowingly developed—the instinct to check in with someone before making plans, the need for external approval before trying something new, and the hesitation to trust my own judgment. It took time, but as I started making decisions *just for me*, I realized how liberating it was to shape my life on my terms.

There's incredible power in knowing that you don't need permission to be happy, successful, or fulfilled. You don't have to wait for someone else's encouragement to take that class, book that trip, or say *yes* to an opportunity that excites you. You can decide.

This week, we're shifting from relying on external validation to standing firm in your choices. You are not waiting for life to happen—you are creating it. The more you trust yourself, the more confident and empowered you will feel.

You are in control. And that's a beautiful thing.

Affirmation for the Month:

"I am complete on my own. My happiness is not dependent on anyone else—I am building a life that is fulfilling, joyful, and uniquely mine."

Affirmation for the Week:

"I am the creator of my own happiness. My choices, my growth, and my future belong to me."

WEEK 2
TAKING OWNERSHIP OF YOUR LIFE JOURNAL ACTIVITIES

———··•··———

Focus: Releasing reliance on external validation and making empowered choices

Visualization:

Find a quiet place and close your eyes. Take a deep breath in... and out.

Now, picture yourself standing in front of a large, blank canvas. In your hand is a paintbrush—smooth, sturdy, and ready. All around you are vibrant colors: bold reds, calming blues, energizing yellows, grounding earth tones. These are your choices. Your ideas. Your values.

With each stroke, you begin painting a life that feels like yours. You add freedom. Independence. Joy. Peace. There's no one directing you—just your own rhythm, your own vision. You don't need permission.

This canvas isn't finished. It doesn't have to be. What matters is that it's yours.

Take another deep breath. Whisper to yourself, *"This is my life, and I'm free to design it."*

When you're ready, open your eyes. Carry this truth into everything you do today.

Daily Practice Reminder:

At the start of each day this week, take a moment to write down and speak aloud:

Your **monthly affirmation:** *"I am complete on my own. My happiness is not dependent on anyone else—I am building a life that is fulfilling, joyful, and uniquely mine."*

Your **weekly affirmation:** *"I am the creator of my own happiness. My choices, my growth, and my future belong to me."*

Let these words guide your healing. Repeating them daily helps shift your thoughts, build emotional resilience, and rewire your self-talk.

Daily Gratitude Reminder:

After completing your journal prompt each day, take a moment to write down 1 to 3 additional things you are grateful for. These could be people, moments, comforts, or anything that brought you peace or warmth today—no matter how small. Gratitude is a gentle yet powerful way to return to the present and remind yourself of what still supports you.

Remember, there is no right way to journal. Write as much or as little as you need. You can follow the prompts exactly or let them take you somewhere else. Let the prompts be a guide—not a rule. If your

heart leads you elsewhere, follow it. These pages are yours. Let them carry what you're holding—no expectations, no perfection required.

DAY 1
RECLAIMING YOUR POWER

Quote: *"No one is coming to save you. This life is 100% your responsibility."* – Brooke Castillo

Journal Prompt: In what areas of your life have you been waiting for external validation? What would change if you gave yourself permission instead?

Activity: Write a permission slip to yourself: *"I give myself permission to..."*

Daily Gratitude: What is one thing you're proud of yourself for doing without anyone's approval?

Let This be Enough: You gave yourself permission to show up fully and claim your space. That truth is enough.

DAY 2
TRUSTING YOURSELF TO MAKE DECISIONS

Quote: *"Confidence comes from making a decision and standing by it."*

Journal Prompt: What is a recent decision you hesitated to make? How can you practice trusting yourself more?

Activity: Make a small but intentional decision today *without* seeking external input. Write about how it felt.

Daily Gratitude: What is one way your own judgment has led to something good in your life?

Let This be Enough: You chose to trust your own voice. That courage is building something unshakable. That is enough.

DAY 3
LETTING GO OF PEOPLE-PLEASING

Quote: *"You are not responsible for how others perceive you."*

Journal Prompt: In what ways do you prioritize other people's feelings over your own needs?

Activity: Set a personal boundary today—whether it's saying "no" to something draining or prioritizing your own needs first.

Daily Gratitude: What is one boundary you've set that you're thankful for?

Let This be Enough: You honored your own needs without guilt. That boundary is an act of self-love. That is enough.

DAY 4
BECOMING THE MAIN CHARACTER OF YOUR LIFE

Quote: *"You are the author of your own story. Make it one you're proud of."*

Journal Prompt: If your life was a movie, who would be in control—the main character or the supporting cast? What does it look like when you step into your own power?

Activity: Make a list of 5 things you can do this week that bring YOU joy.

Daily Gratitude: What's one small decision you made today that reminded you this is *your* life?

Let This be Enough: You stepped into your power, no longer waiting to be chosen. You chose yourself. That is enough.

DAY 5
CELEBRATING SELF-SUFFICIENCY

Quote: *"The best thing you can do is learn to enjoy your own company."*

Journal Prompt: What are some things you used to rely on others for that you can now do on your own?

Activity: Plan a solo activity that excites you—whether it's cooking a meal, going somewhere new, or doing something creative.

Daily Gratitude: What is one thing you enjoy doing by yourself that makes you feel empowered?

Let This be Enough: You did something for you, by you. That confidence is blooming. That is enough.

DAY 6
BREAKING FREE FROM LIMITING BELIEFS

Quote: *"Your only limits are the ones you believe in."*

Journal Prompt: What beliefs have held you back from fully embracing your independence? Where did they come from?

Activity: Rewrite a limiting belief into an empowering statement. Example: *"I can't handle things on my own"* → *"I am more capable than I've ever realized."*

Daily Gratitude: What truth about yourself are you grateful to finally believe?

Let This be Enough: You challenged an old story and made space for something truer. That breakthrough is enough.

DAY 7
WEEKLY REFLECTION – OWNING YOUR LIFE

Reflection Questions:

1. What was the most empowering moment you had this week?
2. How did it feel to make a decision without seeking approval?
3. What's one way you will continue owning your independence moving forward?

Activity: Write yourself a reminder: *"I am in control of my happiness, my choices, and my future."*

Daily Gratitude: What part of your independence are you most grateful for right now?

Somatic Exercise

"Daring to set boundaries is about having the courage to love ourselves, even when we risk disappointing others." – Brené Brown

Boundary Breath – Expansion Practice

This exercise blends movement with intentional breath to strengthen your sense of emotional safety and self-respect.

Instructions

1. Sit or stand comfortably with your spine tall.
2. Extend your arms out to your sides like you're creating an invisible protective circle around you.
3. Take a deep inhale, slowly expanding your arms outward like wings.
4. As you exhale, gently draw your arms in toward your chest, crossing them in a light self-hug.
5. Repeat this movement 5–7 times, breathing deeply and steadily.
6. With each inhale, say (aloud or internally):
7. "I expand with clarity."
8. With each exhale, say:
9. "I protect my peace."
10. On your final repetition, place both hands on your heart. Breathe slowly and say:
11. "My boundaries are sacred. I honor myself."

Optional Reflection Prompt

What did it feel like to physically reinforce your boundaries today?

Let This Be Enough:

You claimed your space. You honored your truth.

That is enough. That is healing.

WEEK 3

INTRODUCTION EXPLORING NEW POSSIBILITIES

Independence isn't just about standing on your own—it's about stepping into new possibilities that weren't available to you before. Now that you're no longer tied to someone else's needs, expectations, or limitations, you have the opportunity to explore what excites you, what challenges you, and what makes you feel alive.

At first, this can feel overwhelming. Maybe you're unsure of what you want, or maybe you've been so focused on surviving heartbreak that you haven't thought about what comes next. But this week, we're shifting from survival to expansion. Instead of just getting through the days, we're asking: *What do I want to do with them?*

For me, stepping into new possibilities wasn't an instant process. I had spent so much time wrapped up in someone else's world that I wasn't sure what my own looked like anymore. But little by little, I started to explore. I tried new things—not because I needed to be great at them, but because they reminded me that life is full of choices. I learned that the best way to build a life I love is to experiment, to say yes to new experiences, and to be open to what's out there.

This week is about curiosity. What have you always wanted to try? What parts of yourself have been waiting to be rediscovered? What if, instead of holding back, you gave yourself permission to step forward—into new dreams, new hobbies, and new adventures?

There is an entire world of possibilities waiting for you. Let's start exploring.

Affirmation for the Month:

"I am complete on my own. My happiness is not dependent on anyone else—I am building a life that is fulfilling, joyful, and uniquely mine."

Affirmation for the Week:

"I am open to new experiences, new opportunities, and new versions of myself. Life is mine to create."

WEEK 3
EXPLORING NEW POSSIBILITIES JOURNAL ACTIVITIES

Focus: Trying new experiences, setting personal goals, and stepping into independence

Visualization:

Close your eyes and take a deep, grounding breath.

Picture yourself standing at the edge of a wide, open field at sunrise. The air is fresh, the horizon stretches far, and in the distance, you see paths winding in many directions—some familiar, some brand new.

You feel the sun on your face, warm and encouraging. With every breath, you release fear and inhale possibility.

You take a step forward. The field doesn't demand a destination—it simply invites you to explore.

There's no right path here, just the freedom to try. To say yes. To see where your curiosity leads.

Let yourself feel excited, not overwhelmed. Life isn't asking you to be perfect—only to be present.

Breathe that in. When you're ready, open your eyes.

Let today be a day of openness and adventure.

Daily Practice Reminder:

At the start of each day this week, take a moment to write down and speak aloud:

Your **monthly affirmation:** *"I am complete on my own. My happiness is not dependent on anyone else—I am building a life that is fulfilling, joyful, and uniquely mine."*

Your **weekly affirmation:** *"I am open to new experiences, new opportunities, and new versions of myself. Life is mine to create."*

Let these words guide your healing. Repeating them daily helps shift your thoughts, build emotional resilience, and rewire your self-talk.

Daily Gratitude Reminder:

After completing your journal prompt each day, take a moment to write down 1 to 3 additional things you are grateful for. These could be people, moments, comforts, or anything that brought you peace or warmth today—no matter how small. Gratitude is a gentle yet powerful way to return to the present and remind yourself of what still supports you.

Remember, there is no right way to journal. Write as much or as little as you need. You can follow the prompts exactly or let them take you somewhere else. Let the prompts be a guide—not a rule. If your heart leads you elsewhere, follow it. These pages are yours. Let them carry what you're holding—no expectations, no perfection required.

DAY 1
SAYING YES TO NEW EXPERIENCES

Quote: *"Life begins at the end of your comfort zone."* – Neale Donald Walsch

Journal Prompt: What is something new you've been curious about but haven't tried yet? What has held you back?

Activity: Choose one small new experience to try this week—whether it's a different workout, a new book genre, or a spontaneous outing.

Daily Gratitude: What's one new thing (big or small) that you're thankful you tried in the past?

Let This be Enough: You said yes to something new, even if it felt small. That willingness to try is enough.

DAY 2
LETTING CURIOSITY LEAD YOU

Quote: *"Follow your curiosity. It knows where you need to go."*

Journal Prompt: If you could take a class, learn a skill, or pursue a dream without any fear of failure, what would it be?

Activity: Write down 3 things you want to explore in the next six months.

Daily Gratitude: What's something that recently sparked your curiosity or wonder?

Let This be Enough: You let curiosity guide you today. That spark is a sign of life returning. That is enough.

DAY 3
DREAMING WITHOUT LIMITS

Quote: *"You are never too old to set another goal or to dream a new dream."* – C.S. Lewis

Journal Prompt: Imagine your ideal life five years from now. What does it look like? How does it feel?

Activity: Write about one bold dream you want to chase—big or small.

Daily Gratitude: What is one dream you're grateful to still hold close?

Let This be Enough: You gave yourself permission to dream again. That hope is powerful. That is enough.

DAY 4
RECONNECTING WITH JOY

Quote: *"Do more of what makes you happy."*

Journal Prompt: What activities bring you joy? Have you stopped doing any of them?

Activity: Reintroduce one joyful habit into your week—something purely for fun, not productivity.

Daily Gratitude: What is one joyful memory that still makes you smile?

Let This be Enough: You made space for joy—not as a reward, but as your right. That is enough.

DAY 6
EXPANDING YOUR COMFORT ZONE

Quote: *"The magic you're looking for is in the work you're avoiding."*

Journal Prompt: What's one thing that makes you nervous but excites you at the same time?

Activity: Take a small step toward something outside your comfort zone today.

Daily Gratitude: What strength are you grateful for that helps you stretch and grow?

Let This be Enough: You stepped toward something unfamiliar with courage. That stretch is enough.

DAY 6
CREATING A LIFE THAT'S YOURS

Quote: *"The best way to predict the future is to create it."* – Abraham Lincoln

Journal Prompt: What does a life designed by YOU look like? What kind of lifestyle, routine, and environment would make you feel fulfilled?

Activity: Make a vision board (physical or digital) or create a simple list of what you want in your life moving forward.

Daily Gratitude: What part of your current life are you most grateful to have created for yourself?

Let This be Enough: You dared to imagine a life designed by you. That vision is the beginning. That is enough.

DAY 7
WEEKLY REFLECTION – OPENING YOURSELF TO LIFE

Reflection Questions:

1. What new experiences or ideas sparked excitement in you this week?
2. Did anything surprise you about stepping outside your routine?
3. How will you continue to keep an open mind moving forward?

Activity: Write a statement of commitment to yourself:

"I am open to the possibilities life has to offer. I trust myself to explore, grow, and create a future that excites me."

Daily Gratitude: What possibility or future idea are you most grateful to be open to?

Somatic Exercise

"And suddenly you know: It's time to start something new and trust the magic of beginnings." – Meister Eckhart

Stepping Into Self-Trust – Grounding Movement

This rhythmic stepping helps regulate your nervous system while reinforcing self-trust through movement and affirmation.

Instructions

1. Find a quiet space where you can stand with your feet hip-width apart.
2. Close your eyes if you feel comfortable. Place one hand on your belly and one hand on your heart.
3. Gently shift your weight from side to side, slowly stepping in place as if you're walking with purpose—but staying grounded.
4. Let each step feel intentional.
5. With each step, repeat (aloud or internally):
6. "I trust myself."
7. "I choose me."
8. "I am steady, I am strong."
9. After 1–2 minutes, bring your feet to stillness.
10. Stand tall, roll your shoulders back, and breathe in deeply through your nose.
11. Exhale slowly through your mouth.
12. End by pressing your palms together at your heart. Whisper to yourself: "I walk in self-trust."

Optional Reflection Prompt

How did it feel to move with purpose and affirm your trust in yourself?

Let This Be Enough:

You stepped forward. You trusted your path.

That is enough. That is healing.

WEEK 4
INTRODUCTION
CULTIVATING INNER STRENGTH

——— · · • · · ———

Independence isn't just about being on your own—it's about trusting yourself to handle whatever life brings. It's about knowing that no matter what happens, you are capable, resilient, and enough.

This week, we shift from exploring new possibilities to strengthening your foundation. You've spent time rediscovering your interests, stepping outside your comfort zone, and embracing solitude. Now, it's time to solidify that growth by reinforcing self-trust, self-care, and emotional resilience.

For me, learning to trust myself again wasn't instant. I had spent years relying on someone else's opinion, validation, and presence to feel secure. At first, making decisions alone felt foreign—like I was waiting for someone to approve them. But over time, I realized that I was capable of leading myself. The more I practiced listening to my own instincts, the more I realized I had always known what was best for me.

Independence isn't about having all the answers. It's about knowing that, even when you don't, you have the strength to figure it out. It's about treating yourself with respect, care, and patience, just as you would a close friend.

This week, we focus on strengthening your self-trust, reinforcing your boundaries, and building confidence in your ability to navigate life on your own terms. Because you don't just deserve a strong foundation—you're already building one.

Affirmation for the Month:

"I am complete on my own. My happiness is not dependent on anyone else—I am building a life that is fulfilling, joyful, and uniquely mine."

Affirmation for the Week:

"I trust myself. I am capable of creating a life that is fulfilling, peaceful, and uniquely mine."

WEEK 4

CULTIVATING INNER STRENGTH JOURNAL ACTIVITIES

Focus: Trusting yourself, prioritizing self-care, and reinforcing your ability to thrive alone

Visualization:

Find a quiet space and close your eyes. Take a slow breath in… and out.

Now, imagine yourself standing at the base of a mountain. Behind you is everything you've overcome—pain, fear, doubt. You glance back and honor it, but you don't stay there. Ahead of you rises a path—winding, strong, steady. It's your journey forward.

With each step you take, you feel your posture lift. Confidence steadies your spine. Peace softens your heart. Strength roots into your feet. You may not have all the answers, but you trust yourself to keep going.

As you climb, you realize you've already made it through the hardest part—beginning.

You reach a quiet overlook. You stand tall, look out over the vast landscape of your life, and smile. You didn't just survive—you grew.

When you're ready, take a deep breath and open your eyes.

Carry this strength with you. You've already proven you can do hard things.

Daily Practice Reminder:

At the start of each day this week, take a moment to write down and speak aloud:

Your **monthly affirmation:** *"I am complete on my own. My happiness is not dependent on anyone else—I am building a life that is fulfilling, joyful, and uniquely mine."*

Your **weekly affirmation:** *"I trust myself. I am capable of creating a life that is fulfilling, peaceful, and uniquely mine."*

Let these words guide your healing. Repeating them daily helps shift your thoughts, build emotional resilience, and rewire your self-talk.

Daily Gratitude Reminder:

After completing your journal prompt each day, take a moment to write down 1 to 3 additional things you are grateful for. These could be people, moments, comforts, or anything that brought you peace or warmth today—no matter how small. Gratitude is a gentle yet powerful way to return to the present and remind yourself of what still supports you.

Remember, there is no right way to journal. Write as much or as little as you need. You can follow the prompts exactly or let them take you somewhere else. Let the prompts be a guide—not a rule. If your heart leads you elsewhere, follow it. These pages are yours. Let them carry what you're holding—no expectations, no perfection required.

DAY 1
TRUSTING YOURSELF AGAIN

Quote: *"Self-trust is the first secret of success."* – Ralph Waldo Emerson

Journal Prompt: What's a moment in your past when you made a great decision for yourself? What does this tell you about your ability to trust yourself now?

Activity: List three small decisions you will trust yourself to make this week—without seeking external validation.

Daily Gratitude: What is one decision you've made recently that you feel proud of?

Let This be Enough: You chose to trust yourself today, even in small ways. That courage is the beginning of everything. That is enough.

DAY 2
THE POWER OF SELF-RESPECT

Quote: *"How you love yourself is how you teach others to love you."* – Rupi Kaur

Journal Prompt: What are three ways you can show yourself more respect in your daily life? (Examples: setting boundaries, speaking kindly to yourself, prioritizing rest)

Activity: Choose one way to actively show yourself respect today.

Daily Gratitude: What is one boundary or self-honoring choice you're grateful you've made?

Let This be Enough: You honored your worth by choosing yourself. That quiet act of respect is enough.

DAY 3
STRENGTHENING YOUR BOUNDARIES

Quote: *"No is a complete sentence."* – Ann Lamott

Journal Prompt: Have you ever felt resentment because you didn't set a boundary? How would things have been different if you had?

Activity: Practice saying "no" today—whether it's to an invitation, an unnecessary obligation, or a negative thought about yourself.

Daily Gratitude: What is one way you've protected your peace recently?

Let This be Enough: You protected your peace, even if it felt hard. That strength is enough.

DAY 4
FINDING PEACE IN YOUR OWN COMPANY

Quote: *"If you make friends with yourself, you will never be alone."* – Maxwell Maltz

Journal Prompt: What do you enjoy most about your own company? What are some ways you can deepen your relationship with yourself?

Activity: Plan a solo experience today—whether it's a walk, a coffee date, or an hour of doing something you love alone.

Daily Gratitude: What's one thing you love about spending time with yourself?

Let This be Enough: You showed up for yourself today. That presence, that love, is enough.

DAY 5
YOUR INDEPENDENCE IS AN ASSET

Quote: *"She remembered who she was, and the game changed."* – Lalah Delia

Journal Prompt: How has embracing your independence changed you? What strengths have you gained from this journey?

Activity: Write down three ways your independence is an asset, not a limitation.

Daily Gratitude: What is one personal strength you now see as a gift?

Let This be Enough: You stood on your own two feet—and realized you were never lacking. That realization is enough.

DAY 6
OWNING YOUR GROWTH

Quote: *"I am not who I was a year ago, and that brings me peace."* – Katina Lee

Journal Prompt: Reflect on how far you've come since the beginning of this journey. What mindset shifts, habits, or realizations have helped you grow the most?

Activity: Write a letter to your past self, reassuring them of the strength they would one day discover.

Daily Gratitude: What part of your healing journey are you most thankful for?

Let This be Enough: You acknowledged how far you've come. That truth, that pride, is more than enough.

DAY 7
WEEKLY REFLECTION – STANDING STRONG

———··●··———

Reflection Questions:

1. What has been the biggest takeaway from embracing your independence?
2. How have you grown emotionally, mentally, or spiritually this month?
3. What are you most proud of?

Activity: Write a final statement of self-trust:

"I am strong, I am whole, and I trust myself to create a life that is fulfilling and joyful."

Daily Gratitude: What is one inner quality you're deeply grateful to have discovered in yourself?

Somatic Exercise

"Within you, there is a stillness and a sanctuary to which you can retreat at any time." – Hermann Hesse

Embodying Inner Peace – Breath + Stillness Practice

This gentle somatic flow blends breath, subtle movement, and affirmation to deepen your connection to inner calm.

Instructions

1. Find a comfortable seated position—on a cushion, chair, or the floor.
2. Rest your hands gently on your knees or heart.
3. Begin with 3 grounding breaths:
4. Inhale through your nose for a count of 4
5. Hold for 4
6. Exhale slowly through your mouth for 6
7. Now, gently sway your upper body side to side like a slow, soothing wave. Let the movement be small and fluid, relaxing your shoulders and jaw.
8. Repeat the following affirmations with each sway:
9. "I am at peace."
10. "I carry calm within me."
11. "Stillness is my strength."
12. After 1–2 minutes, allow your body to come to stillness.
13. Place both hands over your heart. Close your eyes and sit in silence for one final deep breath in and out.
14. Whisper to yourself: "Peace begins in me."

Optional Reflection Prompt

What did stillness reveal to you today?

Let This Be Enough:

You slowed down. You anchored into calm. You remembered your strength.

That is enough. That is healing.

Monthly Reflection: Month 6

What emotions were most present for me this month?

What changes challenged me the most??

How did I support myself through uncertainty?

A moment I'm proud of:

A quote, mantra, or affirmation I want to carry forward:

On a scale of 1–10, how connected do I feel to myself right now?

1 ☐ 2 ☐ 3 ☐ 4 ☐ 5 ☐ 6 ☐ 7 ☐ 8 ☐ 9 ☐ 10

What do I need more of next month?

☐ Rest

☐ Joy

☐ Connection

☐ Confidence

☐ Creativity

☐ Other: _____

One word to guide me next month:

FROM MY HEART TO YOURS: CLOSING OUT MONTH 6

Dear You,

Take a breath and let this moment sink in—you've just completed an entire month dedicated to embracing your independence. And that's no small thing.

Stepping into your independence isn't just about learning how to stand on your own. It's about realizing that you were whole all along. It's about trusting yourself more deeply, honoring your needs without apology, and remembering that your happiness has always been within your reach.

I know there were days when solitude may have felt more like loneliness than empowerment. Moments when the quiet was heavy. But you kept going. You kept showing up. And somewhere along the way, you began to build a life that is truly your own.

This month wasn't about proving you don't need anyone—because we're meant for connection, and desiring love is human. But what you've done is even more powerful: you've proven that *you* are enough. Your life, your voice, your presence—it all matters, whether or not anyone else is standing beside you.

You've reclaimed your time, your energy, your decisions. You've remembered how to enjoy your own company and discovered the strength that comes from being grounded in your own truth. Let this be the foundation you stand on as you move forward. Let it shape the boundaries you protect, the love you welcome, and the life you continue to create.

Because the most radiant version of you is the one who knows she's whole on her own—and who opens her heart from a place of abundance, not emptiness.

So, take a moment to honor all you've done. There's no journal prompt today—just space to breathe, reflect, and take it all in. You've earned that.

I am so proud of the woman rising from these pages.

With love and belief in your strength,

Katina Lee

MONTH 07

RECONNECTING WITH JOY – BOOK SUMMARY

"The reason people can't be happy is because they won't let go of what makes them sad."

Holding onto sadness can feel safer than moving forward, but true healing begins when we loosen our grip. Like a monkey trapped by refusing to release a handful of peanuts, I was the only thing standing in my way. Letting go isn't forgetting—it's creating space for something new.

Finding Joy in Small Moments

Joy isn't found in grand gestures but in everyday moments: a stranger's kindness, a favorite song, or the warmth of the sun. I realized joy hadn't disappeared. I had simply stopped noticing it. The more I paid attention, the more joy found me.

Reclaiming Yourself

Heartbreak often buries the things that once lit us up. Rediscovering old passions—whether a hobby, creative outlet, or new experience—reminds us of who we are beyond the pain. Start small, stay curious, and follow what makes you feel alive.

The Power of Connection

Saying yes to a concert with my siblings turned into one of the happiest nights of my life, proving that joy and pain can coexist. Surrounding yourself with people who uplift you helps rebuild joy, even when it feels out of reach.

Permission to Feel Joy Again

The hardest part wasn't sadness—it was guilt. But joy is not a betrayal of your past; it's proof of your resilience. Smiling, laughing, and choosing happiness isn't letting go of love—it's expanding your story.

The Choice of Joy

Joy doesn't erase pain; it walks alongside it. Choosing joy is choosing life.

Reflection Question: How can I invite more joy into my daily life?

RECONNECTING WITH JOY – MONTH JOURNAL INTRODUCTION

"Happiness is not something you chase—it's something you create." – Unknown

After heartbreak, joy may feel distant, like something reserved for another time in your life. This month is about rediscovering happiness—not through external circumstances, but through intentional choices that bring light back into your life.

Joy isn't about avoiding sadness or forcing yourself to be happy—it's about allowing yourself to experience moments of lightness, laughter, and peace. This chapter will help you reconnect with the things that make you feel alive, reminding you that happiness is always within reach.

What to Expect This Month:

✓ Week 1: Finding Small Moments of Joy – Reconnecting with laughter, creativity, and everyday happiness

✓ Week 2: Releasing Emotional Weight – Letting go of what dims your light and making space for joy

✓ Week 3: Cultivating Gratitude – Recognizing the good in your life and shifting focus toward positivity

✓ Week 4: Designing a Life That Sparks Joy – Creating habits and experiences that support long-term happiness

Each day, you'll practice exercises that help you reclaim joy, whether through gratitude, fun activities, or simple shifts in perspective. By the end of this month, you will have rekindled a sense of excitement, curiosity, and appreciation for life.

Affirmation for the Month:

"I give myself permission to experience joy again. My heart is open to moments of laughter, love, and lightness."

WEEK 1

INTRODUCTION
FINDING SMALL MOMENTS OF JOY

After heartbreak, joy can feel like a distant memory. In the beginning, it's hard to imagine laughing freely or feeling excited about life again. But joy doesn't vanish—it just gets buried beneath the weight of sadness, waiting for you to notice it again. This week is about uncovering joy in its simplest forms: a sunrise, a kind word from a stranger, the warmth of your morning coffee.

The biggest mistake we make in seeking joy is thinking it has to come in big, grand gestures—a life-changing vacation, a new relationship, or a moment of overwhelming happiness. But true joy is often found in the small, unassuming moments. It's the unexpected smile, the comfort of a favorite song, the satisfaction of finishing a book, or the peace of sitting in silence with no expectations.

I remember the first time I laughed—really laughed—after my breakup. It caught me off guard. It wasn't planned or forced; it just happened naturally while talking with my sister. In that moment, I realized that joy hadn't abandoned me. I had just been too weighed down to welcome it in.

This week, we're not forcing happiness, but we *are* inviting it. The smallest sparks of joy can grow into something bigger when you allow yourself to experience them. Joy is not a betrayal of your pain; it's a reminder that life still holds goodness for you.

Let's start by paying attention to those quiet moments of happiness that show up when we least expect them.

Affirmation for the Month:

"I give myself permission to experience joy again. My heart is open to moments of laughter, love, and lightness."

Affirmation for the Week:

"I allow joy to find me in small, unexpected moments. Happiness is always within reach."

WEEK 1
FINDING SMALL MOMENTS OF JOY JOURNAL ACTIVITIES

Focus: Reconnecting with laughter, creativity, and everyday happiness

Visualization:

Close your eyes and take a deep breath. Imagine yourself walking through a quiet garden. The sun is warm on your skin, and you notice the small things—a flower in bloom, a bird singing, the comfort of the breeze.

As you walk, allow yourself to feel the simple joy of this peaceful moment. Let it fill you—softly, gently, without pressure.

Take one more deep breath. Let a small smile come to your face. Joy is still here. You are safe to feel it again.

When you're ready, open your eyes and carry that peace with you today.

Daily Practice Reminder:

At the start of each day this week, take a moment to write down and speak aloud:

Your **monthly affirmation:** *"I give myself permission to experience joy again. My heart is open to moments of laughter, love, and lightness."*

Your **weekly affirmation:** *"I allow joy to find me in small, unexpected moments. Happiness is always within reach."*

Let these words guide your healing. Repeating them daily helps shift your thoughts, build emotional resilience, and rewire your self-talk.

Daily Gratitude Reminder:

After completing your journal prompt each day, take a moment to write down 1 to 3 additional things you are grateful for. These could be people, moments, comforts, or anything that brought you peace or warmth today—no matter how small. Gratitude is a gentle yet powerful way to return to the present and remind yourself of what still supports you.

Remember, there is no right way to journal. Write as much or as little as you need. You can follow the prompts exactly or let them take you somewhere else. Let the prompts be a guide—not a rule. If your heart leads you elsewhere, follow it. These pages are yours. Let them carry what you're holding—no expectations, no perfection required.

DAY 1
THE FIRST STEP TOWARD JOY

Quote: *"Joy is what happens to us when we allow ourselves to recognize how good things really are."* – Marianne Williamson

Journal Prompt: What is one simple thing that has made you smile, even briefly, in the past few days? If nothing comes to mind, what's something that used to bring you joy that you can revisit?

Activity: Take five minutes to intentionally notice something beautiful—whether it's the way the light hits a window, the sound of laughter, or a favorite scent.

Daily Gratitude: What is one thing in your life right now that brings you a sense of comfort or peace?

Let This be Enough: You noticed something beautiful today. That single moment of presence is a seed of joy. That is enough.

DAY 2
LAUGHTER AS MEDICINE

Quote: *"Laughter is a sunbeam of the soul."* – Thomas Mann

Journal Prompt: Think about a time when you laughed until your stomach hurt. What made it so funny? How did it feel in that moment?

Activity: Watch a funny video, listen to a comedy podcast, or call someone who always makes you laugh.

Daily Gratitude: What is a memory that always makes you smile?

Let This be Enough: You let yourself laugh. Even if just for a second, that joy was real. That is enough.

DAY 3
JOY IN SIMPLE PLEASURES

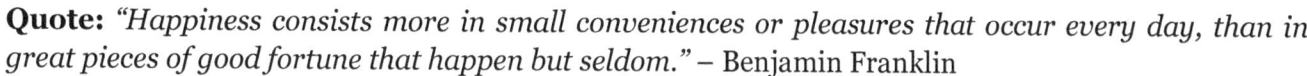

Quote: *"Happiness consists more in small conveniences or pleasures that occur every day, than in great pieces of good fortune that happen but seldom."* – Benjamin Franklin

Journal Prompt: What is one small, everyday thing that brings you comfort or happiness?

Activity: Indulge in something simple that makes you feel good—your favorite cup of tea, a cozy blanket, or a quiet moment alone.

Daily Gratitude: What is something about today that you are thankful for?

Let This be Enough: You embraced a small comfort. That quiet happiness is more powerful than it seems. That is enough.

DAY 4
MUSIC AND MOVEMENT

Quote: *"Music can change the world because it can change people."* – Bono

Journal Prompt: What song always puts you in a good mood? Why do you think it affects you that way?

Activity: Play a song that makes you feel good and move your body—whether it's dancing, walking, or simply swaying in your chair.

Daily Gratitude: What song, artist, or sound brings you happiness?

Let This be Enough: You let joy move through your body. However it looked, however it felt—it counted. That is enough.

DAY 5
THE POWER OF PLAY

Quote: *"We don't stop playing because we grow old; we grow old because we stop playing."* – George Bernard Shaw

Journal Prompt: What's something fun or silly you haven't done in a while?

Activity: Do something playful today—blow bubbles, doodle, play a game, or build something with your hands.

Daily Gratitude: What was something fun you did as a child that you are grateful for experiencing?

Let This be Enough: You remembered what it means to play. That lightness, that freedom—it's part of your healing. That is enough.

DAY 6
NOTICING JOY IN OTHERS

Quote: *"A joyful heart is good medicine."* – Proverbs 17:22

Journal Prompt: Who in your life seems to radiate joy? What can you learn from their approach to life?

Activity: Spend time with someone who lifts your spirits, or simply observe joyful interactions around you.

Daily Gratitude: Who is someone in your life that brings you joy?

Let This be Enough: You saw joy reflected in someone else and let it touch you. That connection, that hope—is enough.

DAY 7
WEEKLY REFLECTION – SMALL JOYS ADD UP

Reflection Questions:

1. What small moments of joy did I notice this week?
2. Did anything surprise me about the way joy showed up?
3. How did it feel to allow myself to experience happiness?

Activity: Write a gratitude list of at least five joyful moments from this past week.

Daily Gratitude: What is one joyful moment from this past week that you want to remember?

Somatic Exercise

"Sometimes letting things go is an act of far greater power than defending or hanging on." – Eckhart Tolle

Shedding the Old – Grounding + Release Practice

This somatic exercise helps you physically and energetically release what you're leaving behind as you step into emotional renewal.

Instructions

1. Stand with your feet hip-width apart and arms relaxed at your sides.
2. Take 3 slow breaths. On each exhale, gently shake out one part of your body—starting with your hands, then arms, then legs. Let your body loosen naturally.
3. Now, close your eyes and imagine you're standing under a gentle waterfall of light. This light washes away old stories, outdated beliefs, and past versions of you that no longer serve.
4. With each breath, imagine letting go of:
5. Regret
6. Guilt
7. The need for perfection
8. Someone else's version of who you should be
9. Say softly or in your mind:
10. "I release what no longer belongs to me."
11. "I return to myself."
12. "This is my new beginning."
13. End by placing both hands over your heart and whisper: "I honor the new version of me that is emerging."

Optional Reflection Prompt

What part of your old self are you ready to thank and release?

Let This Be Enough:

You let go. You honored your growth. You opened space for joy.

That is enough. That is healing.

WEEK 2
INTRODUCTION
RELEASING EMOTIONAL WEIGHT

———··•··———

You've started to reconnect with joy—and now it's time to make more space for it.

Sometimes, what blocks us from feeling happy isn't the absence of joy, but the presence of lingering emotional weight. Guilt. Regret. Resentment. "What ifs" and "should haves." These emotions don't just take up space in your heart—they dim your light and make it harder to fully step into your healing.

This week is about intentional release. It's about noticing the emotional clutter that still lingers in your thoughts, your body, and even your environment—and choosing to let it go.

Letting go doesn't mean forgetting or pretending you were never hurt. It means you're no longer willing to carry what drains your energy or keeps you anchored in the past. It means you're giving yourself permission to heal—not by force, but by making space for peace, presence, and possibility.

You've already survived so much. Now it's time to set down what no longer serves you.

Let's begin the process of clearing space—emotionally, mentally, and even physically—so that joy has room to bloom.

Affirmation for the Month:

"I give myself permission to experience joy again. My heart is open to moments of laughter, love, and lightness."

Affirmation for the Week:

"I release what no longer serves me. I am creating space for peace, joy, and new beginnings."

WEEK 2
RELEASING EMOTIONAL WEIGHT JOURNAL ACTIVITIES

Focus: Letting go of what dims your light and making space for joy

Visualization:

Close your eyes and take a deep breath. Imagine yourself standing beside a flowing river. In your hands, you hold small stones—each one representing a burden you've been carrying: guilt, regret, anger, "what ifs."

One by one, gently toss each stone into the water. Watch the ripples expand and fade as the current carries them away. Feel your shoulders soften, your chest open. You are lighter now—freer.

Take one more deep breath. Let this moment remind you: letting go makes room for peace.

When you're ready, open your eyes. Carry that lightness with you.

Daily Practice Reminder:

At the start of each day this week, take a moment to write down and speak aloud:

Your **monthly affirmation:** *"I give myself permission to experience joy again. My heart is open to moments of laughter, love, and lightness."*

Your **weekly affirmation:** *"I release what no longer serves me. I am creating space for peace, joy, and new beginnings."*

Let these words guide your healing. Repeating them daily helps shift your thoughts, build emotional resilience, and rewire your self-talk.

Daily Gratitude Reminder:

After completing your journal prompt each day, take a moment to write down 1 to 3 additional things you are grateful for. These could be people, moments, comforts, or anything that brought you peace or warmth today—no matter how small. Gratitude is a gentle yet powerful way to return to the present and remind yourself of what still supports you.

Remember, there is no right way to journal. Write as much or as little as you need. You can follow the prompts exactly or let them take you somewhere else. Let the prompts be a guide—not a rule. If your heart leads you elsewhere, follow it. These pages are yours. Let them carry what you're holding—no expectations, no perfection required.

DAY 1
RELEASING THE WEIGHT OF THE PAST

Quote: *"You can't reach for anything new if your hands are still full of yesterday's junk."* – Louise Smith

Journal Prompt: What emotional weight are you still carrying from your past relationship? How does it impact your ability to experience joy?

Activity: Write down one thing you're ready to let go of. Tear up the paper as a symbolic release.

Daily Gratitude: What is something from your past that, even if painful, taught you an important lesson?

Let This be Enough: You took one step toward release. You honored your growth by loosening your grip. That is enough.

DAY 2
LETTING GO OF GUILT

Quote: *"Guilt is a weight that serves no purpose."*

Journal Prompt: Is there guilt lingering from your past relationship or healing process? How can you begin to forgive yourself?

Activity: Write a letter of forgiveness to yourself. Acknowledge that you did the best you could with what you knew at the time.

Daily Gratitude: What is one decision you made that you are proud of?

Let This be Enough: You offered yourself grace. You acknowledged your humanity. That is enough.

DAY 3
RECOGNIZING EMOTIONAL CLUTTER

Quote: *"You will find that it is necessary to let things go; simply for the reason that they are heavy."* – C. JoyBell C.

Journal Prompt: What negative emotions or habits are keeping you from fully stepping into joy?

Activity: Do an "emotional declutter"—list what no longer serves you and commit to releasing one thing today.

Daily Gratitude: What is one habit or thought pattern you have already changed for the better?

Let This be Enough: You cleared space for something better. Even one small shift is a brave beginning. That is enough.

DAY 4
CHOOSING PEACE OVER PAIN

Quote: *"Holding onto anger is like drinking poison and expecting the other person to die."* – Buddha

Journal Prompt: Are you holding onto resentment, anger, or bitterness? How does it feel to imagine setting it down?

Activity: Close your eyes and visualize yourself placing that resentment in a box and walking away from it.

Daily Gratitude: What is something peaceful about today?

Let This be Enough: You let the idea of peace enter your heart, even if only for a moment. That is enough.

DAY 5
LETTING GO OF THE "WHAT IFS"

Quote: *"The only thing more exhausting than holding on to the past is pretending you're okay when you're not."* – Unknown

Journal Prompt: Are you replaying "what if" scenarios in your head? How would your energy shift if you let go of them?

Activity: Write a new mantra: "I release the past, and I open myself to new possibilities." Say it out loud.

Daily Gratitude: What is one possibility for the future that excites you?

Let This be Enough: You paused the questions and chose presence. You opened a door to possibility. That is enough.

DAY 6
DECLUTTERING YOUR PHYSICAL SPACE

Quote: *"Your home is a reflection of your mind."*

Journal Prompt: Does your space reflect a fresh start, or does it hold reminders of heartbreak? How would you feel if it felt lighter?

Activity: Remove one item from your space that no longer serves you.

Daily Gratitude: What is one thing in your home that brings you comfort?

Let This be Enough: You let go of something that no longer aligned with who you are becoming. That choice matters. That is enough.

DAY 7
WEEKLY REFLECTION – CREATING SPACE FOR JOY

Reflection Questions:

1. What emotional weight did I release this week?
2. How did letting go affect my energy and emotions?
3. What do I feel ready to welcome into my life?

Activity: Write a list of at least five things you now have space for in your life—new experiences, emotions, or relationships.

Daily Gratitude: What is one small thing you are grateful for that you might have overlooked before?

Somatic Exercise

"Your task is not to seek for love, but merely to seek and find all the barriers within yourself that you have built against it." – Rumi

Heart Space Expansion – Breath + Posture Practice

This practice invites emotional openness while grounding you in safety and presence.

Instructions

1. Sit comfortably or stand with a straight spine. Gently roll your shoulders back to open the chest.
2. Place both hands over your heart and take 3 deep, slow breaths.
3. As you inhale, imagine your chest expanding—not just with air, but with love, compassion, and inner strength.
4. With each exhale, soften your jaw, your shoulders, your belly. Let go of tightness or emotional pressure.
5. Repeat the following affirmations slowly with your breath:
6. Inhale: "I am open."
7. Exhale: "I am safe."
8. Inhale: "I am allowed to feel."
9. Exhale: "I trust my heart."
10. Now, gently stretch your arms out wide in a gesture of emotional openness. Stay there for a moment and breathe.
11. Close the practice by bringing your hands back to your heart and say: "I allow love to flow in and out of me with ease."

Optional Reflection Prompt

What did your heart need to hear most today?

Let This Be Enough:

You softened. You opened. You made space for joy.

That is enough. That is healing.

WEEK 3
INTRODUCTION
CULTIVATING GRATITUDE

Gratitude isn't about ignoring pain or pretending everything is perfect—it's about choosing to notice what's still good, even in the middle of the mess. It's not always easy, especially after heartbreak. When your world feels heavy, practicing gratitude can feel like one more thing you "should" do. But the truth is, gratitude doesn't deny your pain—it creates space beside it for something softer, something healing.

When I started my gratitude practice, it felt awkward. I wasn't sure how to be thankful while still grieving. But over time, I realized that gratitude wasn't about being happy all the time—it was about anchoring myself in the present and finding small moments of peace. A good cup of coffee. A friend who checked in. The fact that I got out of bed and tried again.

This week is about practicing that shift—learning to see the small gifts that already exist in your life. You're not bypassing what hurts; you're choosing to expand your perspective. Gratitude changes the way you see everything: your past, your present, and even your future.

You're not just healing—you're growing more aware, more grounded, and more capable of holding joy and grief at the same time. Let's begin noticing the good, even if it's just a flicker.

Affirmation for the Month:

"I give myself permission to experience joy again. My heart is open to moments of laughter, love, and lightness."

Affirmation for the Week:

"I choose to see the good. Gratitude grounds me, guides me, and opens my heart to joy."

WEEK 3
CULTIVATING GRATITUDE JOURNAL ACTIVITIES

Focus: Recognizing the good in your life and shifting focus toward positivity

Visualization:

Close your eyes and take a slow, deep breath. Picture yourself standing in a quiet field at sunrise. The air is calm, golden light stretches across the horizon, and the earth beneath your feet feels solid and steady.

With each breath, bring to mind one small thing you're grateful for. See these moments appear like glowing lanterns around you—tiny lights of warmth, comfort, and hope.

Now imagine gathering those lanterns close to your heart, letting their glow fill you with peace.

Breathe in deeply... and when you're ready, open your eyes—carrying that gratitude with you.

Daily Practice Reminder:

At the start of each day this week, take a moment to write down and speak aloud:

Your **monthly affirmation:** *"I give myself permission to experience joy again. My heart is open to moments of laughter, love, and lightness."*

Your **weekly affirmation:** *"I choose to see the good. Gratitude grounds me, guides me, and opens my heart to joy."*

Let these words guide your healing. Repeating them daily helps shift your thoughts, build emotional resilience, and rewire your self-talk.

Daily Gratitude Reminder:

After completing your journal prompt each day, take a moment to write down 1 to 3 additional things you are grateful for. These could be people, moments, comforts, or anything that brought you peace or warmth today—no matter how small. Gratitude is a gentle yet powerful way to return to the present and remind yourself of what still supports you.

Remember, there is no right way to journal. Write as much or as little as you need. You can follow the prompts exactly or let them take you somewhere else. Let the prompts be a guide—not a rule. If your heart leads you elsewhere, follow it. These pages are yours. Let them carry what you're holding—no expectations, no perfection required.

DAY 1
SHIFTING PERSPECTIVE TO GRATITUDE

Quote: *"It is not joy that makes us grateful; it is gratitude that makes us joyful."* – David Steindl-Rast

Journal Prompt: How has your focus been influencing your emotions? What happens when you shift your attention to what is good in your life?

Activity: Start a "Gratitude Jar" (or list). Write one thing each day that you are grateful for and add it to the jar.

Daily Gratitude: What is one thing in your life right now that brings you even the smallest joy?

Let This be Enough: You opened your heart to what is good. Even the smallest shift in focus is a courageous act. That is enough.

DAY 2
FINDING BEAUTY IN THE ORDINARY

Quote: *"Happiness consists more in small conveniences of pleasure that occur every day, than in great pieces of good fortune that happen but seldom."* – Benjamin Franklin

Journal Prompt: What simple, everyday things bring you joy? How can you start paying more attention to them?

Activity: Go for a walk and find one small, beautiful thing you hadn't noticed before—take a picture, describe it, or simply take a moment to appreciate it.

Daily Gratitude: What small daily ritual do you look forward to?

Let This be Enough: You slowed down and noticed the beauty around you. That awareness is a powerful kind of joy. That is enough.

DAY 3
REFRAMING YOUR STORY

Quote: *"The way we tell our stories matters."*

Journal Prompt: How can you reframe your story to highlight growth instead of loss? Instead of "I lost something," how can you say, "I gained something new?"

Activity: Rewrite one painful memory from a perspective of strength—focus on what you learned rather than what you lost.

Daily Gratitude: What is one thing from your past that helped shape you into who you are today?

Let This be Enough: You honored your strength by seeing yourself through the lens of growth. That new perspective is a form of healing. That is enough.

DAY 4
GRATITUDE FOR THE HARD LESSONS

Quote: *"What if we thanked our hardest moments for the wisdom, they gave us?"* – Katina Lee

Journal Prompt: What challenges in your life have turned out to be gifts in disguise?

Activity: Write a letter to one of your past struggles, thanking it for the lessons it taught you.

Daily Gratitude: What personal strength has grown out of your struggles?

Let This be Enough: You turned pain into wisdom. You found meaning in what once hurt. That transformation is more than enough.

DAY 5
GRATITUDE FOR THE PRESENT MOMENT

— ··●·· —

Quote: *"Today is a gift. That's why it's called the present."* – Alice Morse Earle

Journal Prompt: What can you appreciate about where you are right now—even if life isn't perfect?

Activity: Pause every hour today and take a deep breath, reminding yourself: *This moment is enough.*

Daily Gratitude: What is something good that happened today?

Let This be Enough: You breathed deeply into the now. You found peace, even if just for a moment. That is enough.

DAY 6
GRATITUDE FOR YOURSELF

— ··●·· —

Quote: *"You, yourself, as much as anybody in the entire universe, deserve your love and affection."* – Buddha

Journal Prompt: What do you appreciate about yourself? What qualities do you love most?

Activity: Write yourself a short, kind note and place it somewhere visible to read throughout the week.

Daily Gratitude: What is one thing about yourself that you are proud of?

Let This be Enough: You saw yourself with kindness today. You recognized your worth. That simple act is everything. That is enough.

DAY 7
WEEKLY REFLECTION – A MINDSET OF GRATITUDE

Reflection Questions:

1. How has focusing on gratitude shifted your mindset this week?
2. What surprised you about practicing gratitude?
3. How can you continue this practice beyond this week?

Activity: Write a list of 10 things you're grateful for and post it somewhere you'll see often.

Daily Gratitude: What is something you are looking forward to?

Somatic Exercise

"Gratitude turns what we have into enough." – Aesop

Safety in Stillness – Grounding + Touch Practice

This exercise helps soothe the nervous system and reinforces emotional safety through self-contact and breath.

Instructions

1. Find a quiet, comfortable space where you can sit or lie down.
2. Place one hand on your chest and the other on your lower belly. Close your eyes and take five deep, slow breaths, feeling the rise and fall of your body beneath your hands.
3. With each inhale, silently say: "I am here."
4. With each exhale, say: "I am safe."
5. Now bring gentle awareness to your physical body. Press your feet into the floor or let your spine fully rest against a surface. Feel the support beneath you.
6. Slowly begin to tap or gently press your arms, legs, or chest—like you're saying to your body, "You are safe. You are home."
7. Stay in stillness for one more minute, breathing normally, with full presence in your body.
8. Finish by wrapping your arms around yourself in a gentle self-hug and say aloud: "I am grounded in my truth. I belong to myself."

Optional Reflection Prompt

How did gratitude feel in your body today?

Let This Be Enough:

You paused. You connected. You gave thanks.

That is enough. That is healing.

WEEK 4
INTRODUCTION
DESIGNING A LIFE THAT SPARKS JOY

Joy doesn't just happen—it's something you cultivate, shape, and commit to through the choices you make each day. This week is about getting intentional. You've spent the last three weeks rediscovering small joys, releasing emotional weight, and practicing gratitude. Now, it's time to bring all of that together and ask: What kind of life do I want to create?

This isn't about perfection. It's not about building a highlight reel or chasing constant happiness. It's about learning what genuinely brings *you* joy—and finding small, meaningful ways to build more of it into your everyday life.

For me, designing a joy-filled life meant making tiny, consistent shifts. Choosing walks over scrolling. Spending more time on what filled me up instead of drained me. Saying yes to new experiences and no to old patterns. Little by little, joy stopped being something I waited for—and became something I lived into.

This week, you'll explore the people, habits, environments, and rituals that align with your version of happiness. You'll reflect on what lights you up and what weighs you down. And then, you'll begin building a life that feels not just livable—but *beautiful*.

This is your invitation to become the designer of your own joy.

Affirmation for the Month:

"I give myself permission to experience joy again. My heart is open to moments of laughter, love, and lightness."

Affirmation for the Week:

"I am the architect of a joyful life. I choose what stays, what goes, and what grows."

WEEK 4
DESIGNING A LIFE THAT SPARKS JOY JOURNAL ACTIVITIES

Focus: Creating habits and experiences that support long-term happiness

Visualization:

Close your eyes and take a deep, steady breath. Imagine your life as a blank canvas stretched before you. In your hand is a paintbrush—your choices, your dreams, your voice.

With each stroke, you begin to add color: soft tones of peace, bold bursts of joy, calming shades of contentment. There are no rules here. Only what feels right to you.

As the image takes shape, you realize—you're not just healing. You're creating. This is your life, and it can be beautiful.

Breathe in that truth. When you're ready, open your eyes and carry it with you.

Daily Practice Reminder:

At the start of each day this week, take a moment to write down and speak aloud:

Your **monthly affirmation:** *"I give myself permission to experience joy again. My heart is open to moments of laughter, love, and lightness."*

Your **weekly affirmation:** *"I am the architect of a joyful life. I choose what stays, what goes, and what grows."*

Let these words guide your healing. Repeating them daily helps shift your thoughts, build emotional resilience, and rewire your self-talk.

Daily Gratitude Reminder:

After completing your journal prompt each day, take a moment to write down 1 to 3 additional things you are grateful for. These could be people, moments, comforts, or anything that brought you peace or warmth today—no matter how small. Gratitude is a gentle yet powerful way to return to the present and remind yourself of what still supports you.

Remember, there is no right way to journal. Write as much or as little as you need. You can follow the prompts exactly or let them take you somewhere else. Let the prompts be a guide—not a rule. If your heart leads you elsewhere, follow it. These pages are yours. Let them carry what you're holding—no expectations, no perfection required.

DAY 1
THE JOY BLUEPRINT

Quote: *"Happiness is not something ready-made. It comes from your own actions."* – Dalai Lama

Journal Prompt: If joy were a formula, what would yours include? What people, activities, or habits bring you joy?

Activity: Write down five things that consistently make you happy. How can you incorporate them more into your daily or weekly routine?

Daily Gratitude: What is something in your routine that makes you happy?

Let This be Enough: You named what brings you joy—and that clarity is the foundation of your healing. That is enough.

DAY 2
LETTING GO OF WHAT DRAINS YOU

Quote: *"Your time and energy are precious. Spend them wisely."*

Journal Prompt: What habits, relationships, or commitments in your life feel like they are taking away from your joy?

Activity: Identify one thing you can stop doing (or say no to) that will free up energy for what truly makes you happy.

Daily Gratitude: What is one way you have protected your energy recently?

Let This be Enough: You honored your energy by identifying what no longer serves you. That choice is a powerful act of self-respect. That is enough.

DAY 3
CREATING A SPACE THAT FEELS GOOD

— ··●·· —

Quote: *"Your environment influences your mindset."*

Journal Prompt: How does your physical space affect your emotions? What small changes could make it more joyful?

Activity: Declutter or rearrange one area of your home to make it feel lighter and more inviting.

Daily Gratitude: What is one thing in your home that brings you joy?

Let This be Enough: You made space for joy, inside and out. Even the smallest shift can open the door to peace. That is enough.

DAY 4
INVESTING IN EXPERIENCES OVER THINGS

— ··●·· —

Quote: *"Fill your life with experiences, not things. Have stories to tell, not stuff to show."*

Journal Prompt: What experiences (past or future) have brought you the most joy? Why?

Activity: Plan an experience—big or small—that excites you. It could be a trip, a workshop, a fun outing, or even just a simple solo adventure.

Daily Gratitude: What past experience are you grateful to have had?

Let This be Enough: You chose memories over material, connection over clutter. You said yes to life. That is enough.

DAY 5
DESIGNING YOUR IDEAL JOYFUL DAY

— ··●·· —

Quote: *"What you do every day matters more than what you do once in a while."* – Gretchen Rubin

Journal Prompt: If you could design a day that made you feel your happiest, what would it look like?

Activity: Try to incorporate one element of your ideal joyful day into today.

Daily Gratitude: What is one small moment of joy you experienced today?

Let This be Enough: You imagined a day that delights your spirit—and brought a piece of it into your now. That is enough.

DAY 6
JOY AS A DAILY PRACTICE

— ··●·· —

Quote: *"Happiness is a habit—cultivate it."* – Elbert Hubbard

Journal Prompt: What habits or rituals can you build into your daily life to make joy a natural part of your routine?

Activity: Choose one small joy-building habit to start today. Maybe it's a gratitude list before bed, a morning dance session, or sending a kind message to a friend.

Daily Gratitude: What joyful habit have you already started without realizing it?

Let This be Enough: You planted a seed of joy in your everyday life. That rhythm, that intention, that spark—it's enough.

DAY 7
WEEKLY REFLECTION – CREATING A JOY-FILLED LIFE

Reflection Questions:

1. What have you learned about joy this month?
2. How has your perception of happiness changed?
3. What's one joyful habit you will continue?

Activity: Write a personal "Joy Manifesto"—a short statement about how you will prioritize joy in your life moving forward.

Daily Gratitude: What is something that makes life feel meaningful to you?

Somatic Exercise

"Joy is a decision, a really brave one, about how you're going to respond to life." – Wess Stafford

Rising Energy – Movement + Breath Activation

This exercise helps integrate personal power and reinforces the feeling of reclaiming your energy and voice.

Instructions

1. Begin standing tall, feet hip-width apart, arms relaxed at your sides.
2. Take a deep breath in and sweep your arms up overhead slowly.
3. As you exhale, bring your hands down through the center of your body—palms facing inward—like you're gathering energy and grounding it.
4. Repeat this flowing motion 5–7 times, linking breath with movement.
5. Now, gently bounce on your heels for 30 seconds—let your shoulders and arms shake loose. This helps release tension and reset your energy.
6. Then, place one hand on your heart, one on your belly, and say aloud: "My energy is returning. I rise with strength and clarity."
7. End by standing still for a moment with eyes closed. Imagine your energy field expanding around you—strong, clear, and vibrant.

Optional Reflection Prompt

How does joy feel in your body when you choose it intentionally?

Let This Be Enough:

You rose. You moved with purpose. You welcomed joy.

That is enough. That is healing.

Monthly Reflection: Month 7

What emotions were most present for me this month?

What was the hardest part of this month's journey?

What breakthrough or insight did I have?

A moment I'm proud of:

A quote, mantra, or affirmation I want to carry forward:

On a scale of 1–10, how connected do I feel to myself right now?

1 ☐ 2 ☐ 3 ☐ 4 ☐ 5 ☐ 6 ☐ 7 ☐ 8 ☐ 9 ☐ 10

What do I need more of next month?

☐ Rest

☐ Joy

☐ Connection

☐ Confidence

☐ Creativity

☐ Other: _____

One word to guide me next month:

FROM MY HEART TO YOURS: CLOSING OUT MONTH 7

Dear You,

As you close this chapter on *Reconnecting with Joy*, I hope you've come to see that joy isn't something waiting in the distance—it's something you can cultivate, moment by moment, right where you are.

In the beginning, joy may have felt like a stranger. Maybe it felt out of reach—something lost in the aftermath of heartbreak, something reserved for other people, something you weren't sure you were ready to welcome back. But joy has always been here, quietly waiting for you to notice it. It's lived in the small moments—in the laughter that slipped out unexpectedly, in the warmth of connection, in the stillness of a peaceful morning, in the music, the light, the breath.

Letting go of what makes you sad doesn't mean forgetting. It means making space. Space for lightness, for laughter, for love, for excitement. It means allowing yourself to move beyond just surviving... and into something more. Into a life that feels full again—not in spite of your past, but because you chose to grow from it.

As you move forward, remember joy is a practice, not a destination. You don't have to feel happy all the time to live a joyful life. You just have to stay open. Open to noticing the beauty, to welcoming the things that light you up, and to feeling the happiness you so deeply deserve.

You've done something powerful this month. You've given yourself permission to heal through joy. You've created space for beauty to reenter your life. And you've remembered what it feels like to be truly alive.

So, keep choosing joy. Keep saying yes to the things that make you feel like *you*. And never forget you are worthy of happiness—not someday, not when everything is perfect, but right now. Exactly as you are.

There's no journal prompt today—just space to breathe, reflect, and celebrate how far you've come.

With joy and gratitude,

Katina Lee

PS: If you find yourself drawn back to a prompt, a memory, or a moment—you're allowed to return. The pages will meet you where you are, not where you were.

Sometimes, the second time you write it... you hear yourself more clearly. That is healing too.

MONTH 08

EXPANDING YOUR HORIZONS – BOOK SUMMARY

Healing requires stepping beyond the familiar. After heartbreak, it's easy to stay stuck in routines that feel safe but limit your growth. True healing happens when you open yourself to new experiences, challenge old patterns, and step into the unknown—even when it feels uncomfortable.

Shifting Focus from Fear to Possibility

It's natural to fixate on the past, but where you direct your attention shapes your future. Like a racecar driver avoiding a crash by keeping their eyes on the track, you must focus on where you want to go rather than what you've lost. Expanding your horizons starts with shifting your mindset—from fear of the unknown to curiosity about what's ahead.

Facing the Fear of the Unknown

Growth often feels like standing at the base of a mountain, unsure of how to climb it. The "giants" in your life—fear, self-doubt, or the discomfort of change—seem overwhelming, but they are rarely as powerful as they appear. Facing them is not about eliminating fear but about moving forward despite it. Each small step, whether it's trying something new, setting a boundary, or exploring a different perspective, builds confidence and resilience.

Stepping Beyond Your Comfort Zone

The biggest transformations happen when you stop waiting for the right moment and start saying yes to opportunities that challenge you. Whether it's traveling alone, learning a new skill, or simply changing your daily routine, each step beyond your comfort zone expands your sense of self. Growth isn't about rushing into a new life; it's about slowly stretching the boundaries of what you believe is possible.

Preparing for the Unexpected

Encounters with your past—like running into an ex—can stir up emotions, but they don't have to derail your progress. Instead of fearing these moments, focus on how you want to show up: grounded, confident, and unaffected. The real breakthrough isn't in avoiding difficult situations, but in knowing they no longer define you.

By the end of this chapter, you'll have taken intentional steps toward broadening your experiences, embracing change, and proving to yourself that life beyond heartbreak is full of possibility.

Reflection Question: Where have I been playing small, and what is one new experience I can embrace this month to expand my world?

EXPANDING YOUR HORIZONS – MONTH JOURNAL INTRODUCTION

"The best way to grow is to step outside your comfort zone." – Unknown

Growth begins where familiarity ends. This month is about saying yes to new experiences, breaking free from limiting beliefs, and embracing curiosity. Expanding your horizons doesn't mean making drastic changes—it means being open to what life has to offer beyond what you once knew.

When you challenge yourself to try new things, meet new people, and explore new ideas, you step into an expanded version of yourself. This chapter will guide you in taking small but meaningful risks that lead to greater self-discovery and confidence.

What to Expect This Month:

✓ Week 1: Saying Yes to New Experiences – Pushing past fear and embracing new opportunities

✓ Week 2: Breaking Free from Old Patterns – Identifying limiting beliefs and challenging comfort zones

✓ Week 3: Exploring Possibilities – Trying new activities, meeting new people, and expanding your worldview

✓ Week 4: Building a Growth Mindset – Cultivating resilience, adaptability, and an openness to change

Each day, you'll step into new experiences, challenge old narratives, and discover just how much potential lies beyond your comfort zone. By the end of this month, you will have expanded your perspective and strengthened your ability to embrace change.

Affirmation for the Month:

"I welcome new experiences, new opportunities, and new perspectives. I am stepping outside my comfort zone and into a life of endless possibilities."

WEEK 1
INTRODUCTION
SAYING YES TO NEW EXPERIENCES

Healing from heartbreak can make the world feel small. Even if your life looks the same on the outside, everything feels different inside. Suddenly, your routines feel hollow, your energy low, your confidence shaken. You move through the day with caution, unsure if you're ready to trust yourself—or life—again.

In that space, it's easy to say no. No to invitations. No to new ideas. No to the unfamiliar. Because saying no feels safe. But healing doesn't live in the familiar—it lives in what you *haven't* tried yet.

When I was still aching and unsure of who I was without the relationship, the thought of doing something new felt overwhelming. I didn't want to pretend to be okay. But staying in my shell was making me feel stuck. One day, I said yes to something small—lunch with a new friend. That yes turned into a laugh, and that laugh reminded me I was still here. Still growing. Still becoming someone new.

This week is about *those* moments—the tiny, courageous choices that begin to stretch your comfort zone and rebuild your sense of possibility. You're not being asked to leap—you're being asked to *open*. To loosen your grip on what's predictable and let in something different. You don't have to be ready for a brand-new life. But you do have to be willing to say yes to something different than yesterday.

You're not just healing—you're expanding. And every new experience, no matter how small, is a reminder that life is still happening. Still unfolding. Still offering joy, surprise, connection, and purpose.

Let's begin.

Affirmation for the Month:

"I welcome new experiences, new opportunities, and new perspectives. I am stepping outside my comfort zone and into a life of endless possibilities."

Affirmation for the Week:

"I welcome new experiences with an open heart. Each step beyond my comfort zone leads to growth and transformation."

WEEK 1

SAYING YES TO NEW EXPERIENCES JOURNAL ACTIVITIES

Focus: Expanding your comfort zone through intentional yeses. This week focuses on recognizing how small acts of courage—like trying something new or saying yes to unfamiliar opportunities—can become powerful turning points in your healing journey.

Visualization:

Close your eyes and picture a doorway. On one side is your familiar routine; on the other, a world filled with new experiences. Imagine stepping through the door. What do you see, hear, and feel? Let your senses guide you into a future filled with possibility.

Daily Practice Reminder:

At the start of each day this week, take a moment to write down and speak aloud:

Your **monthly affirmation:** *"I welcome new experiences, new opportunities, and new perspectives. I am stepping outside my comfort zone and into a life of endless possibilities."*

Your **weekly affirmation:** *"I welcome new experiences with an open heart. Each step beyond my comfort zone leads to growth and transformation."*

Let these words guide your healing. Repeating them daily helps shift your thoughts, build emotional resilience, and rewire your self-talk.

Daily Gratitude Reminder:

After completing your journal prompt each day, take a moment to write down 1 to 3 additional things you are grateful for. These could be people, moments, comforts, or anything that brought you peace or warmth today—no matter how small. Gratitude is a gentle yet powerful way to return to the present and remind yourself of what still supports you.

Remember, there is no right way to journal. Write as much or as little as you need. You can follow the prompts exactly or let them take you somewhere else. Let the prompts be a guide—not a rule. If your heart leads you elsewhere, follow it. These pages are yours. Let them carry what you're holding—no expectations, no perfection required.

DAY 1
THE POWER OF ONE SMALL STEP

— ∙∙●∙∙ —

Quote: *"A journey of a thousand miles begins with a single step."* – Lao Tzu

Journal Prompt: What is one small action you can take today that pushes you beyond your comfort zone?

Activity: Write down three things you've been hesitant to try. Choose one and commit to doing it this week.

Daily Gratitude: Name one thing you're grateful for about your ability to grow and change.

Let This be Enough: You took a step—no matter how small—toward something new. That willingness to begin is enough.

DAY 2
CURIOSITY OVER FEAR

— ∙∙●∙∙ —

Quote: *"Replace fear of the unknown with curiosity."* – Unknown

Journal Prompt: What is something new you've always wanted to try but fear has held you back? How would it feel to approach it with curiosity instead?

Activity: Challenge yourself to say yes to something new today, even if it's small.

Daily Gratitude: Acknowledge something new you've recently experienced and are grateful for.

Let This be Enough: You looked at fear through the eyes of curiosity. That shift in perspective is a powerful form of courage. That is enough.

DAY 3
SEEING THE WORLD DIFFERENTLY

Quote: *"When you change the way you look at things, the things you look at change."* – Wayne Dyer

Journal Prompt: How do you typically view change—exciting, scary, overwhelming? How can you shift your perspective?

Activity: Do something today that disrupts your usual routine—take a different route to work, try a new coffee shop, or talk to someone new.

Daily Gratitude: What is something about today that felt different in a positive way?

Let This be Enough: You broke your routine and invited change. Even one new way of seeing is a door opening. That is enough.

DAY 4
SAYING YES TO THE UNKNOWN

Quote: *"Life begins at the end of your comfort zone."* – Neale Donald Walsch

Journal Prompt: Reflect on a time when stepping out of your comfort zone led to something positive.

Activity: Say yes to something today that you would normally hesitate to do.

Daily Gratitude: What is one opportunity in your life right now that you're grateful for?

Let This be Enough: You said yes to something unfamiliar—and in doing so, you grew. That is enough.

DAY 5
THE MAGIC OF SPONTANEITY

Quote: *"Some of the best moments in life are the ones you didn't plan."* – Unknown

Journal Prompt: How do you feel about spontaneity? What holds you back from being more spontaneous?

Activity: Do something today that isn't planned—go for an unplanned drive, try a random meal, or take a different path on your walk.

Daily Gratitude: What unexpected joy have you experienced recently?

Let This be Enough: You made space for the unplanned, and in that space, joy found you. That is enough.

DAY 6
TRUSTING YOURSELF TO HANDLE THE UNKNOWN

Quote: *"You are stronger than you think, and braver than you believe."* – Unknown

Journal Prompt: What is one fear you have about stepping outside your comfort zone? How can you remind yourself that you are capable of handling it?

Activity: Write a note of encouragement to yourself about embracing new experiences.

Daily Gratitude: What is one personal strength you are grateful for?

Let This be Enough: You trusted yourself today. You showed up with courage. You are more capable than you know. That is enough.

DAY 7
EXPANDING HORIZONS

Reflection Questions:

1. What new experiences did you say yes to this week?
2. How did stepping outside your comfort zone make you feel?
3. What did you learn about yourself in the process?

Activity: Choose one small way to continue expanding your horizons in the coming week.

Daily Gratitude: Reflect on one moment this week that brought you joy or growth.

Somatic Exercise

"Life begins at the end of your comfort zone." – Neale Donald Walsch

Open to Yes – Chest-Opening Stretch + Breath

This exercise helps you physically embody openness and willingness—core themes of expanding beyond your comfort zone.

Instructions

1. Stand tall or sit comfortably with your spine straight.
2. Inhale deeply and stretch your arms out to the sides like you're opening your heart to the world. Turn your palms upward.
3. As you exhale, bring your hands to your heart and bow your head slightly in gratitude.
4. Repeat 3–5 times, linking breath and movement.
5. Then place both hands over your heart and say aloud or silently:
6. "I am open to new experiences. I welcome life with curiosity and courage."

Optional Reflection Prompt

How did it feel to open your body and mind to something new?

Let This Be Enough:

You opened your arms. You welcomed possibility.

That is enough. That is healing.

WEEK 2

INTRODUCTION
BREAKING FREE FROM OLD PATTERNS

—··•··—

Sometimes the hardest part of growth isn't moving forward—it's letting go of what keeps pulling us back.

This week is about recognizing the patterns that have quietly shaped your life: the stories you tell yourself, the reactions that show up without warning, the habits that feel comfortable even when they're hurting you. These aren't flaws. They're survival strategies—ways your mind and heart tried to keep you safe. But what once protected you may now be the very thing keeping you small.

I remember realizing how often I made myself small in conversations—downplaying my needs, avoiding conflict, or shrinking my dreams so others wouldn't feel uncomfortable. At first, I thought it was politeness. But when I really looked closer, it was fear. Fear of rejection. Fear of being "too much." And fear that if I really showed up, people might leave.

That pattern didn't disappear overnight—but awareness was the beginning of freedom.

This week, you're not trying to change everything at once. You're shining a light on the places where your old story is still running the show. You're choosing to respond differently, even in small ways. That might mean saying no when you'd normally say yes. Speaking up when you'd usually stay silent. Or simply pausing to ask, *is this still serving me?*

You are not broken—you've just outgrown some of your old ways of being. And now, you get to rewrite the rules.

Freedom starts here.

Affirmation for the Month:

"I welcome new experiences, new opportunities, and new perspectives. I am stepping outside my comfort zone and into a life of endless possibilities."

Affirmation for the Week:

"I release the patterns that no longer serve me. I am free to create a new way of living, thinking, and growing."

WEEK 2
BREAKING FREE FROM OLD PATTERNS
JOURNAL ACTIVITIES

Focus: Identifying and dismantling limiting beliefs. This week encourages you to recognize where you've been repeating patterns out of habit, fear, or self-protection, and to begin consciously choosing different paths.

Visualization:

Visualize yourself walking a familiar path and then pausing to take a new one. Along this new road, notice how the scenery changes, how lighter you feel with each step. Imagine leaving old habits behind like stones you no longer need to carry.

Daily Practice Reminder:

At the start of each day this week, take a moment to write down and speak aloud:

Your **monthly affirmation:** *"I welcome new experiences, new opportunities, and new perspectives. I am stepping outside my comfort zone and into a life of endless possibilities."*

Your **weekly affirmation:** *"I release the patterns that no longer serve me. I am free to create a new way of living, thinking, and growing."*

Let these words guide your healing. Repeating them daily helps shift your thoughts, build emotional resilience, and rewire your self-talk.

Daily Gratitude Reminder:

After completing your journal prompt each day, take a moment to write down 1 to 3 additional things you are grateful for. These could be people, moments, comforts, or anything that brought you peace or warmth today—no matter how small. Gratitude is a gentle yet powerful way to return to the present and remind yourself of what still supports you.

Remember, there is no right way to journal. Write as much or as little as you need. You can follow the prompts exactly or let them take you somewhere else. Let the prompts be a guide—not a rule. If your heart leads you elsewhere, follow it. These pages are yours. Let them carry what you're holding—no expectations, no perfection required.

DAY 1
IDENTIFYING THE CYCLES THAT KEEP YOU STUCK

———·••●••·———

Quote: *"We cannot become what we want by remaining what we are."* – Max DePree

Journal Prompt: What old patterns—thoughts, habits, or routines—have been holding you back?

Activity: Write down one pattern you want to change and one small action you can take today to break it.

Daily Gratitude: What is one lesson you've learned from your past that has made you stronger?

Let This be Enough: You named a pattern and imagined a new path. Awareness is the first step toward freedom. That is enough.

DAY 2
THE COMFORT ZONE TRAP

———·••●••·———

Quote: *"Nothing changes if nothing changes."* – Unknown

Journal Prompt: In what ways have you stayed in your comfort zone out of fear? How has this limited you?

Activity: Take one step outside your comfort zone today—big or small. It could be speaking up, setting a boundary, or doing something unfamiliar.

Daily Gratitude: What is one opportunity for growth you are grateful for?

Let This be Enough: You took a step beyond what felt familiar—and that single act is how transformation begins. That is enough.

DAY 3
LETTING GO OF THE PAST

Quote: *"You can't start the next chapter if you keep re-reading the last one."* – Unknown

Journal Prompt: What part of your past are you still holding onto? How is it affecting your ability to move forward?

Activity: Write a "letting go" statement. Example: "I release my attachment to _____ and open myself to new possibilities." Say it out loud.

Daily Gratitude: What is one aspect of your present life that brings you peace?

Let This be Enough: You loosened your grip on yesterday and opened yourself to the possibility of tomorrow. That is enough.

DAY 4
CHALLENGING NEGATIVE BELIEFS

Quote: *"Don't believe everything you think."* – Unknown

Journal Prompt: What limiting beliefs do you have about yourself or your future? Where did they come from?

Activity: Rewrite one limiting belief into an empowering statement. Example: "I am not enough" → "I am whole, worthy, and growing."

Daily Gratitude: What is one positive belief you hold about yourself?

Let This be Enough: You challenged the thoughts that tried to hold you back. That is courage. That is growth. That is enough.

DAY 5
REWRITING THE STORY YOU TELL YOURSELF

Quote: *"The way you tell your story to yourself matters."* – Amy Cuddy

Journal Prompt: What story have you been telling yourself about your heartbreak? Is it a story of loss, failure, or rejection? How can you reframe it as a story of growth and transformation?

Activity: Write your "new story." Instead of "I was abandoned," reframe it as "I am being redirected to something better."

Daily Gratitude: What is one aspect of your story that you're learning to appreciate?

Let This be Enough: You told a truer, kinder story about your life today. That truth is rewriting everything. That is enough.

DAY 6
BREAKING A ROUTINE THAT NO LONGER SERVES YOU

Quote: *"Insanity is doing the same thing over and over again and expecting different results."* – Albert Einstein

Journal Prompt: What daily habits or routines no longer align with who you are becoming?

Activity: Change one small routine today—take a new route to work, rearrange your space, or swap a draining habit for a nourishing one.

Daily Gratitude: What is one daily habit that brings you joy?

Let This be Enough: You dared to do things differently. You are not stuck. You are becoming. That is enough.

DAY 7
WEEKLY REFLECTION – FREEING YOURSELF FROM THE OLD

Reflection Questions:

1. What old patterns did you recognize this week?
2. What was the most challenging part of breaking free from them?
3. How do you feel after making these changes?

Activity: Write a letter to yourself, acknowledging the progress you've made and encouraging yourself to keep going.

Daily Gratitude: What is one personal victory you are grateful for this week?

Somatic Exercise

"You are not a prisoner of your past. You are the architect of your future." – Robin Sharma **Shedding**

Old Layers – Grounding + Gentle Shakeout

This physical release mirrors the emotional release of breaking old patterns and making space for something new.

Instructions

1. Stand with your feet firmly planted on the ground, shoulder-width apart.
2. Close your eyes and take a deep breath in. As you exhale, imagine releasing a layer of old stories, beliefs, or behaviors that no longer serve you.
3. Now begin gently shaking your hands, then your arms, your shoulders, and even your legs—like you're shaking off water. Keep it light and playful.
4. After about 30–60 seconds, bring your movement to stillness. Place one hand on your heart, one on your belly.
5. Say aloud:
6. "I release what I no longer need. I am free to grow into who I am becoming."

Optional Reflection Prompt

What part of your old self did you feel ready to let go of today?

Let This Be Enough:

You shook it off. You stood grounded. You chose your future.

That is enough. That is healing.

WEEK 3

INTRODUCTION EXPLORING POSSIBILITIES

―――・・●・・―――

After heartbreak, it's easy to forget how big life can be.

We get so focused on healing, surviving, and rebuilding that we start to live in a narrow frame—one where our choices feel limited, and our dreams seem far away. But healing doesn't mean returning to who you were. It means becoming someone *more*.

This week is about curiosity. About daring to wonder: *What if my life could be different? What if I'm more capable than I think? What if there's more joy, beauty, and meaning waiting for me than I ever imagined?*

When I first started stepping outside my emotional bubble, I wasn't chasing major transformation. I just needed *something* to help me feel alive again. I tried little things—visiting a new café, signing up for a class I'd always been curious about, having deeper conversations with new people. None of it was life-changing in itself—but collectively, it sparked something in me. I started to remember that my world was bigger than my pain.

This week, you're not trying to figure everything out. You're just exploring. You're choosing expansion over fear, and discovery over routine. This is your permission slip to try something new—not because you have to, but because you *can*.

Joy, creativity, connection—they all live on the other side of curiosity. Step toward them.

Affirmation for the Month:

"I welcome new experiences, new opportunities, and new perspectives. I am stepping outside my comfort zone and into a life of endless possibilities."

Affirmation for the Week:

"I am open to new experiences and opportunities. My life is full of endless possibilities."

WEEK 3
EXPLORING POSSIBILITIES JOURNAL ACTIVITIES

Focus: Awakening curiosity and rediscovering possibility. This week invites you to explore new people, places, and perspectives, helping you remember that your world is bigger than your pain and your story is far from over.

Visualization:

Picture yourself standing in a wide-open field. Each direction represents a possibility. Walk toward one that excites you, even if it's unfamiliar. Notice how your body feels as you move toward curiosity instead of fear.

Daily Practice Reminder:

At the start of each day this week, take a moment to write down and speak aloud:

Your **monthly affirmation:** *"I welcome new experiences, new opportunities, and new perspectives. I am stepping outside my comfort zone and into a life of endless possibilities."*

Your **weekly affirmation:** *"I am open to new experiences and opportunities. My life is full of endless possibilities."*

Let these words guide your healing. Repeating them daily helps shift your thoughts, build emotional resilience, and rewire your self-talk.

Daily Gratitude Reminder:

After completing your journal prompt each day, take a moment to write down 1 to 3 additional things you are grateful for. These could be people, moments, comforts, or anything that brought you peace or warmth today—no matter how small. Gratitude is a gentle yet powerful way to return to the present and remind yourself of what still supports you.

Remember, there is no right way to journal. Write as much or as little as you need. You can follow the prompts exactly or let them take you somewhere else. Let the prompts be a guide—not a rule. If your heart leads you elsewhere, follow it. These pages are yours. Let them carry what you're holding—no expectations, no perfection required.

DAY 1
SAYING YES TO SOMETHING NEW

Quote: *"Do one thing every day that scares you."* – Eleanor Roosevelt

Journal Prompt: What is something new you've been curious about but haven't tried? What has held you back?

Activity: Try something new today—big or small. It could be a new food, a new route home, or reaching out to someone new.

Daily Gratitude: What is one opportunity you are grateful for today?

Let This be Enough: You opened a door to something new. Curiosity led the way—and that brave yes is enough.

DAY 2
THE MAGIC OF SPONTANEITY

Quote: *"Life is either a daring adventure or nothing at all."* – Helen Keller

Journal Prompt: When was the last time you were truly spontaneous? How did it feel?

Activity: Do something unplanned today—go for a walk without a destination, start a creative project, or take a last-minute trip somewhere new.

Daily Gratitude: What is one unexpected joy you experienced today?

Let This be Enough: You let go of the plan and followed the moment. In that space, you found freedom. That is enough.

DAY 3
EXPANDING YOUR SOCIAL CIRCLE

Quote: *"Surround yourself with people who inspire you."* – Unknown

Journal Prompt: What kind of people do you want to attract into your life? What qualities do they have?

Activity: Introduce yourself to someone new or reach out to someone you haven't spoken to in a while.

Daily Gratitude: Who in your life are you grateful for today?

Let This be Enough: You reached toward connection with openness and hope. Even the smallest outreach is growth. That is enough.

DAY 4
EXPLORING A NEW PERSPECTIVE

Quote: *"Change the way you look at things, and the things you look at change."* – Wayne Dyer

Journal Prompt: What is one belief you've always held that you're open to challenging?

Activity: Read an article, watch a documentary, or have a conversation that expands your perspective on something.

Daily Gratitude: What is one new idea or insight you are grateful for?

Let This be Enough: You challenged what you thought you knew. Shifting perspective is powerful. That is enough.

DAY 5
A SOLO ADVENTURE

Quote: *"Go confidently in the direction of your dreams."* – Henry David Thoreau

Journal Prompt: What is something you would love to do alone but have hesitated to try?

Activity: Plan and take yourself on a solo date—go to a coffee shop, see a movie, or explore a new place on your own.

Daily Gratitude: What is one thing you love about your own company?

Let This be Enough: You chose your own company and found peace there. That quiet courage is more than enough.

DAY 6
DARING TO DREAM BIGGER

Quote: *"If your dreams don't scare you, they aren't big enough."* – Ellen Johnson Sirleaf

Journal Prompt: If there were no limits, what would your dream life look like? Describe it in detail.

Activity: Take one step toward your dream—research something, sign up for a class, or make a vision board.

Daily Gratitude: What is one dream you are grateful to be working toward?

Let This be Enough: You allowed yourself to dream again. Big, wild, hopeful dreams. That is enough.

DAY 7
WEEKLY REFLECTION – EMBRACING POSSIBILITIES

Reflection Questions:

1. What new experiences did you say yes to this week?
2. What surprised you about stepping outside your comfort zone?
3. How did it feel to explore new perspectives and connections?

Activity: Write a letter to your future self, describing how you want to continue embracing new possibilities.

Daily Gratitude: What is one moment of joy from this week that you are grateful for?

Somatic Exercise

"When nothing is certain, anything is possible." – Margaret Drabble

Expanding Possibility – Open-Heart Stretch + Visualization

This stretch activates your heart center and signals to your nervous system that it's safe to trust, explore, and expand.

Instructions

1. Stand or sit tall in a comfortable space. Take a deep breath in, then slowly exhale.
2. Now, open your arms wide to either side like you're welcoming the world. Let your chest gently lift and your shoulders relax back.
3. As you hold this open posture for 1–2 minutes, visualize a light radiating from your chest—expanding outward with every breath.
4. Say aloud or internally:
5. "I am open to new experiences."
6. "Possibility surrounds me."
7. "I welcome what's next."
8. When you're ready, gently lower your arms and place both hands over your heart.
9. Take one more breath, anchoring this openness in your body.

Optional Reflection Prompt

What did openness feel like in your body today?

Let This Be Enough:

You expanded. You welcomed the unknown. You chose possibility.

That is enough. That is healing.

WEEK 4

INTRODUCTION: BUILDING A GROWTH MINDSET

———·· • ··———

Growth doesn't come from having all the answers—it comes from staying open when the answers change.

This week is about cultivating a mindset that supports lasting transformation. A mindset that allows you to stumble without shame, to try without perfection, and to see every challenge as an invitation to expand.

In the past, you may have been conditioned to fear failure or setbacks. Maybe someone made you feel like mistakes were evidence of weakness, or like you had to prove your worth by getting everything "right." But that's not how real growth works.

The most resilient people I know aren't fearless—they're just willing to keep going. They treat life like a practice: trying, adjusting, learning, and repeating. They know that discomfort isn't a stop sign—it's a signal that something powerful is unfolding.

This week, you're not aiming for flawless progress. You're choosing to lean in. To show up for your journey with compassion, flexibility, and courage. Whether you're navigating change, processing emotions, or simply trying something new, your mindset is your greatest asset.

You can grow from anything. Not because life is easy—but because you're committed to evolving.

This is the week you stop asking, *Can I do this?* and start telling yourself, *I'll figure it out as I go.*

You're becoming stronger, wiser, and more grounded with every step.

Affirmation for the Month:

"I welcome new experiences, new opportunities, and new perspectives. I am stepping outside my comfort zone and into a life of endless possibilities."

Affirmation for the Week:

"I embrace change and growth. Every challenge is an opportunity to become stronger, wiser, and more resilient."

WEEK 4

BUILDING A GROWTH MINDSET – JOURNAL ACTIVITIES

Focus: Shifting your mindset from fixed to growth oriented. This week is about learning to see setbacks as lessons, discomfort as a sign of progress, and resilience as a skill you've already been building all while staying kind to yourself in the process.

Visualization:

See yourself climbing a gentle hill. With each step, you carry a lesson learned, a strength discovered. At the top, you look out over everything you've overcome and everything still ahead. Let the view remind you: growth is already in motion.

Daily Practice Reminder:

At the start of each day this week, take a moment to write down and speak aloud:

Your **monthly affirmation:** *"I welcome new experiences, new opportunities, and new perspectives. I am stepping outside my comfort zone and into a life of endless possibilities."*

Your **weekly affirmation:** *"I embrace change and growth. Every challenge is an opportunity to become stronger, wiser, and more resilient."*

Let these words guide your healing. Repeating them daily helps shift your thoughts, build emotional resilience, and rewire your self-talk.

Daily Gratitude Reminder:

After completing your journal prompt each day, take a moment to write down 1 to 3 additional things you are grateful for. These could be people, moments, comforts, or anything that brought you peace or warmth today—no matter how small. Gratitude is a gentle yet powerful way to return to the present and remind yourself of what still supports you.

Remember, there is no right way to journal. Write as much or as little as you need. You can follow the prompts exactly or let them take you somewhere else. Let the prompts be a guide—not a rule. If your heart leads you elsewhere, follow it. These pages are yours. Let them carry what you're holding—no expectations, no perfection required.

DAY 1
FAILURE AS A TEACHER

Quote: *"There is no failure. Only feedback."* – Robert Allen

Journal Prompt: What is one time in your life when you failed at something, but it led to growth or a better opportunity?

Activity: Reframe a recent "failure" as a learning experience. What did it teach you?

Daily Gratitude: What is one lesson from failure you are grateful for?

Let This be Enough: You chose to see failure as wisdom, not weakness. That shift in mindset is growth. That is enough.

DAY 2
ADAPTING TO CHANGE

Quote: *"It is not the strongest of the species that survive, nor the most intelligent, but the one most responsive to change."* – Charles Darwin

Journal Prompt: How do you typically respond to change? What is one way you can become more adaptable?

Activity: Do something today that pushes you out of your usual routine—change up your schedule, try a new habit, or take a new approach to a problem.

Daily Gratitude: What is one change in your life that turned out to be a blessing?

Let This be Enough: You moved with the moment instead of resisting it. In that flexibility, strength bloomed. That is enough.

DAY 3
THE POWER OF RESILIENCE

Quote: *"Rock bottom became the solid foundation on which I rebuilt my life."* – J.K. Rowling

Journal Prompt: What is something difficult you have overcome? How did it shape you into who you are today?

Activity: Write a letter to your past self, reminding them of how strong and resilient they are.

Daily Gratitude: What is one challenge that made you stronger?

Let This be Enough: You honored the strength it took to make it through. You are standing—resilient, wiser. That is enough.

DAY 4
CULTIVATING A POSITIVE MINDSET

Quote: *"Your thoughts shape your reality."* – Unknown

Journal Prompt: What negative thoughts or beliefs have been holding you back? How can you reframe them into something more empowering?

Activity: Choose one limiting belief you have about yourself and rewrite it as a positive affirmation. Repeat it throughout the day.

Daily Gratitude: What is one positive belief about yourself that you are grateful for?

Let This be Enough: You caught the thought and chose a kinder one. That's not small—that's transformation. That is enough.

DAY 5
CHOOSING GROWTH OVER COMFORT

Quote: *"A comfort zone is a beautiful place, but nothing ever grows there."* – Unknown

Journal Prompt: Where in your life have you been staying comfortable instead of growing? What is one step you can take to challenge yourself?

Activity: Take one action today that pushes you outside your comfort zone—whether it's starting a conversation, sharing your work, or trying something new.

Daily Gratitude: What is one uncomfortable experience that led to growth?

Let This be Enough: You stretched today—even just a little. That edge, that nudge forward, that decision to try—it's enough.

DAY 6
EMBRACING THE JOURNEY

Quote: *"The journey of a thousand miles begins with a single step."* – Lao Tzu

Journal Prompt: How have you grown in the past month? What have you learned about yourself?

Activity: Write down three things you are proud of from this month's journey of expanding your horizons.

Daily Gratitude: What is one part of your journey you are grateful for?

Let This be Enough: You reflected. You saw how far you've come. You honored your journey with love. That is enough.

DAY 7
WEEKLY REFLECTION – GROWTH IN ACTION

Reflection Questions:
1. What new perspectives have you gained about yourself?
2. What challenge did you face this month, and how did you overcome it?
3. What habits or mindset shifts will you carry forward?

Activity: Write a commitment to yourself for the next month—one way you will continue to expand your horizons and embrace growth.

Daily Gratitude: What is one lesson from this month that you are grateful for?

Somatic Exercise

"The oak fought the wind and was broken, the willow bent when it must and survived."

– Robert Jordan

Rooted and Ready – Grounding Breath + Power Posture

This exercise combines breath with posture to reinforce a grounded, resilient mindset as you close out the month of growth.

Instructions
1. Stand tall with both feet planted firmly on the ground, about hip-width apart. Soften your knees and let your arms hang loosely at your sides.
2. Close your eyes (or soften your gaze) and imagine strong roots growing from the soles of your feet deep into the earth.
3. With each inhale, feel energy rising through those roots.
4. With each exhale, release tension or doubt.
5. After a few grounding breaths, bring your hands to your hips or stretch your arms out in a wide V shape—your power posture.
6. Say internally or aloud:
7. "I am grounded in who I am."
8. "I trust myself to grow."
9. "I move forward with strength."
10. Hold this position for at least 1 minute. Feel the confidence settle into your body.
11. When you're ready, bring your hands back to your heart or sides and take one final, steady breath.

Optional Reflection Prompt

What part of you feels stronger today than it did at the beginning of the month?

Let This Be Enough:

You stood tall. You grounded your growth. You embodied strength.

That is enough. That is healing.

Monthly Reflection: Month 8

What emotions were most present for me this month?

What was the hardest part of this month's journey?

What breakthrough or insight did I have?

A moment I'm proud of:

A quote, mantra, or affirmation I want to carry forward:

On a scale of 1–10, how connected do I feel to myself right now?

1 ☐ 2 ☐ 3 ☐ 4 ☐ 5 ☐ 6 ☐ 7 ☐ 8 ☐ 9 ☐ 10

What do I need more of next month?

☐ Rest

☐ Joy

☐ Connection

☐ Confidence

☐ Creativity

☐ Other: _____

One word to guide me next month:

FROM MY HEART TO YOURS: CLOSING OUT MONTH 8

Dear You,

You've done something incredible this month. You stepped beyond what was familiar, challenged the limits of what you thought was possible, and stretched yourself in ways you may not have believed you could. *Expanding your horizons* isn't just about trying new things—it's about becoming someone who embraces growth, change, and the beauty of possibility.

I know how tempting it can be to stay in the comfort zone—to cling to what's predictable, to avoid the risk of uncertainty. But you? You chose the brave path. You looked beyond the walls of your past and dared to imagine something more. That is powerful. That is life-changing.

This month, you've proven to yourself that you are capable of facing fears, pushing boundaries, and saying yes to life in a way that declares *I am not settling for small*. Whether it was trying something new, shifting your perspective, or simply choosing courage over comfort—every step you took became a bold act of expansion.

But remember, this doesn't end here. Growth isn't a destination—it's a way of living. Keep saying yes to life. Keep showing up for your dreams. Keep believing that your future is bigger, brighter, and more beautiful than you've ever imagined.

And if fear shows up again (because it will), remind yourself of this: the best things in life often begin right where your comfort zone ends.

You're expanding in ways you may not even fully see yet... and the world is rising up to meet you.

There's no prompt today—just space to reflect, celebrate, and breathe in how far you've come.

With so much love and belief in you,

Katina Lee

PS: If you find yourself drawn back to a prompt, a memory, or a moment—you're allowed to return. The pages will meet you where you are, not where you were.

Sometimes, the second time you write it... you hear yourself more clearly. That is healing too.

MONTH 09

STRENGTHENING YOUR MINDSET – BOOK SUMMARY

Heartbreak isn't just emotional—it takes a physical toll. Grief settles into your body, affecting your muscles, energy levels, and overall well-being. Healing requires more than emotional processing; it demands restoring balance and strength in both body and mind.

Recognizing Heartbreak in the Body

Emotional pain triggers physical symptoms like muscle tension, fatigue, brain fog, and digestive issues. Acknowledging this connection allows you to approach healing holistically.

Healing Through Movement and Breath

The body stores heartbreak, but intentional movement—whether walking, yoga, or dancing—releases stored pain and helps regulate stress. Deep breathing calms the nervous system, lifting mood and restoring a sense of vitality.

Rebuilding Mental Strength

Posture, breathing, and mindset shape emotional resilience. Standing tall, practicing affirmations, and reframing negative thoughts help rewire the brain for healing. Small shifts in how you carry yourself can create lasting changes in how you feel.

Nourishing the Body for Healing

Grief depletes essential nutrients, impacting mood and energy. Hydration, balanced meals, and key supplements like magnesium and omega-3s support emotional stability and recovery. Even simple acts like preparing a healthy meal reinforce self-worth.

Prioritizing Rest and Recovery

Sleep is essential for emotional and physical healing. Creating a calming bedtime routine and reducing screen time improves sleep quality, helping the mind and body reset.

Releasing Emotional Triggers

Triggers—whether a song, place, or memory—can pull you back into the past. Instead of avoiding them, shift how you respond. Grounding techniques and mindful breathing help reclaim inner peace.

By the end of this chapter, you'll have explored how to reconnect with your body, strengthen your mind, and rebuild resilience. Healing is about more than overcoming pain—it's about creating a foundation for lasting strength.

Reflection Question: How can I support my body and mind this month in ways that strengthen my healing?

STRENGTHENING YOUR MINDSET – MONTH JOURNAL INTRODUCTION

―――― ··●·· ――――

"Healing isn't just about emotions—it's about restoring balance in your mind and body." – Unknown

Heartbreak doesn't just affect your emotions; it impacts your physical health, energy levels, and overall well-being. This month is about strengthening both your mind and body, recognizing how deeply they are connected, and creating habits that support your healing.

When you prioritize physical wellness, you boost mental resilience. Movement, nourishment, rest, and self-care aren't just about feeling better physically—they are essential components of emotional healing. This chapter will guide you in restoring your strength, improving your mindset, and reclaiming your energy from the inside out.

What to Expect This Month:

✓ Week 1: Recognizing the Mind-Body Connection – Understanding how emotional pain manifests physically

✓ Week 2: Healing Through Movement – Using exercise, breathwork, and grounding techniques to release stored pain

✓ Week 3: Nourishing Your Body – Prioritizing hydration, nutrition, and self-care practices that fuel recovery

✓ Week 4: Rest and Rebuilding – Improving sleep, managing stress, and creating a foundation for lasting well-being

Each day, you'll engage in simple, effective practices that strengthen your mind and body. By the end of this month, you will have created habits that support your healing and empower you to move forward with greater vitality and confidence.

Affirmation for the Month:

"My thoughts shape my reality. I choose to cultivate a mindset of resilience, gratitude, and possibility."

WEEK 1

INTRODUCTION RECOGNIZING THE MIND-BODY CONNECTION

———·· • ·· ———

Heartbreak doesn't just break your heart—it affects your whole body.

You might notice your shoulders aching with tension, your stomach feeling unsettled, your energy levels dipping without explanation. Sleep becomes elusive. Your appetite changes. Even breathing can feel different—shallower, tighter. That's because emotional pain doesn't stay in the mind—it seeps into your muscles, your nervous system, your gut, your bones. It becomes part of how you move through the world.

When I went through heartbreak, I felt it physically in ways I hadn't expected. My chest was tight. My limbs felt heavy. I was constantly exhausted, even after rest. I had read that the body stores trauma, but it wasn't until I experienced it that I understood how true that was. I knew I needed to heal emotionally—but what I didn't realize was that my body needed healing just as much.

This week is about noticing the ways your body is carrying your pain—and beginning to care for it with compassion.

You may have spent a lot of time trying to "think your way" through healing. But true healing asks us to *feel* our way through. To tune into the messages our bodies have been whispering (or screaming) at us. Your body is not your enemy—it's doing its best to protect you, even when it feels like it's shutting down. It's holding the weight of everything you've been through, often without being asked.

But here's the good news: just as the body holds pain, it also holds the power to release it.

This week, we'll begin a conversation with the body. Not to fix everything all at once—but to listen. To breathe. To gently release. Whether it's through noticing where you hold tension, softening your breath, scanning your body for stress, or simply offering gratitude to the parts of you that are still holding on— you are invited to reconnect.

Healing happens when we treat the body not as a burden, but as a sacred space. A partner in recovery. A source of wisdom.

Let this week be your return to that connection.

Affirmation for the Month:

"My thoughts shape my reality. I choose to cultivate a mindset of resilience, gratitude, and possibility."

Affirmation for the Week:

"I listen to my body's needs and give it the care it deserves. Healing is happening within me."

WEEK 1
RECOGNIZING THE MIND-BODY CONNECTION JOURNAL ACTIVITIES

Focus: Understanding how emotional pain manifests physically and learning to listen to your body's signals.

Visualization:

Close your eyes and imagine scanning your body from head to toe. As you pass over each part, visualize warm light easing any tightness, pain, or fatigue. Thank each area for carrying you through heartbreak.

Daily Practice Reminder:

At the start of each day this week, take a moment to write down and speak aloud:

Your **monthly affirmation:** *"My thoughts shape my reality. I choose to cultivate a mindset of resilience, gratitude, and possibility."*

Your **weekly affirmation:** *"I listen to my body's needs and give it the care it deserves. Healing is happening within me."*

Let these words guide your healing. Repeating them daily helps shift your thoughts, build emotional resilience, and rewire your self-talk.

Daily Gratitude Reminder:

After completing your journal prompt each day, take a moment to write down 1 to 3 additional things you are grateful for. These could be people, moments, comforts, or anything that brought you peace or warmth today—no matter how small. Gratitude is a gentle yet powerful way to return to the present and remind yourself of what still supports you.

Remember, there is no right way to journal. Write as much or as little as you need. You can follow the prompts exactly or let them take you somewhere else. Let the prompts be a guide—not a rule. If your heart leads you elsewhere, follow it. These pages are yours. Let them carry what you're holding—no expectations, no perfection required.

DAY 1
HEARTBREAK IN THE BODY

Quote: *"Your body keeps score of your pain."* – Bessel van der Kolk

Journal Prompt: Where do you feel emotional pain in your body? Describe any physical symptoms of heartbreak you've noticed.

Activity: Do a body scan meditation—close your eyes and mentally check in with each part of your body.

Daily Gratitude: What is one thing your body has done for you today, even if it feels small?

Let This be Enough: You showed up. You listened inward. You honored your process. That is enough. That is healing.

DAY 2
THE WEIGHT OF STRESS AND TENSION

Quote: *"Tension is who you think you should be. Relaxation is who you are."* – Chinese Proverb

Journal Prompt: Where do you hold tension in your body? How does stress physically manifest for you?

Activity: Try a gentle stretching session or progressive muscle relaxation to release tension.

Daily Gratitude: What is one physical sensation that feels good or comforting to you?

Let This be Enough: You noticed where your body holds tension—and chose to soften. That awareness is a kindness. That is enough.

DAY 3
UNDERSTANDING THE GUT-BRAIN CONNECTION

Quote: *"Your gut is your second brain."* – Dr. Michael Gershon

Journal Prompt: How has heartbreak affected your eating habits? Do you notice changes in digestion, appetite, or cravings?

Activity: Nourish your body today—eat something nutrient-rich and drink plenty of water.

Daily Gratitude: What is one meal or drink that brings you comfort?

Let This be Enough: You offered nourishment with intention. You listened to what your body asked for. That is enough.

DAY 4
HEALING THROUGH BREATH

Quote: *"Breathing in, I calm my body. Breathing out, I smile."* – Thích Nhất Hạnh

Journal Prompt: How does your breathing feel when you're anxious or overwhelmed? What changes when you consciously slow it down?

Activity: Practice 4-4-6 breathing (inhale 4 seconds, hold 4 seconds, exhale 6 seconds) to regulate your nervous system.

Daily Gratitude: What is one breath of fresh air you've enjoyed today?

Let This be Enough: You slowed down. You breathed through the noise. You returned to yourself. That is enough.

DAY 5
RECOGNIZING SLEEP DISRUPTIONS

Quote: *"Sleep is the best meditation."* – Dalai Lama

Journal Prompt: How has your sleep changed since the breakup? What patterns do you notice?

Activity: Tonight, create a calming bedtime ritual (dim lights, no screens, deep breathing).

Daily Gratitude: What is one small comfort that helps you relax at night?

Let This be Enough: You made space for rest. You honored your need for stillness. That is enough.

DAY 6
NOTICING ENERGY SHIFTS

Quote: *"Your energy introduces you before you even speak."*

Journal Prompt: How has your energy felt lately? What activities drain you, and what restores you?

Activity: Do one thing today that replenishes your energy (even if it's just sitting in the sun for 5 minutes).

Daily Gratitude: What is one thing that made you feel lighter today?

Let This be Enough: You paid attention to what lifted and what drained you. You protected your energy. That is enough.

DAY 7
WEEKLY REFLECTION – LISTENING TO YOUR BODY

— ··●·· —

Reflection Questions:

1. What body signals have I been ignoring?
2. What is one small thing I can do to take better care of myself physically?

Activity: Write a thank-you note to your body for all that it has carried you through.

Daily Gratitude: What is one way your body has supported you, even through challenging times?

Somatic Exercise

"Your body hears everything your mind says. Stay kind." – Unknown

Body Gratitude Scan – Touch + Awareness Practice

This practice rebuilds trust between your mind and body, helping you recognize how much your body has carried you through, even in pain.

Instructions

1. Find a quiet space to sit or lie down comfortably. Close your eyes and take three slow, deep breaths.
2. Gently place your hands on different parts of your body—your heart, your stomach, your legs, your shoulders—as you move through this simple gratitude ritual.
3. With each placement, say (aloud or silently):
4. "Thank you, [body part], for supporting me."
5. Example:
6. "Thank you, feet, for carrying me."
7. "Thank you, heart, for beating even when it hurts."
8. "Thank you, shoulders, for holding so much."
9. Move slowly, with presence. Let each touch be soft and intentional.
10. End with your hands over your heart. Whisper:
11. "My body is my ally. I honor it with care and compassion."

Optional Reflection Prompt

How did your body respond to being acknowledged with kindness?

Let This Be Enough:

You listened. You honored. You offered compassion.

That is enough. That is healing.

WEEK 2
INTRODUCTION
HEALING THROUGH MOVEMENT

"Motion is the language of the body—and healing begins when we listen."

When we go through heartbreak, our bodies often freeze. We hold our breath. We stay curled inward. We carry tension in our shoulders, clench our jaws, and feel heavy in our steps. That's not weakness—it's the body doing its best to protect you. But healing asks for something different. It asks us to move.

This week is about reconnecting with your body through intentional movement—not for performance, but for presence. Whether it's a gentle walk, a stretch, dancing in your kitchen, or even just shaking out your hands, movement helps the body release what words can't. It's one of the most powerful tools we have for shifting emotion, rebalancing the nervous system, and inviting healing to land.

When I was in the depths of heartbreak, I found myself stuck—both mentally and physically. I couldn't sit still, but I also didn't want to move. What finally helped me was walking. Just 10 minutes at a time. No expectations, no rules. It wasn't exercise—it was *release*. Every step helped clear space for peace to return.

This week, try to think of movement as medicine. Let your body guide you. Some days might call for stillness, others for energy. But every time you move with intention, you send a message to your body: *I'm here. I'm listening. I'm healing.*

Your body has carried so much. Now it's time to help it let go.

Affirmation for the Month:

"My thoughts shape my reality. I choose to cultivate a mindset of resilience, gratitude, and possibility."

Affirmation for the Week:

"Movement is healing. I honor my body by listening to what it needs and allowing it to release what it no longer has to carry."

WEEK 2

HEALING THROUGH MOVEMENT JOURNAL ACTIVITIES

Focus: Using physical movement to release stored emotions and restore energy.

Visualization:

Visualize yourself walking through a forest or along a beach, with each step helping you release a piece of pain or tension. Picture your breath syncing with your movement, grounding you in the present moment.

Daily Practice Reminder:

At the start of each day this week, take a moment to write down and speak aloud:

Your **monthly affirmation:** *"My thoughts shape my reality. I choose to cultivate a mindset of resilience, gratitude, and possibility."*

Your **weekly affirmation:** *"Movement is healing. I honor my body by listening to what it needs and allowing it to release what it no longer has to carry."*

Let these words guide your healing. Repeating them daily helps shift your thoughts, build emotional resilience, and rewire your self-talk.

Daily Gratitude Reminder:

After completing your journal prompt each day, take a moment to write down 1 to 3 additional things you are grateful for. These could be people, moments, comforts, or anything that brought you peace or warmth today—no matter how small. Gratitude is a gentle yet powerful way to return to the present and remind yourself of what still supports you.

Remember, there is no right way to journal. Write as much or as little as you need. You can follow the prompts exactly or let them take you somewhere else. Let the prompts be a guide—not a rule. If your heart leads you elsewhere, follow it. These pages are yours. Let them carry what you're holding—no expectations, no perfection required.

DAY 1
MOVING THROUGH HEARTBREAK

Quote: *"Movement is medicine."*

Journal Prompt: How has your body responded to grief? What physical sensations do you notice?

Activity: Go for a 10-minute walk outside. Breathe deeply and take in your surroundings.

Daily Gratitude: What is one part of your body you're grateful for—simply because it keeps going, even when you feel low?

Let This be Enough: You took a step. You moved forward—physically and emotionally. That is enough.

DAY 2
THE POWER OF BREATHWORK

Quote: *"Breathing deeply brings us back to ourselves."*

Journal Prompt: What happens to your breathing when you feel stressed or overwhelmed?

Activity: Practice 4-7-8 breathing (inhale for 4 seconds, hold for 7, exhale for 8).

Daily Gratitude: What is one moment today when your breath helped calm or ground you?

Let This be Enough You came home to your breath. You grounded yourself in presence. That is enough.

DAY 3
SHAKING OFF STAGNANT ENERGY

Quote: *"Sometimes, you just need to shake it out."* -Unknown

Journal Prompt: When was the last time you moved just for fun?

Activity: Put on your favorite song and dance, jump, or shake your arms and legs for two minutes.

Daily Gratitude: What is one way movement helped shift your mood or mindset today?

Let This be Enough: You let your body move the emotion. You made space for release. That is enough.

DAY 4
GENTLE MOVEMENT FOR HEALING

Quote: *"Be gentle with yourself."*

Journal Prompt: What kind of movement feels good to your body right now?

Activity: Try five minutes of stretching or yoga. Focus on releasing tension.

Daily Gratitude: What is one gentle act of care you offered your body today?

Let This be Enough: You chose softness. You honored what your body could do today. That is enough.

DAY 5
NATURE AS A HEALER

———··•··———

Quote: *"Go outside. Your soul will thank you."*

Journal Prompt: How do you feel when you spend time in nature?

Activity: Spend 10 minutes outside, whether it's a park, backyard, or a quiet space near a tree.

Daily Gratitude: What is one thing in nature you noticed today that brought you peace or beauty?

Let This be Enough: You touched stillness beneath the sky. You let the earth hold a little of your weight. That is enough.

DAY 6
STRENGTHENING THE BODY, STRENGTHENING THE MIND

———··•··———

Quote: *"The mind and body heal together."*

Journal Prompt: How do you feel after moving your body this week?

Activity: Do one simple strength-building movement (push-ups, squats, or lunges).

Daily Gratitude: What is one physical action—no matter how small—that made you feel stronger today?

Let This be Enough: You showed up for your strength. You reminded yourself of your resilience. That is enough.

DAY 7
WEEKLY REFLECTION – NOTICING THE SHIFT

Reflection Questions:

1. How did movement affect my mood this week?
2. What types of movement felt the best?
3. What is one movement I can commit to doing regularly?

Activity: Write a letter to your body, thanking it for carrying you through healing.

Daily Gratitude: What is one physical ability you are grateful for today?

Somatic Exercise

"Movement is a medicine for creating change in a person's physical, emotional, and mental states."
–Carol Welch

Release Through Rhythm – Movement + Breath

This rhythmic movement helps clear energetic residue from the body, grounding you in the present.

Instructions

1. Find a private space where you can move freely.
2. Start by standing still, eyes closed, and take three deep breaths.
3. Begin a gentle shaking movement—start with your hands, then your arms, shoulders, legs, and feet. Let your whole body join in. Keep it soft and loose.
4. As you shake, exhale through your mouth with a "haaa" sound or a sigh. Imagine stress and stuck emotions falling away.
5. Repeat a phrase as you move:
6. "I release what my body no longer needs."
7. "I shake off the past. I welcome what's new."
8. Continue for 1–2 minutes, then come to stillness.
9. Place one hand on your heart, the other on your belly. Feel your breath settle.
10. Finish by whispering: "I am here, I am whole, I am healing."

Optional Reflection Prompt

What shifted in your body or mind after this rhythmic release?

Let This Be Enough:

You moved what needed moving. You cleared space for new energy.

That is enough. That is healing.

WEEK 3
INTRODUCTION
NOURISHING YOUR BODY

"You can't heal a hurting heart with an empty body."

After heartbreak, it's easy to forget your own needs. Meals get skipped. Coffee becomes a stand-in for sleep. You grab whatever's convenient or comforting—not because it's what your body needs, but because you're just trying to make it through the day. I've been there—running on caffeine, ignoring hunger cues, surviving on snacks and stress. At the time, I didn't realize how much my emotional pain was affecting the way I cared for my body.

But here's what I learned: *nourishment is healing.* What you put into your body shapes how you feel—physically, emotionally, and mentally. Food is more than fuel—it's information. It tells your body whether it's safe, supported, and strong enough to heal. And when you choose to nourish yourself intentionally, even in small ways, you're sending a powerful message to yourself: *I matter. I am worthy of care. I am still healing, and I deserve to feel good while I do it.*

To be honest, I never considered myself a good cook. I used to feel intimidated in the kitchen, like I needed to be some kind of culinary expert to prepare a healthy meal. But I've learned you don't need great skills to eat well or follow a recipe. It doesn't have to be complicated to be healing—and I'm starting to realize I'm better at it than I thought.

This week, we're not focusing on diets or perfection. This is about reconnecting with your body's needs. Drinking more water. Adding color to your plate. Slowing down and noticing how food makes you feel. It might look like making a simple meal from scratch, sipping a warm tea, or sitting down to eat without distractions. These small acts of nourishment are also acts of *self-respect.*

I remember the first time I cooked for myself after my heartbreak. It wasn't fancy—just fresh vegetables, a handful of quinoa, some olive oil and lemon. But as I sat down and took that first bite, something shifted. It wasn't just food—it was care. Not from someone else—from *me.*

This week, you are invited to nourish not just your body, but your sense of worth. Let your meals become rituals of healing. Let your hydration be a form of presence. Let your food choices remind you that you are rebuilding strength from the inside out.

Your body is your home. Let's treat it like a sacred space.

Affirmation for the Month:

"My thoughts shape my reality. I choose to cultivate a mindset of resilience, gratitude, and possibility."

Affirmation for the Week:

"I nourish my body with kindness and care. Every choice I make supports my healing."

WEEK 3
NOURISHING YOUR BODY JOURNAL ACTIVITIES

Focus: Prioritizing hydration, nutrition, and self-care practices that fuel recovery.

Visualization:

Imagine preparing a nourishing meal for yourself with love and intention. Visualize the colors, textures, and smells. As you take a bite in your mind, feel your body absorbing energy, comfort, and healing.

Daily Practice Reminder:

At the start of each day this week, take a moment to write down and speak aloud:

Your **monthly affirmation:** *"My thoughts shape my reality. I choose to cultivate a mindset of resilience, gratitude, and possibility.":*

Your **weekly affirmation:** *"I nourish my body with kindness and care. Every choice I make supports my healing."*

Let these words guide your healing. Repeating them daily helps shift your thoughts, build emotional resilience, and rewire your self-talk.

Daily Gratitude Reminder:

After completing your journal prompt each day, take a moment to write down 1 to 3 additional things you are grateful for. These could be people, moments, comforts, or anything that brought you peace or warmth today—no matter how small. Gratitude is a gentle yet powerful way to return to the present and remind yourself of what still supports you.

Remember, there is no right way to journal. Write as much or as little as you need. You can follow the prompts exactly or let them take you somewhere else. Let the prompts be a guide—not a rule. If your heart leads you elsewhere, follow it. These pages are yours. Let them carry what you're holding—no expectations, no perfection required.

DAY 1
HYDRATION AND HEALING

— • • ● • • ———— •

Quote: *"Water is life."* – Lakota Proverb

Journal Prompt: How much water do you drink daily? How do you feel when you're well-hydrated?

Activity: Drink an extra glass of water today. Notice how it makes you feel.

Daily Gratitude: What is one refreshing drink you enjoy that reminds you to care for yourself?

Let This be Enough: You chose to pour back into yourself. One glass. One moment. One choice to care. That is enough.

DAY 2
EATING FOR ENERGY

— • • ● • • ———— •

Quote: *"Food is fuel, not just comfort."*

Journal Prompt: What foods make you feel energized? What foods drain you?

Activity: Plan one meal today with whole, nutrient-rich ingredients.

Daily Gratitude: What food makes you feel energized, loved, or comforted?

Let This be Enough: You fed your body with intention. You honored its need for fuel, not just comfort. That is enough.

DAY 3
THE GUT-BRAIN CONNECTION

Journal Prompt: Have you noticed changes in your digestion or appetite since your heartbreak?

Activity: Add a probiotic or fiber-rich food to your diet today.

Daily Gratitude: What is one way your body communicates its needs to you that you're thankful for?

Let This be Enough: You listened inward. You paid attention to what your body was trying to tell you. That is enough.

DAY 4
COOKING AS SELF-CARE

Quote: *"Preparing food is an act of self-love."*

Journal Prompt: How do you feel about cooking for yourself?

Activity: Make a meal from scratch today, even if it's something simple.

Daily Gratitude: What is one meal, dish, or ingredient that brings you joy or a sense of home?

Let This be Enough: You turned a task into tenderness. You created something nourishing. That is enough.

DAY 5
SUGAR, CAFFEINE, AND EMOTIONAL BALANCE

Quote: *"What you consume affects your mood."*

Journal Prompt: Do you notice mood swings after sugar or caffeine?

Activity: Reduce one processed food or drink today and notice the difference.

Daily Gratitude: What is one small healthy swap you've made that you're proud of?

Let This be Enough: You noticed how what you consume shapes how you feel. You chose with care. That is enough.

DAY 6
SUPPLEMENTS FOR EMOTIONAL HEALTH

Quote: *"Give your body what it needs."*

Journal Prompt: Are there any vitamins or supplements that might support your mood and energy?

Activity: Research or start taking a supplement that supports healing (e.g., magnesium, omega-3s).

Daily Gratitude: What is one habit, supplement, or nutrient that helps you feel more balanced?

Let This be Enough: You considered what your body needs to thrive. You made space for support. That is enough.

DAY 7
WEEKLY REFLECTION – HONORING YOUR BODY

Reflection Questions:
1. How did my energy levels shift this week?
2. What foods or drinks made me feel better or worse?
3. How can I continue to make nourishing choices?

Activity: Write down five foods or habits that make you feel strong and healthy.

Daily Gratitude: What is one way your body supported you this week?

Somatic Exercise

"Caring for your body, mind, and spirit is your greatest and grandest responsibility. It's about listening to the needs of your soul and then honoring them." – Kristi Ling

Nourishment Grounding – Presence + Touch

This gentle practice reconnects you to your body through loving attention and sensory grounding.

Instructions

1. Sit comfortably in a chair or on the floor. Close your eyes and place your hands gently on your stomach or over your heart.
2. Take three deep breaths—in through your nose, out through your mouth.
3. With each breath, repeat softly:
4. "I nourish my body."
5. "I honor my healing."
6. "I am worthy of care."
7. Now, gently massage your hands, then your arms and shoulders. Move to your legs and feet if comfortable. Let your touch be slow and intentional, like a thank-you to your body.
8. Finish by wrapping your arms around yourself in a gentle self-hug. Hold for a few breaths.
9. Say out loud or silently:
10. "Thank you, body. I choose to care for you."

Optional Reflection Prompt

What does nourishment mean to you today—physically, emotionally, and spiritually?

Let This Be Enough:

You honored your body. You listened with care.

That is enough. That is healing.

WEEK 4

INTRODUCTION
REST AND REBUILDING

Sometimes, the most productive thing you can do is rest.

We live in a world that glorifies hustle—where productivity is often treated like a badge of honor and rest is seen as weakness or laziness. But after heartbreak, that mindset can become a trap. When your body and mind are already in survival mode, pushing through only deepens the burnout. True healing—physically, mentally, emotionally—requires deep, intentional rest.

This has been one of the hardest lessons for me. I've struggled with insomnia for most of my life. Even as a child, sleep didn't come easily. I always felt like there was something else I should be doing—some task to complete, some emotion to keep buried. After heartbreak, that lifelong struggle with sleep got even worse. Some nights I ran on two or three hours of rest if that. And no matter how tired I was, I couldn't let myself stop. I didn't know how.

But I'm learning.

Slowly, I've started creating practices and rituals to help my body settle. A warm cup of tea. Screens off early. Breathing exercises. Journaling before bed. They haven't "fixed" everything—I still have nights when sleep feels far away—but I no longer see rest as a luxury or something I need to earn. I see it as a vital part of my healing.

This week is about redefining rest—not as doing nothing, but as something deeply restorative. It's about giving yourself permission to slow down, to pause, and to *receive* care instead of constantly giving it. Whether that's sleeping a little longer, taking a mindful walk, or simply lying down and breathing deeply for a few minutes, these small acts of rest are not indulgences—they're necessities.

We'll explore calming bedtime routines, managing emotional stress, creating mental space, and tuning into what your body really needs. You've done so much emotional work. Let this be the week your body catches up.

Let rest be your rebellion. Let it be your healing.

You don't have to have it all figured out. You just have to begin honoring the parts of you that are asking for peace.

Affirmation for the Month:

"My thoughts shape my reality. I choose to cultivate a mindset of resilience, gratitude, and possibility."

Affirmation for the Week:

"I give myself permission to rest, heal, and restore my energy. My body and mind deserve care."

WEEK 4

REST AND REBUILDING JOURNAL ACTIVITIES

———··●··———

Focus: Improving sleep, managing stress, and creating a foundation for long-term well-being.

Visualization:

Picture yourself wrapped in a warm, soft blanket, lying peacefully in a space that feels deeply safe. Visualize each breath bringing calm and each moment of stillness restoring strength to your body and mind.

Daily Practice Reminder:

At the start of each day this week, take a moment to write down and speak aloud:

Your **monthly affirmation:** *"My thoughts shape my reality. I choose to cultivate a mindset of resilience, gratitude, and possibility."*

Your **weekly affirmation:** *"I give myself permission to rest, heal, and restore my energy. My body and mind deserve care."*

Let these words guide your healing. Repeating them daily helps shift your thoughts, build emotional resilience, and rewire your self-talk.

Daily Gratitude Reminder:

After completing your journal prompt each day, take a moment to write down 1 to 3 additional things you are grateful for. These could be people, moments, comforts, or anything that brought you peace or warmth today—no matter how small. Gratitude is a gentle yet powerful way to return to the present and remind yourself of what still supports you.

Remember, there is no right way to journal. Write as much or as little as you need. You can follow the prompts exactly or let them take you somewhere else. Let the prompts be a guide—not a rule. If your heart leads you elsewhere, follow it. These pages are yours. Let them carry what you're holding—no expectations, no perfection required.

DAY 1
THE IMPORTANCE OF SLEEP

Quote: *"Sleep is the best meditation."* – Dalai Lama

Journal Prompt: How has your sleep been affected by heartbreak? Do you notice patterns of insomnia, restlessness, or exhaustion?

Activity: Create a calming nighttime routine—turn off screens an hour before bed, dim the lights, and relax with deep breathing.

Daily Gratitude: What is one simple comfort that makes bedtime feel more peaceful?

Let This be Enough: You gave yourself permission to unwind. You honored the quiet. That is enough.

DAY 2
MANAGING STRESS AND OVERWHELM

Quote: *"Your nervous system deserves kindness."*

Journal Prompt: What are your biggest sources of stress right now? How do you typically handle stress?

Activity: Try a 5-minute body scan meditation to relax tension and reset your nervous system.

Daily Gratitude: What is one thing that brought you peace today, even for a moment?

Let This be Enough: You paused. You breathed. You allowed peace to find its way in. That is enough.

DAY 3
RELEASING EMOTIONAL TRIGGERS

Quote: *"You are not your past. You are healing in the present."*

Journal Prompt: What are some triggers that still bring up strong emotions? How can you shift your response to them?

Activity: When a trigger arises today, practice deep breathing and grounding rather than reacting immediately.

Daily Gratitude: What is something in your life right now that feels safe and steady?

Let This be Enough: You noticed the hurt but didn't become it. You chose presence. That is enough.

DAY 4
THE POWER OF INTENTIONAL REST

Quote: *"Rest is not a reward; it's a necessity."*

Journal Prompt: How often do you let yourself fully rest without guilt? What is your relationship with downtime?

Activity: Schedule 30 minutes today for intentional rest—whether it's napping, reading, or just being still.

Daily Gratitude: What is something restful that you genuinely enjoy?

Let This be Enough: You let go. You stopped chasing and simply *were*. That is enough.

DAY 5
CREATING A SELF-CARE PLAN

Quote: *"Taking care of yourself is part of the healing."*

Journal Prompt: What are three things that help you feel nurtured and cared for? How can you make them part of your weekly routine?

Activity: Write down a simple self-care routine for yourself—things you can do daily, weekly, and monthly to maintain well-being.

Daily Gratitude: What is one act of self-care you've done recently that made you feel good?

Let This be Enough: You thought about what you need. You made space for care. That is enough.

DAY 6
RECOGNIZING PROGRESS IN HEALING

Quote: *"You are stronger than you think."* – AA Milne

Journal Prompt: What is something you can do now that you couldn't at the beginning of your healing journey?

Activity: Look back at previous journal entries and reflect on your progress.

Daily Gratitude: What is one way your mind or body has become stronger through this journey?

Let This be Enough: You looked back—and saw just how far you've come. You gave yourself credit. That is enough.

DAY 7
WEEKLY REFLECTION – REBUILDING STRENGTH

Reflection Questions:

1. How has prioritizing rest and recovery affected me this week?
2. What habits or routines will I continue to support my well-being?
3. In what ways do I feel more in tune with my body?

Activity: Write yourself a letter of encouragement, reminding yourself of all the ways you've taken care of your body and mind this month.

Daily Gratitude: What is one lesson about healing that you've learned from this month?

Somatic Exercise

"Rest is not idleness, and to lie sometimes on the grass under the trees… is by no means a waste of time." – John Lubbock

Rest Ritual – Breath + Stillness

This somatic rest ritual affirms that true healing includes moments of stillness, softness, and surrender.

Instructions

1. Lie down on your back or sit in a supported position with your hands resting over your heart or belly.
2. Close your eyes and take 5 slow breaths, counting to 4 on the inhale and 6 on the exhale.
3. With each exhale, repeat:
4. "I release."
5. "I receive."
6. "I restore."
7. Bring your attention to your body. Feel the weight of your limbs, the support beneath you, the ease of being held without effort.
8. Stay here for 3–5 minutes. If thoughts come, acknowledge them and return to the breath.
9. End with this affirmation, whispered or said aloud:
10. "I have done enough. I am enough. I am at peace."

Optional Reflection Prompt

How did it feel to choose rest as an act of strength?

Let This Be Enough:

You rested. You received. You restored.

That is enough. That is healing.

Monthly Reflection: Month 9

What emotions were most present for me this month?

What was the hardest part of this month's journey?

What breakthrough or insight did I have?

A moment I'm proud of:

A quote, mantra, or affirmation I want to carry forward:

On a scale of 1–10, how connected do I feel to myself right now?
1 ☐ 2 ☐ 3 ☐ 4 ☐ 5 ☐ 6 ☐ 7 ☐ 8 ☐ 9 ☐ 10

What do I need more of next month?

☐ Rest

☐ Joy

☐ Connection

☐ Confidence

☐ Creativity

☐ Other: _____

One word to guide me next month:

FROM MY HEART TO YOURS: CLOSING OUT MONTH 9

Dear You,

This month, you did something powerful—you chose to care for your body and your mind with intention. You tuned in to how heartbreak lives in your physical self, and you met that pain with kindness. Through movement, nourishment, rest, and mindful self-care, you've shown up for your healing in a whole new way.

Take a moment and really let that sink in. Maybe you didn't do it perfectly (whatever that means). Maybe there were hard days, slow starts, or skipped steps. But none of that matters because you kept going. You made choices—big and small—that reminded your body and mind that healing is not just possible... it's already happening.

You've proven to yourself that you are capable of rebuilding. Not just in how you carry yourself physically, but in how you keep rising emotionally. Strength isn't about pushing through—it's about showing up, listening in, and honoring what you need.

Let this be your reminder: your body is your ally. Your mind is learning how to trust again. Healing is happening in all of you—one breath, one stretch, one choice at a time.

So, keep going. Keep listening. Keep trusting the quiet, steady strength that's rising within you.

There's no prompt today—just space to reflect on what you've done and how far you've come.

With love and encouragement,

Katina Lee

PS: If you find yourself drawn back to a prompt, a memory, or a moment—you're allowed to return. The pages will meet you where you are, not where you were.

Sometimes, the second time you write it... you hear yourself more clearly. That is healing too.

MONTH 10

CREATING A VISION FOR YOUR FUTURE – BOOK SUMMARY

After heartbreak, the future may feel uncertain, as if the life you once imagined is no longer possible. In the early days, survival is the focus—but true healing comes when you shift from simply getting by to intentionally creating a future that excites and fulfills you.

Imagining a New Future

Loss can leave you feeling directionless, but your story isn't over. Visualization helps you move from reacting to life's circumstances to designing a future that aligns with your values and desires.

Reframing Setbacks as Redirection

A breakup isn't just an ending—it's an opportunity to realign with who you truly are. Instead of focusing on what's lost, ask yourself: What does this make possible for me? This mindset shift allows you to take control of your narrative.

Expanding Possibilities: The Power of "Yet"

Doubt can limit your vision before you even begin. Adding yet to self-defeating thoughts turns them into possibilities:

1. Instead of "I'll never be happy again," say "I haven't found happiness yet."

Building Your Future with Small Steps

Big dreams take shape through consistent, intentional action. Start with one area—career, relationships, personal growth—and take a small step:

1. Create a vision board or write down one dream with a first action step.
2. Align daily choices with the future you want.

Embracing Fear and Moving Forward Anyway

Fear often accompanies change, but it doesn't have to hold you back. Courage isn't the absence of fear—it's choosing to move forward despite it.

By the end of this chapter, you'll have begun shaping a future beyond heartbreak, guided by your dreams and resilience. The life you want isn't something you have to wait for—it's something you can start creating now.

Reflection Question: What is one dream I am ready to pursue, and what small step can I take toward it this month?

CREATING A VISION FOR YOUR FUTURE – MONTH JOURNAL INTRODUCTION

"Your future is not defined by your past—it is created by the choices you make today." – **Unknown**

After heartbreak, the future can feel uncertain, as if the life you once envisioned is no longer possible. This month is about shifting from merely surviving to actively designing a life that excites and fulfills you.

Healing isn't just about letting go of the past—it's about looking ahead with hope and intention. This chapter will guide you in visualizing your ideal future, setting meaningful goals, and taking small steps to create a life that aligns with your dreams.

What to Expect This Month:

✓ Week 1: Imagining a New Future – Allowing yourself to dream beyond heartbreak

✓ Week 2: Reframing Setbacks – Seeing challenges as redirection, not failure

✓ Week 3: Taking Small Steps – Aligning daily choices with your long-term vision

✓ Week 4: Embracing Possibility – Overcoming fear and moving forward with confidence

Each day, you'll engage in journaling prompts and exercises designed to help you clarify your vision and take action toward the future you want. By the end of this month, you will have shifted from uncertainty to excitement, knowing that your best days are still ahead.

Affirmation for the Month:

"I am the architect of my life. I dream boldly, plan intentionally, and take inspired action toward the future I desire."

WEEK 1
INTRODUCTION
IMAGINING A NEW FUTURE

———·· • ·· ———

After heartbreak, it's common to feel like the future you once pictured has been erased. All the plans, dreams, and quiet hopes tied to another person can suddenly feel meaningless—and that can leave you feeling lost. But just because the path changed doesn't mean the journey is over. This week is about picking up the pieces not to rebuild what was, but to create something new—something that's fully and beautifully yours.

It can be hard to give yourself permission to dream again. There's a vulnerability in it, especially if life hasn't gone the way you hoped. Maybe you're afraid to want too much. Maybe you're scared of being disappointed again. But dreaming is a vital part of healing. It's how we remember that there's more ahead than there is behind. It's how we begin to shift from surviving to thriving.

This week, we'll explore the power of visualization, imagination, and clarity. You'll begin to uncover what you truly want—independent of anyone else's story. Maybe you want a peaceful home, a fulfilling job, deeper friendships, or solo adventures. Your dreams don't have to be perfect or practical—they just have to be yours.

Let this be a gentle invitation to believe in your own future again. Not because everything will go exactly as planned—but because you are worthy of joy, possibility, and a life that lights you up from the inside out.

Affirmation for the Month:

"I am the architect of my life. I dream boldly, plan intentionally, and take inspired action toward the future I desire."

Affirmation for the Week:

"I give myself permission to dream again. My future is full of possibilities, and I am ready to explore them."

WEEK 1

IMAGINING A NEW FUTURE JOURNAL ACTIVITIES

---·· • ··---

Focus: Allowing yourself to dream beyond heartbreak, visualizing possibilities

Visualization:

Close your eyes and picture a version of your life that feels aligned with your truest self—free, fulfilled, and joyful. See the space you're in, the people around you, how you feel in your body. Let yourself imagine without limitation or fear. Let the vision unfold, even if it's not fully clear yet—just let your heart lead.

Daily Practice Reminder:

At the start of each day this week, take a moment to write down and speak aloud:

Your **monthly affirmation:** *"I am the architect of my life. I dream boldly, plan intentionally, and take inspired action toward the future I desire."*

Your **weekly affirmation:** *"I give myself permission to dream again. My future is full of possibilities, and I am ready to explore them."*

Let these words guide your healing. Repeating them daily helps shift your thoughts, build emotional resilience, and rewire your self-talk.

Daily Gratitude Reminder:

After completing your journal prompt each day, take a moment to write down 1 to 3 additional things you are grateful for. These could be people, moments, comforts, or anything that brought you peace or warmth today—no matter how small. Gratitude is a gentle yet powerful way to return to the present and remind yourself of what still supports you.

Remember, there is no right way to journal. Write as much or as little as you need. You can follow the prompts exactly or let them take you somewhere else. Let the prompts be a guide—not a rule. If your heart leads you elsewhere, follow it. These pages are yours. Let them carry what you're holding—no expectations, no perfection required.

DAY 1
THE BLANK SLATE

—··•··—

Quote: *"Every day is a new beginning. Take a deep breath and start again."* – Unknown

Journal Prompt: If you could start fresh with no limitations, what would your dream life look like? Write freely, without worrying about what's realistic.

Activity: Find an image or quote that represents the kind of future you'd love to create. Save it as your phone background or place it somewhere you'll see it daily.

Daily Gratitude: What is one thing about today that made you feel hopeful?

Let This be Enough: You took a step. You showed up. You chose growth. That is enough. That is healing.

DAY 2
LETTING GO OF THE OLD VISION

—··•··—

Quote: *"Sometimes the hardest part isn't letting go but learning to start over."* – Nicole Sobon

Journal Prompt: What parts of the future you imagined with your ex still linger? Are there dreams you can reshape to fit your life now?

Activity: Write a goodbye letter to the version of your future that included them. Thank it for what it taught you and release it with love.

Daily Gratitude: What is one thing about yourself that you appreciate?

Let This be Enough: You released something heavy. You made space for peace. That is enough. That is healing.

DAY 3
THE POWER OF VISUALIZATION

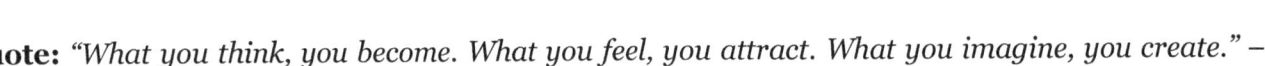

Quote: *"What you think, you become. What you feel, you attract. What you imagine, you create."* – Buddha

Journal Prompt: Close your eyes and visualize your happiest future. Where are you? What are you doing? Who is with you? Describe it in detail.

Activity: Set a timer for five minutes and daydream about your ideal day five years from now. Let yourself feel the excitement of what's possible.

Daily Gratitude: What is one thing in your life right now that brings you joy?

Let This be Enough: You took a step. You showed up. You chose growth. That is enough. That is healing.

DAY 4
IDENTIFYING YOUR CORE DESIRES

Quote: *"Clarity about what matters provides clarity about what does not."* – Cal Newport

Journal Prompt: What do you genuinely want in life—beyond relationships? What dreams, experiences, or accomplishments matter to you?

Activity: Make a list of five things you want to experience in the next five years. Big or small, it doesn't matter—just let yourself dream.

Daily Gratitude: What is one thing about your personality that you love?

Let This be Enough: You took a step. You showed up. You chose growth. That is enough. That is healing.

DAY 5
RECOGNIZING THAT THE BEST IS YET TO COME

Quote: *"What if everything you're going through is preparing you for what you asked for?"* – Unknown

Journal Prompt: If you knew for certain that your best days were still ahead, how would that change the way you feel today?

Activity: Write yourself a letter from your future self, encouraging you to keep moving forward.

Daily Gratitude: What is one lesson from your past that has made you stronger?

Let This be Enough: You took a step. You showed up. You chose growth. That is enough. That is healing.

DAY 6
TRUSTING THE JOURNEY

Quote: *"The universe is not punishing you or blessing you. The universe is responding to the vibration you are offering."* – Abraham Hicks

Journal Prompt: What would it feel like to fully trust that you are on the right path, even if you can't see the full picture yet?

Activity: Take a moment to reflect on where you were five years ago and how much has changed. Use that as proof that transformation is always possible.

Daily Gratitude: What is one small moment today that made you smile?

Let This be Enough: You claimed your space. You chose yourself. That is enough. That is healing.

DAY 7
WEEKLY REFLECTION – SEEING THE BIGGER PICTURE

Reflection Questions:

1. What new possibilities have you allowed yourself to imagine this week?
2. How does it feel to shift your focus from the past to the future?
3. What's one small step you can take next week to move toward the vision you created?

Activity: Create a one-sentence vision statement for your future. Example: "I am creating a life filled with purpose, adventure, and deep connections."

Daily Gratitude: What is one thing you're excited about for the future?

Somatic Exercise

"The future belongs to those who believe in the beauty of their dreams." – Eleanor Roosevelt

Future Self Embodiment – Visualization + Posture

This exercise anchors your dreams into your body, helping your nervous system begin to trust the possibility of that future.

Instructions

1. Stand tall with your feet grounded and your hands relaxed by your sides. Take a few deep breaths.
2. Close your eyes and visualize your future self—confident, joyful, peaceful. Notice:
3. How does she stand?
4. How does she walk?
5. What does her face look like when she smiles?
6. Now begin to embody her posture. Gently lift your chin, soften your shoulders, open your chest. Stand like her. Breathe like her.
7. Walk around your space as your future self for 1–2 minutes. Say to yourself with each step:
8. "I am her."
9. "I am becoming."
10. "My future begins now."
11. Finish by placing your hand over your heart and repeating:
12. "I believe in the life I am creating."

Optional Reflection Prompt

What did you feel when you embodied your future self?

Let This Be Enough:

You envisioned. You embodied. You stepped forward.

That is enough. That is healing.

WEEK 2
INTRODUCTION REFRAMING SETBACKS

When you start building a new vision for your life, it's easy to assume the road forward will be clear and smooth. But the truth is, healing and growth come with challenges. You'll face moments of doubt, frustration, and fear. And when those moments happen, it can be tempting to believe you're failing or slipping backward. But what if those setbacks weren't roadblocks—but redirections?

This week, we'll practice reframing what it means to "mess up" or "fall behind." Setbacks are not signs that you've gone the wrong way—they're simply reminders that you're still human. They're invitations to pause, reflect, and shift. Sometimes what feels like rejection is actually protection. Sometimes what looks like delay is preparation. You haven't failed—you're being guided.

The key to resilience isn't avoiding hard things—it's learning how to meet them with grace. When something doesn't work out the way you hoped, ask: "What is this here to teach me?" or "How can I use this to grow stronger?" These simple questions can help you reclaim your power and keep moving forward with purpose.

Let this be the week where you stop being hard on yourself for the detours and start trusting the path—even when it's winding. You're not off-track. You're evolving.

Affirmation for the Month:

"I am the architect of my life. I dream boldly, plan intentionally, and take inspired action toward the future I desire."

Affirmation for the Week:

"Every challenge I face is shaping me into a stronger, wiser version of myself. Setbacks do not define me—I define how I move forward."

WEEK 2
REFRAMING SETBACKS JOURNAL ACTIVITIES

———··•··———

Focus: Seeing challenges as redirection, not failure

Visualization:

Visualize yourself on a winding path. Along the way are small obstacles—rocks, puddles, hills—but instead of stopping you, each one strengthens your step. See yourself overcoming each one with ease, growing taller and more confident with every move forward. Let yourself feel proud of the journey, not just the destination.

Daily Practice Reminder:

At the start of each day this week, take a moment to write down and speak aloud:

Your **monthly affirmation:** *"I am the architect of my life. I dream boldly, plan intentionally, and take inspired action toward the future I desire."*

Your **weekly affirmation:** *"Every challenge I face is shaping me into a stronger, wiser version of myself. Setbacks do not define me—I define how I move forward."*

Let these words guide your healing. Repeating them daily helps shift your thoughts, build emotional resilience, and rewire your self-talk.

Daily Gratitude Reminder:

After completing your journal prompt each day, take a moment to write down 1 to 3 additional things you are grateful for. These could be people, moments, comforts, or anything that brought you peace or warmth today—no matter how small. Gratitude is a gentle yet powerful way to return to the present and remind yourself of what still supports you.

Remember, there is no right way to journal. Write as much or as little as you need. You can follow the prompts exactly or let them take you somewhere else. Let the prompts be a guide—not a rule. If your heart leads you elsewhere, follow it. These pages are yours. Let them carry what you're holding—no expectations, no perfection required.

DAY 1
EMBRACING THE DETOURS

Quote: *"Sometimes when things are falling apart, they may actually be falling into place."* – Shannon L. Alder

Journal Prompt: Think of a time in your life when something didn't go as planned but ultimately led to something better. What did that experience teach you?

Activity: Write down one current challenge you're facing and brainstorm three potential ways it could lead to growth or opportunity.

Daily Gratitude: What is one challenge that has helped you grow?

Let This be Enough: You took a step. You showed up. You chose growth. That is enough. That is healing.

DAY 2
THE LESSONS IN HEARTBREAK

Quote: *"A breakup is not the end of your story—it's the start of a new chapter."*

Journal Prompt: What has this breakup taught you about yourself, love, or what you genuinely want in life?

Activity: Write a letter to your past self, sharing the lessons you've learned and encouraging yourself to keep going.

Daily Gratitude: What is one lesson from your past relationship that will help you in your future?

Let This be Enough: You took a step. You showed up. You chose growth. That is enough. That is healing.

DAY 3
REFRAMING "FAILURE"

Quote: *"Failure is simply the opportunity to begin again, this time more intelligently."* – Henry Ford

Journal Prompt: What is one thing in your life you've labeled as a "failure"? How can you reframe it as a learning experience?

Activity: Make a list of three things you once struggled with but have since improved on. Use this as proof that growth is always possible.

Daily Gratitude: What is one thing you once struggled with that now comes easily?

Let This be Enough: You faced the fear. You softened the story. That is enough. That is healing.

DAY 4
THE POWER OF "YET"

Quote: *"You may not be where you want to be, but you're not where you used to be either."* – Joel Osteen

Journal Prompt: Rewrite three self-limiting beliefs by adding the word "yet." (Example: Instead of "I'm not healed," write "I'm not healed yet.")

Activity: Say each of your new "yet" statements out loud. Notice how it shifts your mindset from limitation to possibility.

Daily Gratitude: What is one thing you're making progress on, even if it's slow?

Let This be Enough: You took a step. You showed up. You chose growth. That is enough. That is healing.

DAY 5
LETTING GO OF THE "WHAT IFS"

Quote: *"You can't start the next chapter if you keep re-reading the last one."*

Journal Prompt: Are you holding onto any "what if" thoughts about the past? How do they keep you stuck?

Activity: Write a statement of release, such as: "I let go of what could have been and open myself to what is meant to be." Say it out loud as a commitment to yourself.

Daily Gratitude: What is one opportunity or blessing in your life right now?

Let This be Enough: You released something heavy. You made space for peace. That is enough. That is healing.

DAY 6
REDEFINING SUCCESS

Quote: *"Success is not final; failure is not fatal: it is the courage to continue that counts."* – Winston Churchill

Journal Prompt: How do you define success in this season of your life? What would it look like to succeed in your healing journey?

Activity: Create a new definition of success that isn't about perfection, but about progress.

Daily Gratitude: What is one personal strength that has helped you overcome difficulties?

Let This be Enough: You took a step. You showed up. You chose growth. That is enough. That is healing.

DAY 7
WEEKLY REFLECTION – FINDING STRENGTH IN SETBACKS

Reflection Questions:
1. What setback this week challenged you the most?
2. How did you choose to reframe it in a positive way?
3. What's one belief about failure or setbacks that you're ready to let go of?

Activity: Write a short mantra to remind yourself that setbacks are part of the journey. Example: "Every challenge is shaping me for something greater."

Daily Gratitude: What is one thing about yourself that you're proud of?

Somatic Exercise

"Rock bottom became the solid foundation on which I rebuilt my life." – J.K. Rowling

Shake Off the Setback – Nervous System Reset + Movement

This practice supports emotional release through gentle movement and resets your body after a week of reflecting on challenges and reframing setbacks.

Instructions
1. Stand up with feet shoulder-width apart. Take a deep breath in through your nose, exhale slowly through your mouth.
2. Begin by shaking out your hands, then your arms. Gradually move into your shoulders, torso, hips, legs, and feet. Let the movement be loose and unstructured.
3. As you shake, imagine you are releasing fear, frustration, regret, or disappointment. You can say:
4. "I let go."
5. "I'm moving it through."
6. "This does not define me."
7. Continue shaking gently for 1–2 minutes.
8. When you're done, stand still. Place one hand on your heart and one on your belly. Take three deep breaths.
9. Whisper:
10. "I am grounded. I am learning. I am growing."

Optional Reflection Prompt

What did your body feel like it needed to let go of today?

Let This Be Enough:

You released. You breathed. You chose to keep going.

That is enough. That is healing.

WEEK 3
INTRODUCTION
TAKING SMALL STEPS

——— ··●·· ———

Dreaming big is powerful—but turning those dreams into reality can feel overwhelming. You may wonder: Where do I even begin? What if I get it wrong? The truth is, most transformations don't happen in one sweeping motion—they unfold through small, intentional steps taken consistently over time.

This week is about shifting from vision to action. You'll focus on how your everyday choices, habits, and routines either support your future—or pull you away from it. And you'll learn to start where you are, using what you have. There is no perfect time, and you don't need to have it all figured out to move forward. Progress begins the moment you decide to act, even if the action feels small.

Maybe your first step is waking up earlier, journaling for five minutes, reaching out to a new friend, or saying no to something that no longer serves you. Every time you take a step that aligns with your future, you're casting a vote for the person you're becoming. That matters.

Let this week be a celebration of imperfect, beautiful progress. You're not just dreaming about the life you want—you're building it, one meaningful step at a time.

Affirmation for the Month:

"I am the architect of my life. I dream boldly, plan intentionally, and take inspired action toward the future I desire."

Affirmation for the Week:

"Every small step I take is a step toward the future I am creating. I trust the process and embrace the journey."

WEEK 3

TAKING SMALL STEPS JOURNAL ACTIVITIES

—··•··—

Focus: Aligning daily choices with your long-term vision

Visualization:

Picture your future self living a life you love—engaged in meaningful work, surrounded by love, grounded in purpose. Now trace that life backward step by step, until you reach where you are today. Visualize each small action you can take to close that gap. See your steps building a bridge from now to next.

Daily Practice Reminder:

At the start of each day this week, take a moment to write down and speak aloud:

Your **monthly affirmation:** *"I am the architect of my life. I dream boldly, plan intentionally, and take inspired action toward the future I desire."*

Your **weekly affirmation:** *"Every small step I take is a step toward the future I am creating. I trust the process and embrace the journey."*

Let these words guide your healing. Repeating them daily helps shift your thoughts, build emotional resilience, and rewire your self-talk.

Daily Gratitude Reminder:

After completing your journal prompt each day, take a moment to write down 1 to 3 additional things you are grateful for. These could be people, moments, comforts, or anything that brought you peace or warmth today—no matter how small. Gratitude is a gentle yet powerful way to return to the present and remind yourself of what still supports you.

Remember, there is no right way to journal. Write as much or as little as you need. You can follow the prompts exactly or let them take you somewhere else. Let the prompts be a guide—not a rule. If your heart leads you elsewhere, follow it. These pages are yours. Let them carry what you're holding—no expectations, no perfection required.

DAY 1
THE POWER OF SMALL ACTIONS

Quote: *"You don't have to see the whole staircase, just take the first step."* – Martin Luther King Jr.

Journal Prompt: What small step can you take today that aligns with the future you want?

Activity: Identify one action, no matter how small, and commit to doing it today.

Daily Gratitude: What is one small decision you made recently that had a positive impact?

Let This be Enough: You took a step. You showed up. You chose growth. That is enough. That is healing.

DAY 2
BUILDING A MORNING ROUTINE FOR SUCCESS

Quote: *"How you start your day determines how you live your day."* – Louise Hay

Journal Prompt: What does your ideal morning routine look like? How would it support your goals?

Activity: Make one small improvement to your morning routine (e.g., drinking water first thing, setting an intention, or stretching).

Daily Gratitude: What is one thing you appreciate about your mornings?

Let This be Enough: You took a step. You showed up. You chose growth. That is enough. That is healing.

DAY 3
CHOOSING PROGRESS OVER PERFECTION

Quote: *"Done is better than perfect."* – Sheryl Sandberg

Journal Prompt: Where in your life are you waiting for the "perfect" moment instead of just starting?

Activity: Take one imperfect step forward today, whether it's starting a project, making a decision, or taking care of yourself in a new way.

Daily Gratitude: What progress have you made, even if it feels small?

Let This be Enough: You took a step. You showed up. You chose growth. That is enough. That is healing.

DAY 4
THE COMPOUND EFFECT OF SMALL CHOICES

Quote: *"Every choice you make either moves you closer to or further from your goals."*

Journal Prompt: Think of one habit that, if practiced consistently, would improve your future. What small action can you take daily to build that habit?

Activity: Start a habit tracker for the week. Choose one habit and track your consistency.

Daily Gratitude: What is one habit you already practice that benefits you?

Let This be Enough: You took a step. You showed up. You chose growth. That is enough. That is healing.

DAY 5
SAYING YES TO WHAT ALIGNS, NO TO WHAT DOESN'T

Quote: *"Every 'yes' is a no to something else. Choose wisely."* – Greg McKeown

Journal Prompt: What are you currently saying "yes" to that doesn't align with your goals? What would happen if you said "no" instead?

Activity: Practice saying no to one thing today that drains your energy or distracts you from your goals.

Daily Gratitude: What is something you said "yes" to that has enriched your life?

Let This be Enough: You took a step. You showed up. You chose growth. That is enough. That is healing.

DAY 6
VISUALIZING YOUR IDEAL DAY

Quote: *"Your future depends on what you do today."* – Mahatma Gandhi

Journal Prompt: If you could design your perfect day, what would it look like? How would you spend your time?

Activity: Write out your "ideal day" in detail. Then, find one small way to bring part of that vision into today.

Daily Gratitude: What is one part of your current routine that brings you joy?

Let This be Enough: You took a step. You showed up. You chose growth. That is enough. That is healing.

DAY 7
WEEKLY REFLECTION – CELEBRATING SMALL WINS

Reflection Questions:

1. What small steps did you take this week toward your future?
2. How did those actions make you feel?
3. What's one thing you learned about yourself this week?

Activity: Write a note to yourself celebrating your progress. Remind yourself that every step, no matter how small, matters.

Daily Gratitude: What is one personal quality that has helped you move forward?

Somatic Exercise

"Success is the sum of small efforts, repeated day in and day out." – Robert Collier

Root Into Action – Grounding + Future-Oriented Movement

This somatic practice helps integrate the small steps you've taken throughout the week by anchoring them physically and emotionally into your body.

Instructions

1. Stand barefoot (if possible) with both feet planted firmly on the ground. Close your eyes.
2. Visualize roots growing from the soles of your feet into the earth—deep, strong, supportive.
3. Take three slow, grounding breaths, inhaling through the nose and exhaling through the mouth. With each breath, feel more centered.
4. Begin shifting your weight slowly from one foot to the other, gently swaying. With each shift, say aloud or internally:
5. "I take small steps."
6. "Each step matters."
7. "I am building the life I desire."
8. After a few minutes, return to stillness. Place your hands over your heart and say:
9. "I am rooted. I am growing. I am moving forward."

Optional Reflection Prompt

What small win are you most proud of today?

Let This Be Enough:

You moved with purpose. You celebrated your steps.

That is enough. That is healing.

WEEK 4

INTRODUCTION
EMBRACING POSSIBILITY

——— ··●·· ———

The final week of this chapter is about stepping fully into your power. You've spent the past few weeks envisioning, releasing, and acting. Now, it's time to widen your lens and embrace the truth: anything is possible when you believe in yourself.

Fear might still be there—fear of failure, fear of rejection, fear of the unknown. That's okay. Fear doesn't mean you're unready—it means you're expanding. You're moving beyond what's comfortable and choosing to believe that you are capable of more. That belief is everything. Because the future you want won't arrive all at once—but it *will* come to those who keep showing up for it.

This week is your invitation to imagine boldly, dream courageously, and take action rooted in faith rather than fear. You'll practice trusting the timing of your life, seeing challenges as part of the unfolding story, and letting yourself want *more*. Not because you're not already enough—but because you finally realize how worthy you are of all the goodness that life has to offer.

You don't have to settle. You're allowed to dream bigger. You're allowed to want things that light you up. And you're absolutely allowed to go after them.

Affirmation for the Month:

"I am the architect of my life. I dream boldly, plan intentionally, and take inspired action toward the future I desire."

Affirmation for the Week:

"I trust in the possibilities ahead. I am open to new experiences, new opportunities, and new growth."

WEEK 4
EMBRACING POSSIBILITY JOURNAL ACTIVITIES

Focus: Overcoming fear, expanding your vision, and moving forward with confidence

Visualization:

Imagine standing at the edge of a cliff, looking out over a vast, beautiful landscape that represents your future. Every color, sound, and detail reflect something you deeply desire. As you inhale, feel the energy of that vision. As you exhale, release fear. Visualize yourself stepping forward—not with certainty, but with faith. Trust that the path will rise to meet you.

Daily Practice Reminder:

At the start of each day this week, take a moment to write down and speak aloud:

Your **monthly affirmation:** *"I am the architect of my life. I dream boldly, plan intentionally, and take inspired action toward the future I desire."*

Your **weekly affirmation:** *"I trust in the possibilities ahead. I am open to new experiences, new opportunities, and new growth."*

Let these words guide your healing. Repeating them daily helps shift your thoughts, build emotional resilience, and rewire your self-talk.

Daily Gratitude Reminder:

After completing your journal prompt each day, take a moment to write down 1 to 3 additional things you are grateful for. These could be people, moments, comforts, or anything that brought you peace or warmth today—no matter how small. Gratitude is a gentle yet powerful way to return to the present and remind yourself of what still supports you.

Remember, there is no right way to journal. Write as much or as little as you need. You can follow the prompts exactly or let them take you somewhere else. Let the prompts be a guide—not a rule. If your heart leads you elsewhere, follow it. These pages are yours. Let them carry what you're holding—no expectations, no perfection required.

DAY 1
CHOOSING COURAGE OVER COMFORT

Quote: *"Everything you want is on the other side of fear."* – Jack Canfield

Journal Prompt: What fears are holding you back from stepping into your future?

Activity: Take one small action today that challenges your comfort zone (e.g., reaching out to someone, trying a new experience, or speaking your truth).

Daily Gratitude: What is one time in your past when you were brave?

Let This be Enough: You took a step. You showed up. You chose growth. That is enough. That is healing.

DAY 2
RELEASING THE FEAR OF FAILURE

Quote: *"You miss 100% of the shots you don't take."* – Wayne Gretzky

Journal Prompt: What is one thing you've avoided doing because you're afraid of failing? What if failure was simply part of the learning process?

Activity: Take the first step toward something you've been afraid to pursue. It doesn't have to be perfect—just start.

Daily Gratitude: What is one lesson you've learned from a past failure?

Let This be Enough: You released something heavy. You made space for peace. That is enough. That is healing.

DAY 3
SEEING SETBACKS AS SETUPS

Quote: *"Sometimes life doesn't give you what you want, not because you don't deserve it, but because you deserve more."*

Journal Prompt: Think about a time something didn't go as planned but ended up leading to something better. How can you apply that perspective to challenges you face now?

Activity: Write a letter to your future self, reassuring them that setbacks are part of the journey and will lead to growth.

Daily Gratitude: What is one challenge that helped shape you into who you are today?

Let This be Enough: You took a step. You showed up. You chose growth. That is enough. That is healing.

DAY 4
TRUSTING THE TIMING OF YOUR LIFE

Quote: *"What is meant for you will not pass you by."* – Irish Proverb

Journal Prompt: Are you trying to force a timeline, or are you allowing things to unfold naturally? How can you surrender to the process while still taking action?

Activity: Write down three things you want to manifest in your future. Then, let go of the need to control *when* they happen, trusting they will come at the right time.

Daily Gratitude: What is one thing in your life that happened at the perfect time, even if you didn't see it that way at first?

Let This be Enough: You claimed your space. You chose yourself. That is enough. That is healing.

DAY 5
ALLOWING YOURSELF TO DREAM BIGGER

Quote: *"If your dreams don't scare you, they're not big enough."* – Ellen Johnson Sirleaf

Journal Prompt: If you had no limitations (money, time, fear), what would you pursue? What is stopping you from going after it now?

Activity: Make a list of "impossible" dreams, then pick one and brainstorm a first step to make it feel more real.

Daily Gratitude: What is one dream you are excited to work toward?

Let This be Enough: You took a step. You showed up. You chose growth. That is enough. That is healing.

DAY 6
LIVING IN ALIGNMENT WITH YOUR VISION

Quote: *"The future depends on what you do today."* – Mahatma Gandhi

Journal Prompt: If your future self could give you advice, what would they say? How can you start embodying that version of yourself now?

Activity: Act *as if* your dream life is already unfolding. Dress the part, think the part, or take an action that aligns with your highest vision.

Daily Gratitude: What is one thing you love about who you are becoming?

Let This be Enough: You imagined something more. You believed again. That is enough. That is healing.

DAY 7
WEEKLY REFLECTION – STEPPING INTO THE FUTURE

Reflection Questions:

1. How has your mindset shifted over the past month?
2. What steps have you taken toward your vision?
3. What are you most excited about in your future?

Activity: Write a commitment to yourself: What promise do you want to make about how you'll continue growing and embracing new possibilities?

Daily Gratitude: What is one thing about your future that excites you?

Somatic Exercise

"Go confidently in the direction of your dreams. Live the life you have imagined." – Henry David Thoreau

Open to Possibility – Expansive Stretching + Breath

This final practice of the month embodies openness, hope, and trust in the future you're stepping into.

Instructions

1. Begin by standing tall with feet shoulder-width apart. Close your eyes and take three deep breaths, grounding yourself in the present.
2. As you inhale, raise your arms up and out into a wide V-shape, chest open. Feel your heart lifting toward the sky.
3. As you exhale, gently lower your arms back down, imagining you are releasing fear or limitation with your breath.
4. Repeat this movement slowly for 1–2 minutes, saying aloud or internally with each inhale:
5. "I am open."
6. "I am ready."
7. "I welcome what's next."
8. End by bringing your palms together at your heart, bowing your head slightly, and saying:
9. "I trust myself and the path ahead."

Optional Reflection Prompt

What does it feel like in your body to welcome your future?

Let This Be Enough:

You opened. You released. You welcomed what's next.

That is enough. That is healing.

Monthly Reflection: Month 10

What emotions were most present for me this month?
_____

What was the hardest part of this month's journey?
_____

What breakthrough or insight did I have?
_____

A moment I'm proud of:
_____

A quote, mantra, or affirmation I want to carry forward:
_____

On a scale of 1–10, how connected do I feel to myself right now?

1 ☐ 2 ☐ 3 ☐ 4 ☐ 5 ☐ 6 ☐ 7 ☐ 8 ☐ 9 ☐ 10

What do I need more of next month?

☐ Rest

☐ Joy

☐ Connection

☐ Confidence

☐ Creativity

☐ Other: _____

One word to guide me next month:
_____

FROM MY HEART TO YOURS: CLOSING OUT MONTH 10

———··•··———

Dear You,

Look at how far you've come.

There was a time when you didn't know if you'd make it through the heartbreak—when every day felt like a battle just to keep going. But here you are, standing at the edge of something new. Something filled with possibility.

This journey hasn't been easy. It's required you to sit with your pain, face the unknown, let go of what was, and slowly open your heart to what could be. There were days when doubt crept in, when old wounds whispered familiar lies, when the future felt too uncertain to trust. But still—you kept going. And that is the clearest proof of your strength.

You've rewritten your story. Not by erasing the past, but by choosing how you move forward. You've reclaimed your mind, your body, your heart, and your vision. You've learned that healing isn't about forgetting—it's about transforming.

And now, the road ahead is wide open.

You are no longer defined by what hurt you. You are no longer tied to the version of yourself that lived in survival. You are free to shape your future—with intention, with clarity, and with a heart that knows its own worth.

So, take the dreams you've rediscovered, the lessons you've learned, and the strength you've built... and walk boldly into the life that is waiting for you.

You are not just surviving anymore.

You are thriving.

And the best part? This is only the beginning.

There's no prompt today—just space. Write what's on your heart. Celebrate how far you've come.

With all my love and belief in you,

Katina Lee

PS: If you find yourself drawn back to a prompt, a memory, or a moment—you're allowed to return. The pages will meet you where you are, not where you were.

Sometimes, the second time you write it... you hear yourself more clearly. That is healing too.

MONTH 11

OPENING YOUR HEART AGAIN – BOOK SUMMARY

Loving again after heartbreak is an act of courage. The walls built for protection can also keep love out, making trust and vulnerability feel like risks. But opening your heart isn't about rushing into a new relationship—it's about rediscovering your ability to give and receive love, starting with yourself.

Healing Before Love

Love should never be a distraction from healing. True readiness comes when you no longer seek love to fill a void but to complement the life you've built.

Knowing Your Worth

Heartbreak teaches what you don't want—healing helps define what you do. The right love won't require proving your worth, shrinking yourself, or sacrificing your peace. Love should uplift, not deplete.

Reframing Rejection

Rejection isn't a measure of your worth but a redirection toward better alignment. Trusting again starts with trusting yourself—your instincts, boundaries, and ability to walk away when something isn't right.

Balancing Boundaries & Vulnerability

Boundaries protect your heart; vulnerability allows it to connect. The right person won't challenge your boundaries but will respect and honor them while welcoming your openness.

Love as an Addition, not a Fix

A fulfilling relationship enhances, not completes, your life. Focus on becoming the person who naturally attracts the love you seek.

Taking Small Steps

Opening your heart doesn't mean rushing—it starts with small acts of trust: strengthening friendships, embracing joy, and allowing meaningful connections.

By the end of this chapter, you'll understand that love isn't something you chase—it's something you allow when the time is right.

Reflection Question: How can I open my heart while protecting my peace and honoring my worth?

OPENING YOUR HEART AGAIN – MONTH JOURNAL INTRODUCTION

"The bravest thing you can do after heartbreak is believe in love again." – Unknown

After experiencing deep hurt, opening your heart again can feel risky—even impossible. This month is about exploring what it means to trust, connect, and embrace love again, whether in friendships, family, or future relationships.

Loving again isn't about rushing into something new—it's about healing the barriers that keep love out. This chapter will help you rebuild trust in yourself, set healthy boundaries, and recognize what you truly deserve in love and relationships.

What to Expect This Month:

- ✓ Week 1: Understanding Your Readiness – Recognizing emotional wounds and fears around love
- ✓ Week 2: Rebuilding Trust – Strengthening trust in yourself and recognizing safe connections
- ✓ Week 3: Setting Boundaries in Love – Protecting your heart while staying open to connection
- ✓ Week 4: Attracting Healthy Love – Defining what you want and stepping forward with confidence

Each day, you'll reflect on past patterns, explore what healthy love looks like, and practice opening your heart in small, intentional ways. By the end of this month, you will feel more secure in your ability to love and be loved—on your terms, at your own pace.

Affirmation for the Month:

"Love begins with me. I trust in my ability to give and receive love, knowing that my heart is strong, whole, and ready for new connections."

WEEK 1

INTRODUCTION UNDERSTANDING YOUR READINESS

—··•··—

Opening your heart again after heartbreak isn't about leaping into a new relationship. It's about turning inward and asking, "Am I ready—not to love someone else, but to love *myself* enough to try again?" This week is about checking in with your emotional readiness, not to rush the process, but to bring honesty and compassion to wherever you are right now. Healing is not linear. There's no race. Readiness isn't about being "perfectly healed"—it's about being present with your truth.

When we've been hurt, our instinct is often to protect—to close off, to avoid vulnerability, to retreat into emotional safety. But the same walls that kept pain out can also keep love out. Readiness begins with being willing to gently examine those walls. What are they made of? Fear? Self-doubt? Grief? You don't have to tear them down all at once—you just have to peek over them, slowly and with care.

This week, you'll explore the stories you still carry about love and your capacity to receive it. You'll identify any lingering beliefs that might be holding you back—such as "love always ends in pain" or "I can't trust myself to choose wisely." And you'll begin to rewrite those beliefs from a place of strength and growth. You are not who you were when you were hurt. You are someone who has learned, who is evolving, and who is capable of creating a different kind of love moving forward.

Whether you feel completely open or still a little cautious, this week is not about judgment—it's about curiosity. Be gentle with yourself. You don't need to be "ready" to love someone tomorrow. You just need to be ready to listen to your heart today.

Affirmation for the Month:

"Love begins with me. I trust in my ability to give and receive love, knowing that my heart is strong, whole, and ready for new connections."

Affirmation for the Week:

"I release fear and welcome love in all its forms. My heart is healing, and I trust in my ability to love again."

WEEK 1
UNDERSTANDING YOUR READINESS JOURNAL ACTIVITIES

Focus: Exploring emotional readiness by identifying lingering fears, beliefs, and stories that affect your capacity to give and receive love again.

Visualization:

Close your eyes and take a deep breath. Picture your heart as a gentle light glowing in your chest. It's not too bright, not too dim—just steady. Let yourself notice how it feels without judgment. Maybe it's tender, guarded, hopeful, or still healing.

Now imagine placing your hands over your heart and whispering, "I'm listening." You're not rushing your heart—you're honoring it. Let that light glow a little warmer, knowing it doesn't have to be fully open to be loved.

Take another deep breath. You are allowed to take your time. When you're ready, gently open your eyes and carry that sense of compassion with you.

Daily Practice Reminder:

At the start of each day this week, take a moment to write down and speak aloud:

Your **monthly affirmation:** *"Love begins with me. I trust in my ability to give and receive love, knowing that my heart is strong, whole, and ready for new connections."*

Your **weekly affirmation:** *"I release fear and welcome love in all its forms. My heart is healing, and I trust in my ability to love again."*

Let these words guide your healing. Repeating them daily helps shift your thoughts, build emotional resilience, and rewire your self-talk.

Daily Gratitude Reminder:

After completing your journal prompt each day, take a moment to write down 1 to 3 additional things you are grateful for. These could be people, moments, comforts, or anything that brought you peace or warmth today—no matter how small. Gratitude is a gentle yet powerful way to return to the present and remind yourself of what still supports you.

Remember, there is no right way to journal. Write as much or as little as you need. You can follow the prompts exactly or let them take you somewhere else. Let the prompts be a guide—not a rule. If your heart leads you elsewhere, follow it. These pages are yours. Let them carry what you're holding—no expectations, no perfection required.

DAY 1
ACKNOWLEDGING WHERE YOU ARE

Quote: *"The first step toward change is awareness. The second step is acceptance."* – Nathaniel Branden

Journal Prompt: Where do you feel you are in your journey of healing? Are there areas where you still feel guarded or afraid to love again?

Activity: Write a compassionate letter to yourself, acknowledging the progress you've made and the areas that still need healing.

Daily Gratitude: Write down one way your heart has shown resilience throughout your healing journey.

Let This be Enough: You took a step. You showed up. You chose growth. That is enough. That is healing.

DAY 2
RECOGNIZING EMOTIONAL BARRIERS

Quote: *"The walls we build around us to keep out sadness also keep out joy."* – Jim Rohn

Journal Prompt: What emotional barriers have you built to protect yourself from getting hurt again? How have they helped you, and how might they be holding you back?

Activity: Draw a wall on paper. Inside, write the fears keeping you from love. On the outside, write the benefits of opening your heart again.

Daily Gratitude: List one loving relationship in your life (friendship, family, self-love) that brings you joy and security.

Let This be Enough: You took a step. You showed up. You chose growth. That is enough. That is healing.

DAY 3
RELEASING FEAR OF BEING HURT AGAIN

Quote: *"You can't start the next chapter of your life if you keep rereading the last one."*

Journal Prompt: What scares you most about loving again? Is it fear of rejection, betrayal, or losing yourself? How can you remind yourself that you are stronger now?

Activity: Write a list of affirmations counteracting each fear (e.g., "I am worthy of love that is safe and fulfilling").

Daily Gratitude: Think of a time you showed bravery in love, whether by expressing feelings, setting a boundary, or letting go of the wrong person.

Let This be Enough: You released something heavy. You made space for peace. That is enough. That is healing.

DAY 4
LETTING GO OF PAST HURTS

Quote: *"Holding onto anger is like drinking poison and expecting the other person to die."* – Buddha

Journal Prompt: Are there any lingering resentments from past relationships that still affect you? What would it feel like to release them?

Activity: Write a letter to someone from your past (you don't have to send it) expressing anything left unsaid. When finished, tear it up or burn it as a symbol of release.

Daily Gratitude: Acknowledge one way the pain from your past has led to personal growth.

Let This be Enough: You released something heavy. You made space for peace. That is enough. That is healing.

DAY 5
REDEFINING LOVE ON YOUR TERMS

Quote: *"Love is not about finding the right person but becoming the right person."* – Dr. Neil Clark Warren

Journal Prompt: What does love mean to you now? How has your understanding of love changed since your last relationship?

Activity: Create a "New Definition of Love" statement for yourself. What kind of love do you want to attract, and what will it feel like?

Daily Gratitude: List one way you show love to yourself every day.

Let This be Enough: You opened your heart. You honored what you need. That is enough. That is healing.

DAY 6
EMBRACING THE POSSIBILITY OF LOVE AGAIN

Quote: *"The heart is a muscle. The more you use it, the stronger it gets."*

Journal Prompt: Imagine yourself in a future relationship that is safe, healthy, and fulfilling. What does it look and feel like? How is it different from past relationships?

Activity: Close your eyes and visualize this version of love. Breathe into the feeling of safety and joy.

Daily Gratitude: Write down one thing about your life today that would make you a great partner in the future.

Let This be Enough: You opened your heart. You honored what you need. That is enough. That is healing.

DAY 7
WEEKLY REFLECTION – AM I READY TO LOVE AGAIN?

Quote: *"Healing doesn't mean the damage never existed. It means the damage no longer controls you."* – Akshay Dubey

Reflection Questions:

1. What emotions surfaced this week as you explored love and fear?
2. Where do you still feel blocked, and how can you work through it?
3. What small steps can you take to open your heart in a way that feels safe and authentic?

Activity: Write a message to your future self about what you hope for in love and relationships.

Daily Gratitude: Express appreciation for your heart's ability to heal and love again.

Somatic Exercise

"Healing doesn't mean the damage never existed. It means the damage no longer controls you." – Akshay Dubey

Release & Recenter – Neck, Jaw, and Shoulder Tension Reset

This somatic reset encourages physical softness and emotional release—helping your body unlearn the habit of tension and re-learn the safety of ease.

Instructions

1. Find a comfortable seated position, with your spine upright and relaxed.
2. Begin with three deep breaths, inhaling through the nose and exhaling through the mouth. As you exhale, sigh it out audibly to release pressure.
3. Gently roll your shoulders backward in slow circles, then forward. Do this 5 times each direction, breathing steadily.
4. Place your hands on your jaw, and softly open and close your mouth, noticing any clenching. Then, massage your jawline with your fingertips, saying silently:
5. "I release."
6. "I soften."
7. "I let go."
8. Tilt your head gently from side to side, ear toward shoulder. Hold each side for a few seconds. Then let your head hang slightly forward, relaxing your neck.
9. End by placing your hands over your heart. Close your eyes and repeat:
10. "I don't have to control everything. I am safe to surrender."

Optional Reflection Prompt

Where in your body do you feel resistance when it comes to love—and how did that shift during this practice?

Let This Be Enough:

You softened. You released. You reminded your body that love begins with safety.

That is enough. That is healing.

WEEK 2

INTRODUCTION REBUILDING TRUST

—————•••••—————

Trust—once broken—doesn't rebuild overnight. And it doesn't just apply to trusting others. One of the most overlooked parts of healing after heartbreak is learning to trust *yourself* again. This week is about rebuilding that inner foundation. It's about learning to believe that you can listen to your instincts, honor your needs, and protect your peace without shutting yourself off from the possibility of connection.

You may be asking: How do I trust again when the last time I did, I was hurt? That's a valid question—and one rooted in self-preservation. But healing isn't about making sure you never get hurt again. It's about building the inner strength to know that if hurt happens, you'll handle it with wisdom and resilience. You'll see the signs. You'll choose differently. And most importantly, you'll trust that your worth isn't determined by someone else's ability to honor it.

This week, you'll reflect on the times you silenced your inner voice for the sake of love. You'll explore where your boundaries were crossed and why, and begin rewriting the story that says, "I can't trust myself." Because you can. You've already come so far—and that progress is proof that you're capable of making empowered, self-honoring choices moving forward.

You don't have to trust blindly. In fact, healthy trust is built slowly and with discernment. Let this week be a return to yourself—a quiet, confident reminder that you know what love feels like when it's right. You're not rebuilding trust to be naïve again. You're doing it so you can love again—with both courage and clarity.

Affirmation for the Month:

"Love begins with me. I trust in my ability to give and receive love, knowing that my heart is strong, whole, and ready for new connections."

Affirmation for the Week:

"I trust myself to recognize love that is safe, healthy, and aligned with my worth. I release fear and open my heart to new possibilities."

WEEK 2

REBUILDING TRUST JOURNAL ACTIVITIES

———··●··———

Focus: Strengthening your inner trust, identifying past moments of self-abandonment, and choosing to believe in your ability to recognize and nurture safe, respectful connections.

Visualization:

Take a deep breath in… and exhale slowly. Imagine yourself standing on solid ground, feet planted, spine tall. You are steady, even if the world has shifted around you.

Now, bring your awareness inward. Picture a small flame at the center of your chest—this is your inner trust. Maybe it flickers. Maybe it burns strong. Whatever it looks like, it's still there. Still alive. Still yours.

Breathe into that flame and say silently, "I trust myself to choose what's right for me." Let that flame grow just a little stronger. When you're ready, open your eyes, carrying that quiet strength forward.

Daily Practice Reminder:

At the start of each day this week, take a moment to write down and speak aloud:

Your **monthly affirmation:** *"Love begins with me. I trust in my ability to give and receive love, knowing that my heart is strong, whole, and ready for new connections."*

Your **weekly affirmation:** *"I trust myself to recognize love that is safe, healthy, and aligned with my worth. I release fear and open my heart to new possibilities."*

Let these words guide your healing. Repeating them daily helps shift your thoughts, build emotional resilience, and rewire your self-talk.

Daily Gratitude Reminder:

After completing your journal prompt each day, take a moment to write down 1 to 3 additional things you are grateful for. These could be people, moments, comforts, or anything that brought you peace or warmth today—no matter how small. Gratitude is a gentle yet powerful way to return to the present and remind yourself of what still supports you.

Remember, there is no right way to journal. Write as much or as little as you need. You can follow the prompts exactly or let them take you somewhere else. Let the prompts be a guide—not a rule. If your heart leads you elsewhere, follow it. These pages are yours. Let them carry what you're holding—no expectations, no perfection required.

DAY 1
REBUILDING TRUST IN YOURSELF

Quote: *"Trust yourself. You've survived a lot, and you'll survive whatever comes next."*

Journal Prompt: Have you ever ignored red flags in past relationships? How can you rebuild trust in yourself to recognize when something isn't right in the future?

Activity: Write a list of five ways you will honor your intuition moving forward.

Daily Gratitude: Acknowledge one decision you made in the past that showed you were capable of trusting yourself.

Let This be Enough: You claimed your space. You chose yourself. That is enough. That is healing.

DAY 2
RELEASING THE FEAR OF BEING HURT AGAIN

Quote: *"Fear and trust cannot coexist. Choose trust."* – Sue Dyer

Journal Prompt: What past experiences make it difficult for you to trust others? What would it take for you to release those fears?

Activity: Write a letter to your past self, offering reassurance that even if trust was broken before, you are wiser and stronger now.

Daily Gratitude: Write one lesson you've learned about trust that will help you in future relationships.

Let This be Enough: You released something heavy. You made space for peace. That is enough. That is healing.

DAY 3
IDENTIFYING SAFE AND UNSAFE LOVE

Quote: *"Love should not require losing yourself to keep it."*

Journal Prompt: What does a safe relationship feel like to you? What are signs of love that is secure, honest, and nurturing?

Activity: Create a list of qualities that define a safe and trustworthy partner. Compare it to past experiences and recognize patterns you want to avoid.

Daily Gratitude: List one person in your life who has proven to be trustworthy.

Let This be Enough: You opened your heart. You honored what you need. That is enough. That is healing.

DAY 4
STRENGTHENING YOUR BOUNDARIES

Quote: *"Boundaries are the distance at which I can love you and me simultaneously."* – Prentis Hemphill

Journal Prompt: Have you ever compromised your boundaries in relationships? How did it impact your ability to trust?

Activity: Write down three non-negotiable boundaries you will uphold in future relationships to protect your emotional well-being.

Daily Gratitude: Acknowledge one time you stood up for yourself, even if it was difficult.

Let This be Enough: You claimed your space. You chose yourself. That is enough. That is healing.

DAY 5
LEARNING TO TRUST LOVE AGAIN

Quote: *"You don't have to trust everyone, but you do have to trust that love still exists for you."*

Journal Prompt: What would it feel like to fully trust love again? What fears come up when you think about opening your heart?

Activity: Write an affirmation that reminds you love is still possible, such as: *"I trust that love will find me when I am ready."*

Daily Gratitude: Name one example of love that you witness in the world (it can be romantic, platonic, or self-love).

Let This be Enough: You claimed your space. You chose yourself. That is enough. That is healing.

DAY 6
TRUSTING WITHOUT LOSING YOURSELF

Quote: *"Trust takes years to build, seconds to break, and a lifetime to repair. Choose wisely."*

Journal Prompt: How can you remain open to love without losing yourself in the process? What does balance look like in a healthy relationship?

Activity: Visualize a future relationship where trust exists. How do you feel? What makes it feel safe? Write about that vision in detail.

Daily Gratitude: Write one way you honor your individuality in relationships.

Let This be Enough: You claimed your space. You chose yourself. That is enough. That is healing.

DAY 7
WEEKLY REFLECTION – REBUILDING TRUST IN LOVE

Reflection Questions:

1. How has your view of trust changed this week?
2. What small steps can you take to rebuild trust in yourself and others?
3. What boundaries will help you maintain trust in future relationships?

Activity: Write a commitment statement to yourself about how you will approach trust moving forward.

Daily Gratitude: Express gratitude for your heart's resilience and ability to trust again, even after pain.

Somatic Exercise

"I am not what happened to me, I am what I choose to become." – Carl Jung

Inner Compass – Grounding + Chest Opening Sequence

This sequence grounds you while opening your heart to self-trust—the foundation of strong inner guidance.

Instructions

1. Stand barefoot, feet shoulder-width apart. Feel the ground beneath you. Wiggle your toes and gently shift your weight side to side.
2. Close your eyes and take three deep belly breaths. Inhale through the nose, expanding your stomach. Exhale through the mouth with a soft "haaa" sound.
3. As you inhale, reach both arms out and up toward the sky, stretching your chest and lifting your heart.
4. As you exhale, bring your arms down slowly, palms facing the earth. Repeat this movement 3 times, visualizing yourself calling in clarity and releasing confusion.
5. Then place one hand on your heart, one hand on your belly. Ask silently:
6. "What is true for me right now?"
7. "What do I already know deep within?"
8. Breathe gently into this moment, trusting what arises.
9. End by softly whispering or thinking:
10. "My body is wise. I trust my inner knowing."

Optional Reflection Prompt

What truth did your body reveal to you when you gave it a moment to speak?

Let This Be Enough:

You asked. You listened. You trusted your own wisdom.

That is enough. That is healing.

WEEK 3
INTRODUCTION
SETTING BOUNDARIES IN LOVE

When it comes to love, boundaries are not barriers—they're bridges to healthier, more fulfilling relationships. Many of us were taught that setting boundaries means we're being difficult, selfish, or unloving. But the truth is, boundaries are one of the most loving things you can offer—not just to yourself, but to others. They clarify what you need to feel safe, respected, and emotionally connected.

This week, we shift from seeing boundaries as rules to seeing them as self-respect in action. You'll examine the ways you've compromised in past relationships—maybe tolerating inconsistent behavior, accepting emotional unavailability, or silencing your own needs in the name of "keeping the peace." These patterns may have protected you temporarily, but they ultimately kept you disconnected from your truth.

Now, you're writing a new story—one where your "no" is honored as much as your "yes." One where your voice, needs, and space matter. Boundaries allow you to stay open *without* losing yourself. They create the conditions for healthy, mutual love to flourish. And when someone truly values you, they won't resist your boundaries—they'll respect them.

This week is your opportunity to get clear on what you want and need in future relationships. What's non-negotiable for your peace? What behavior crosses the line? Where do you need more structure to feel emotionally safe? And perhaps most importantly: Can you give yourself permission to enforce those boundaries with love, not guilt?

Affirmation for the Month:

"Love begins with me. I trust in my ability to give and receive love, knowing that my heart is strong, whole, and ready for new connections."

Affirmation for the Week:

"My boundaries are an expression of self-love. I protect my heart while staying open to love that aligns with my worth."

WEEK 3

SETTING BOUNDARIES IN LOVE JOURNAL ACTIVITIES

—··•·· ———·

Focus: Defining and reinforcing boundaries that honor your emotional needs, protect your peace, and support relationships that align with your worth.

Visualization:

Close your eyes and breathe in deeply. Visualize a soft glow forming around your body, like a protective bubble. It's warm, light, and firm. This is your boundary—your sacred space.

Now imagine someone approaching. You're calm, grounded. You kindly hold up your hand and say, "I choose what I allow into my life." The light around you pulses gently, not as a wall, but as a shield of love and self-respect.

Take another breath. Let this boundary support you as you move through your day. When you're ready, open your eyes with clarity and strength.

Daily Practice Reminder:

At the start of each day this week, take a moment to write down and speak aloud:

Your **monthly affirmation:** *"Love begins with me. I trust in my ability to give and receive love, knowing that my heart is strong, whole, and ready for new connections."*

Your **weekly affirmation:** *"My boundaries are an expression of self-love. I protect my heart while staying open to love that aligns with my worth."*

Let these words guide your healing. Repeating them daily helps shift your thoughts, build emotional resilience, and rewire your self-talk.

Daily Gratitude Reminder:

After completing your journal prompt each day, take a moment to write down 1 to 3 additional things you are grateful for. These could be people, moments, comforts, or anything that brought you peace or warmth today—no matter how small. Gratitude is a gentle yet powerful way to return to the present and remind yourself of what still supports you.

Remember, there is no right way to journal. Write as much or as little as you need. You can follow the prompts exactly or let them take you somewhere else. Let the prompts be a guide—not a rule. If your heart leads you elsewhere, follow it. These pages are yours. Let them carry what you're holding—no expectations, no perfection required.

DAY 1
DEFINING YOUR RELATIONSHIP BOUNDARIES

—••●•• —

Quote: *"The right person will never make you feel guilty for protecting your peace."*

Journal Prompt: What boundaries are most important to you in a romantic relationship? Why?

Activity: Write a list of five boundaries that will help you maintain emotional well-being in future relationships.

Daily Gratitude: Reflect on one past relationship (romantic or platonic) that respected your boundaries and how that felt.

Let This be Enough: You claimed your space. You chose yourself. That is enough. That is healing.

DAY 2
UNDERSTANDING THE COST OF COMPROMISING YOUR BOUNDARIES

—••●•• —

Quote: *"Every time you compromise your boundaries for the wrong person, you step further away from yourself."*

Journal Prompt: Have you ever compromised your boundaries to keep a relationship? What did you learn from that experience?

Activity: Write a letter to your past self, forgiving them for times they ignored their own needs, and committing to doing better moving forward.

Daily Gratitude: Identify one situation where you upheld a boundary and felt empowered because of it.

Let This be Enough: You claimed your space. You chose yourself. That is enough. That is healing.

DAY 3
BOUNDARIES AS A FORM OF SELF-RESPECT

Quote: *"Boundaries teach others how to love you."*

Journal Prompt: How do you want to be treated in love? How can your boundaries reflect that?

Activity: Write an affirmation about your boundaries, such as: *"I do not have to explain or defend my boundaries. I set them with confidence and self-respect."*

Daily Gratitude: List one way you show respect to yourself and your needs.

Let This be Enough: You claimed your space. You chose yourself. That is enough. That is healing.

DAY 4
LEARNING TO SAY NO WITHOUT GUILT

Quote: *"No is a complete sentence."* – Anne Lamott

Journal Prompt: Why does saying no sometimes feel difficult? How can you reframe it as an act of self-care?

Activity: Write three examples of situations where saying no would have protected your energy. Then, rewrite how you will respond in similar situations in the future.

Daily Gratitude: Acknowledge one way saying no has brought you peace in the past.

Let This be Enough: You took a step. You showed up. You chose growth. That is enough. That is healing.

DAY 5
BOUNDARIES AND EMOTIONAL AVAILABILITY

Quote: *"You should not have to beg for love, attention, or respect."* -Unknown

Journal Prompt: Have you ever accepted emotional unavailability in a partner? What will you do differently moving forward?

Activity: Write a commitment statement to yourself about not settling for inconsistent or unavailable love.

Daily Gratitude: Identify one example of emotional availability (from a friend, family member, or past partner) that made you feel safe and valued.

Let This be Enough: You claimed your space. You chose yourself. That is enough. That is healing.

DAY 6
BOUNDARIES IN COMMUNICATION AND CONFLICT

Quote: *"Healthy love does not require walking on eggshells."*

Journal Prompt: How do you typically handle conflict in relationships? What would a healthy approach look like for you?

Activity: Write three boundary statements for how you will handle conflict moving forward. Examples:
1. "I will not engage in conversations that involve yelling or disrespect."
2. "If I feel emotionally overwhelmed, I will take a break and revisit the discussion later."
3. "I will not allow anyone to dismiss my feelings or manipulate my emotions."

Daily Gratitude: List one person in your life who respects your communication boundaries.

Let This be Enough: You claimed your space. You chose yourself. That is enough. That is healing.

DAY 7
WEEKLY REFLECTION – SETTING BOUNDARIES FOR HEALTHY LOVE

Reflection Questions:

1. What was the biggest lesson you learned about boundaries this week?
2. How can you stay firm in your boundaries while remaining open to love?
3. What boundary do you feel most proud of setting for yourself?

Activity: Write a personal declaration: *"I am worthy of love that honors my boundaries. I will no longer shrink myself to be loved."*

Daily Gratitude: Express gratitude for the clarity and strength that boundaries bring into your life.

Somatic Exercise

"Boundaries are not walls. They are the bridge to love that is safe and fulfilling."

Embodied Boundaries – Arm Extension + Grounding Stance

This somatic practice supports boundary setting by engaging your physical space. It helps you feel the difference between self and other—where you begin and where others end.

Instructions

1. Stand with your feet grounded, hips-width apart. Feel your weight evenly distributed.
2. Slowly extend both arms out to your sides, palms facing outward. Imagine you are pressing against an invisible wall, gently but firmly.
3. Hold this position for 3–5 deep breaths, and with each exhale, repeat:
4. "This is my space."
5. "I protect my energy."
6. "My boundaries are clear and kind."
7. Next, slowly bring your arms inward, crossing them over your chest in a self-hug. Breathe deeply here, acknowledging the safety you are creating for yourself.
8. *Optional:* Walk slowly around your space while imagining a soft, protective bubble around you—your emotional boundary made visible.
9. End by placing your hands over your heart and saying:
10. "I am allowed to protect my peace. My boundaries are sacred."

Optional Reflection Prompt

What does it feel like in your body when you stand firm in your boundaries?

Let This Be Enough:

You claimed your space. You honored your energy.

That is enough. That is healing.

WEEK 4

INTRODUCTION ATTRACTING HEALTHY LOVE

---·••●••·---

Healthy love is not something you find by chasing—it's something you invite by becoming. This final week is about stepping fully into your self-worth and aligning with the kind of love that mirrors your growth. It's not about proving your value to someone else. It's about living in a way that reflects your worth so clearly, that the love you attract naturally honors and uplifts it.

So many people enter new relationships trying to "be enough" for someone else. But here's the shift: You *already are* enough. The work now is to believe that, embody that, and only entertain relationships that reinforce it. Healthy love won't ask you to shrink, settle, or self-abandon. It will meet you where you are—with care, clarity, and consistency.

This week, you'll define the kind of relationship you want to build, not just in theory but in practice. What kind of partnership would support your dreams, respect your boundaries, and challenge you to grow? Who do you need to become to naturally attract and sustain that love? The more aligned you are with your truth, the more naturally aligned your relationships will become.

You don't have to be perfect to attract healthy love. You just have to be authentic. Show up as yourself. Honor your values. Keep your standards high and your heart open. Love will come—not because you chased it, but because you *became* the version of yourself who attracts it effortlessly.

Affirmation for the Month:

"Love begins with me. I trust in my ability to give and receive love, knowing that my heart is strong, whole, and ready for new connections."

Affirmation for the Week:

"I attract love that reflects my worth. I am open to healthy, aligned connections that nourish my soul."

WEEK 4

ATTRACTING HEALTHY LOVE JOURNAL ACTIVITIES

———··•··———

Focus: Clarifying the kind of love you desire, embodying your worth, and allowing love to find you naturally by staying true to your values and authenticity.

Visualization:

Take a moment to breathe deeply. Picture your heart like a flower gently beginning to open. No rush, no force—just soft unfolding.

With each breath, feel warmth expanding in your chest. You are safe. You are ready to receive love that honors who you are.

Now, imagine someone meeting that love with their own light—equal, steady, kind. There's no chase, no fear, only mutual care and respect.

Breathe in one more time. Whisper to yourself, "I welcome love that sees me, values me, and grows with me." When you're ready, open your eyes—open to possibility.

Daily Practice Reminder:

At the start of each day this week, take a moment to write down and speak aloud:

Your **monthly affirmation:** *"Love begins with me. I trust in my ability to give and receive love, knowing that my heart is strong, whole, and ready for new connections."*

Your **weekly affirmation:** *"I attract love that reflects my worth. I am open to healthy, aligned connections that nourish my soul."*

Let these words guide your healing. Repeating them daily helps shift your thoughts, build emotional resilience, and rewire your self-talk.

🍃 Daily Gratitude Reminder:

After completing your journal prompt each day, take a moment to write down 1 to 3 additional things you are grateful for. These could be people, moments, comforts, or anything that brought you peace or warmth today—no matter how small. Gratitude is a gentle yet powerful way to return to the present and remind yourself of what still supports you.

Remember, there is no right way to journal. Write as much or as little as you need. You can follow the prompts exactly or let them take you somewhere else. Let the prompts be a guide—not a rule. If your

heart leads you elsewhere, follow it. These pages are yours. Let them carry what you're holding—no expectations, no perfection required.

DAY 1
DEFINING THE LOVE YOU WANT

Quote: *"You don't attract what you want—you attract what you believe you deserve."*

Journal Prompt: If you could design your ideal relationship, what would it look like? How would it make you feel?

Activity: Create a list of *non-negotiables* and *desirable traits* in a future partner.

Daily Gratitude: Reflect on past experiences that have shown you what you truly want (even if it came through learning what you *don't* want).

Let This be Enough: You opened your heart. You honored what you need. That is enough. That is healing.

DAY 2
BECOMING THE LOVE YOU SEEK

Quote: *"The love you seek begins with the love you give yourself."*

Journal Prompt: How can you embody the qualities you want in a partner?

Activity: Write five ways you can show yourself the kind of love, care, and respect you would want from someone else.

Daily Gratitude: Identify one way you already nurture and care for yourself.

Let This be Enough: You opened your heart. You honored what you need. That is enough. That is healing.

DAY 3
RELEASING FEAR AROUND LOVE

Quote: *"Fear and love cannot coexist. To let love in, you must let fear go."*

Journal Prompt: What fears do you have about opening your heart again? How can you release them?

Activity: Write a letter to your fear, acknowledging its presence but choosing to let it go. Then, write a second letter to your future self, reminding yourself that love is safe, joyful, and meant for you.

Daily Gratitude: Recognize one past experience where you felt truly loved and safe.

Let This be Enough: You released something heavy. You made space for peace. That is enough. That is healing.

DAY 4
TRUSTING LOVE TO FIND YOU

Quote: *"When you stop chasing, what's meant for you will find you."*

Journal Prompt: Have you ever chased love or validation? How did that feel? How would it feel instead to *allow* love to come naturally?

Activity: Write a mantra to remind yourself that love will come when the time is right, such as: *"I do not chase; I attract. What is meant for me will find me."*

Daily Gratitude: Express gratitude for the timing of your life—even if things didn't go as planned, trust they are unfolding perfectly.

Let This be Enough: You claimed your space. You chose yourself. That is enough. That is healing.

DAY 5
RECOGNIZING SAFE & HEALTHY LOVE

Quote: *"The right love won't make you anxious—it will make you feel safe."*

Journal Prompt: How can you recognize the difference between a *healthy* love and a love that simply *feels familiar*?

Activity: Write a list of signs that a relationship is safe, nurturing, and built on mutual respect.

Daily Gratitude: Appreciate one person in your life who makes you feel emotionally safe.

Let This be Enough: You opened your heart. You honored what you need. That is enough. That is healing.

DAY 6
DATING & CONNECTION WITH INTENTION

Quote: *"I am not looking for someone to complete me—I am looking for someone to complement me."*

Journal Prompt: How can you approach dating or new relationships from a place of confidence and self-worth?

Activity: Write three dating or connection *intentions*—not rules but guiding principles that will help you navigate relationships in a way that feels good for you.

Daily Gratitude: Recognize one past moment where you showed up for yourself in a relationship.

Let This be Enough: You opened your heart. You honored what you need. That is enough. That is healing.

DAY 7
WEEKLY REFLECTION –
OPENING YOUR HEART TO THE RIGHT LOVE

Reflection Questions:

1. What was the biggest realization you had about love this week?
2. How do you feel about opening your heart now compared to when you started this journey?
3. What commitment will you make to yourself as you move forward?

Activity: Write a personal affirmation for love, such as: *"I trust love to find me at the right time. I am worthy of deep, fulfilling love that honors my soul."*

Daily Gratitude: Express gratitude for the love that already exists in your life—whether through friendships, family, or self-love.

Somatic Exercise

"When you honor your worth, love becomes a reflection of that."

Integration Flow – Breath, Touch, and Stillness

This somatic practice is designed to help you integrate everything you've explored this month—emotional honesty, body awareness, and boundary setting—into a sense of wholeness and calm.

Instructions

1. Sit or lie down in a comfortable position. Let your body settle.
2. Place one hand on your heart and one on your belly. Take a slow, full breath in through your nose, allowing both areas to rise.
3. Exhale gently through your mouth, and repeat for 5 deep breaths.
4. Now, gently tap or brush your body from head to toe—scalp, face, shoulders, arms, torso, legs. Use light, intentional pressure. This tells your nervous system:
5. "I am here."
6. "I am safe."
7. "I belong in my body."
8. Finish by placing both hands over your heart and saying:
9. "I am whole."
10. "I honor my healing."
11. "I trust myself to keep going."
12. Sit in stillness for one more minute. Let everything settle.

Optional Reflection Prompt

What does wholeness feel like in your body today?

Let This Be Enough:

You arrived. You honored your journey. You opened to love.

That is enough. That is healing.

Monthly Reflection: Month 11

What emotions were most present for me this month?
_____

What was the hardest part of this month's journey?
_____

What breakthrough or insight did I have?
_____

A moment I'm proud of:
_____

A quote, mantra, or affirmation I want to carry forward:
_____

On a scale of 1–10, how connected do I feel to myself right now?

1 ☐ 2 ☐ 3 ☐ 4 ☐ 5 ☐ 6 ☐ 7 ☐ 8 ☐ 9 ☐ 10

What do I need more of next month?

☐ Rest

☐ Joy

☐ Connection

☐ Confidence

☐ Creativity

☐ Other: _____

One word to guide me next month:
_____

FROM MY HEART TO YOURS: CLOSING OUT MONTH 11

Dear You,

You've walked through fire and emerged stronger.

You've faced heartbreak, uncertainty, and the fear of trusting again—and yet here you are, standing in the light of a new beginning. Opening your heart again isn't just about finding love. It's about rediscovering your capacity for joy, connection, and hope. It's about choosing to live fully, even when love has hurt you before.

I know this hasn't been an easy road. There were moments when you questioned whether love was worth the risk, whether your heart could truly mend. You've faced fears, broken patterns, and learned to trust yourself in ways you never had before. And even if you're not quite ready yet—that's okay. Healing doesn't happen all at once. Growth isn't measured by how fast you move forward, but by how intentionally you do so.

Love will come when the time is right—but the most important love, the love you've cultivated within yourself, is already here. You've learned to protect your heart without closing it. To set boundaries without building walls. And most importantly, you've realized that you are already whole, already enough, just as you are.

You don't need to chase love. You don't need to prove your worth. You don't need to shrink yourself to fit someone else's story. The love that's meant for you will meet you with ease, honor, and authenticity—never force.

So, if doubt ever returns… if you ever wonder whether you're lovable, or whether you'll find the connection you seek—I hope you remember this:

You are love. You radiate love.

And the right love—the kind that honors you, values you, and nourishes your soul—will never pass you by.

Keep your heart open—not for just anyone, but for the right one. And until that love finds you, keep becoming the person you were always meant to be.

There's no prompt today—just space. Use your journal to reflect on where you are and what you're still becoming.

With all my heart,

Katina Lee

MONTH 12

CELEBRATING YOUR GROWTH – BOOK SUMMARY

Healing isn't just about moving on—it's about recognizing your progress and embracing the person you've become. This chapter is a moment to honor your strength, resilience, and growth.

Reflecting on Your Journey

Growth happens quietly, and sometimes we don't see it until we look back. The pain that once felt unbearable has softened, and even if you're not fully healed, you're no longer where you started.

Gratitude & Letting Go

Gratitude helps shift your focus from what was lost to what was gained—strength, wisdom, boundaries, and self-worth. Letting go of bitterness is an act of self-love, freeing you from what no longer serves you.

Embracing the New You

Heartbreak has reshaped you, revealing strengths you didn't know you had. The next step is living intentionally making choices that align with your values and vision.

The Power of Mantras

Mantras reinforce self-belief and focus on what's ahead. Choose one that resonates, such as:

1. "I am worthy of love and happiness."
2. "My past does not define me; I create my future."

Turning Pain into Purpose

Your journey holds wisdom that can uplift others. Whether through sharing your story, mentoring, or simply being present, you can turn your experience into something meaningful.

Celebrating Your Wins

Every step forward is worth celebrating—the first time you smiled again, set a boundary, or felt hopeful about the future. Acknowledge these moments and let them fuel your next chapter.

Stepping Into the Light

This isn't just about healing from the past—it's about stepping forward with confidence, knowing you are stronger, wiser, and ready for all that life has to offer.

Reflection Question: How can I celebrate my growth and carry this strength into the next chapter of my life?

CELEBRATING YOUR GROWTH – MONTH JOURNAL INTRODUCTION

———・・●・・———

"You are not the same person you were at the start of this journey. And that is something worth celebrating." – Unknown

You've spent the last year rebuilding, healing, and rediscovering yourself. This month is about pausing to recognize just how far you've come. It's easy to focus on what still needs healing, but true growth comes when you acknowledge the strength, wisdom, and resilience you've gained.

Healing isn't about reaching a perfect destination—it's about honoring every step of the journey. This final chapter will help you reflect on your progress, celebrate your wins, and step forward with confidence into the life you've built.

What to Expect This Month:

✓ Week 1: Recognizing Your Growth – Looking back at where you started and honoring how far you've come

✓ Week 2: Embracing Gratitude – Shifting your perspective to appreciate the lessons and strengths gained

✓ Week 3: Turning Pain into Purpose – Exploring how your journey can inspire and uplift others

✓ Week 4: Stepping into Your Next Chapter – Setting intentions for the future and celebrating your transformation

Each day, you'll engage in reflection exercises that reinforce your confidence and gratitude. By the end of this month, you will not only feel proud of your healing but also empowered to continue growing, thriving, and embracing the limitless possibilities ahead.

Affirmation for the Month:

"I honor the journey that has brought me here. I am proud of my growth, my resilience, and the person I have become."

WEEK 1

INTRODUCTION RECOGNIZING YOUR GROWTH

———··•··———

There was a time you didn't think you'd make it through. The pain was too raw. The nights stretched endlessly. Even the simplest tasks—getting out of bed, eating, breathing—felt monumental. You might not have believed it back then, but you kept going. You survived heartbreak, sat in the silence, held space for your grief—and somehow, step by step, you found your way forward.

You're not the same person who began this journey. Maybe you're not fully "over it," and maybe you never will be in the way you once imagined. But you're no longer where you started. And that matters more than you know.

Healing doesn't always arrive with fireworks or big breakthroughs. Often, it shows up quietly—in your ability to say no without guilt, to hold space for your emotions without drowning in them, or to sit with uncertainty and still trust your path. It's in how you speak to yourself now. How you hold your boundaries. How you breathe a little easier in moments that used to break you.

Too often, we minimize our progress because it doesn't fit into a before-and-after narrative. But healing isn't about reaching some final destination—it's about integration. It's about who you're becoming in the process. And you? You've become someone who chose to keep showing up. Who honored their truth. Who made space for discomfort and still moved forward.

This week, you're invited to pause and witness that growth. Not to relive the pain, but to celebrate the courage it took to move through it. You'll reflect on the choices, shifts, and inner strength that carried you to this moment. This is your time to say: *I've come so far. And I'm proud of myself for it.*

You don't need anyone else to tell you how strong you are—you know it in your bones. Let this week be your moment of acknowledgment. Of celebration. Of standing still just long enough to say: *I did that. I became this.*

Affirmation for the Month:

"I honor the journey that has brought me here. I am proud of my growth, my resilience, and the person I have become."

Affirmation for the Week:

"I honor how far I've come. I am proud of the person I've become."

WEEK 1
RECOGNIZING YOUR GROWTH JOURNAL ACTIVITIES

Focus: Reflection, self-recognition, emotional milestones

Visualization:

Close your eyes and picture a path behind you, filled with steppingstones. Each stone represents a moment of growth - some small, some monumental. Pause on one that feels significant. See yourself standing on it now, strong and grounded. Breathe in pride. Breathe out doubt. You have come so far.

Daily Practice Reminder:

At the start of each day this week, take a moment to write down and speak aloud:

Your **monthly affirmation:** *"I honor the journey that has brought me here. I am proud of my growth, my resilience, and the person I have become."*

Your **weekly affirmation:** *"I honor how far I've come. I am proud of the person I've become."*

Let these words guide your healing. Repeating them daily helps shift your thoughts, build emotional resilience, and rewire your self-talk.

Daily Gratitude Reminder:

After completing your journal prompt each day, take a moment to write down 1 to 3 additional things you are grateful for. These could be people, moments, comforts, or anything that brought you peace or warmth today—no matter how small. Gratitude is a gentle yet powerful way to return to the present and remind yourself of what still supports you.

Remember, there is no right way to journal. Write as much or as little as you need. You can follow the prompts exactly or let them take you somewhere else. Let the prompts be a guide—not a rule. If your heart leads you elsewhere, follow it. These pages are yours. Let them carry what you're holding—no expectations, no perfection required.

DAY 1
LOOKING BACK WITHOUT SHAME

Quote: *"You may not be proud of everything you've done, but you can be proud of how far you've come."*

Journal Prompt: Think back to who you were at the beginning of this journey. What did she need? What would you want to say to her now?

Activity: Write a kind letter to your past self—acknowledging her strength, grace, and grit.

Daily Gratitude: What part of your growth are you most grateful for?

Let This be Enough: You showed up. You listened inward. You honored your process. That is enough. That is healing.

DAY 2
SMALL WINS MATTER

Quote: *"Healing isn't loud. Sometimes it's just breathing through a moment you once would have drowned in."* – Katina Lee

Journal Prompt: What are three small wins you've had during this healing journey that others might not even notice—but you know were huge?

Activity: Write each one on a sticky note or small piece of paper. Put them somewhere you'll see this week.

Daily Gratitude: What quiet victory are you celebrating today?

Let This be Enough: You celebrated the quiet victories. You recognized your strength.

DAY 3
YOUR HEALING MILESTONES

Quote: *"You might not have noticed it as it happened, but one day you realized—you were lighter."*

Journal Prompt: What moments made you realize you were healing, even just a little? Describe one that surprised you.

Activity: Create a timeline of 5 moments that marked progress (even if it wasn't linear).

Daily Gratitude: What is something you can do now that felt impossible at the beginning?

Let This be Enough: You noticed the shift. You named your progress.
That is enough. That is healing.

DAY 4
PRIDE WITHOUT PERFECTION

Quote: *"You don't have to be fully healed to be proud of your progress."*

Journal Prompt: Are there parts of you that are still tender, still working through things? How can you honor your healing even in the middle of it?

Activity: Write down 3 things you're proud of—no qualifiers or disclaimers.

Daily Gratitude: What is one way you've shown up for yourself recently?

Let This be Enough: You allowed yourself to be proud—even in progress.
That is enough. That is healing.

DAY 5
CELEBRATING YOUR STRENGTH

Quote: *"You didn't get stronger because you wanted to. You got stronger because you had to. And you did."*

Journal Prompt: What inner strength have you discovered or deepened in the past year?

Activity: Name your strengths as if you were writing your own character bio. Be bold. Be honest. Brag a little.

Daily Gratitude: What are you most grateful for in your own character?

Let This be Enough: You honored the power within you. You stood in your truth.
That is enough. That is healing.

DAY 6
WHAT YOU'VE OUTGROWN

Quote: *"Sometimes growth looks like walking away from what once felt comfortable."* - Unknown

Journal Prompt: What habits, beliefs, or patterns have you outgrown in the past year?

Activity: Light a candle and sit with a list of these patterns. Fold the list and say, "Thank you for serving me. I no longer need you."

Daily Gratitude: What is something new you've made space for?

Let This be Enough: You acknowledged what no longer fits. You thanked it. You released it.
That is enough. That is healing.

DAY 7
WEEKLY REFLECTION – HONORING YOUR JOURNEY

Reflection Questions:

1. What part of your growth are you most proud of?
2. What would your past self be most amazed by?
3. How can you keep celebrating progress without needing it to be perfect?

Activity: Record a voice memo or short video to yourself saying, "I'm proud of you." Save it to revisit when you need it.

Daily Gratitude: What makes you feel proud today?

Somatic Exercise

"Gratitude turns what we have into enough, and more. It turns denial into acceptance, chaos into order, confusion into clarity… it makes sense of our past, brings peace for today, and creates a vision for tomorrow." – Melody Beattie

Grounding Through Gratitude – Breath + Touch Integration

This week has been about embracing gratitude—not just as a mindset, but as a lived, embodied experience. This somatic exercise helps you anchor that gratitude in your body.

Instructions

1. Sit or stand comfortably with both feet planted firmly on the ground.
2. Close your eyes. Take a deep breath in and slowly exhale. Do this three times.
3. Begin to gently press or tap on each part of your body as you name something you're grateful for. For example:
4. As you tap your arms: "I'm grateful for the strength that's carried me through."
5. As you rest your hand over your heart: "I'm grateful for my courage to keep going."
6. As you touch your legs or feet: "I'm grateful for the steps I've taken forward."
7. Work your way from head to toe or wherever you feel called. Let the rhythm of touch and gratitude sync with your breath.
8. Finish by hugging yourself or placing your hands over your heart. Say:
9. "I am thankful for this body."
10. "I am thankful for this life."
11. "I am thankful for the journey."

Optional Reflection Prompt

How does your body respond when you offer it gratitude without conditions?

Let This Be Enough:

You gave thanks. You honored the journey. You softened into pride.

That is enough. That is healing.

WEEK 2
INTRODUCTION
EMBRACING GRATITUDE

———··•··———

Gratitude is one of the most powerful forces in healing—not because it erases pain, but because it teaches you how to hold the pain and the beauty at the same time. After heartbreak, it can feel impossible to find anything to be thankful for. The loss is loud. The silence is sharp. But as time passes and your heart begins to soften, you start to notice you are still here. You are still becoming. And that is something to be grateful for.

This week is not about pretending everything is okay. Gratitude isn't a bypass—it's a bridge. It allows you to acknowledge what was hard *and* honor what was gained. You've spent so much time grieving what could have been. Now it's time to honor what *is*. The strength you've built. The boundaries you've enforced. The self-respect you've reclaimed. None of that came easily. But it came. And you earned every bit of it.

Gratitude doesn't mean denying your grief—it means seeing the beauty that emerged alongside it. It's the peace you found on a day that used to trigger you. The friend who showed up unexpectedly. The night you laughed without feeling guilty. It's realizing that even in the middle of your pain, your heart kept beating, your spirit kept trying, and your growth never stopped.

You'll use this week to explore what you've learned, what you've gained, and how gratitude can shift your perspective. These aren't silver linings—they're signposts of your healing. Studies show that gratitude can increase hope, improve sleep, ease anxiety, and even strengthen the immune system. But more than that, it helps you reclaim joy—without waiting for life to be perfect first.

You're not here to be grateful *instead* of being real. You're here to be grateful *because* you've lived fully, loved deeply, and learned something sacred in the process. Let this week anchor you in appreciation—for the journey, for the people who walked it with you, and for the version of yourself that showed up, even when it was hard.

Affirmation for the Month:

"I honor the journey that has brought me here. I am proud of my growth, my resilience, and the person I have become."

Affirmation for the Week:

"I am grateful for my journey, my growth, and the strength I've discovered along the way."

WEEK 2

EMBRACING GRATITUDE JOURNAL ACTIVITIES

Focus: This week is about changing the way you see challenges—not as signs of failure, but as sacred pauses and powerful redirections. Every setback holds wisdom. You'll learn to meet obstacles with compassion and curiosity and uncover the hidden strength in what didn't go as planned. This is where resilience is rewritten.

Visualization:

Take a deep breath and imagine your heart as a garden. With every inhale, see it blooming with the people, lessons, and moments that brought light into your life this year. With each exhale, offer quiet thanks. Let gratitude soften your heart and expand your joy.

Daily Practice Reminder:

At the start of each day this week, take a moment to write down and speak aloud:

Your **monthly affirmation:** *"I honor the journey that has brought me here. I am proud of my growth, my resilience, and the person I have become."*

Your **weekly affirmation:** *"I am grateful for my journey, my growth, and the strength I've discovered along the way."*

Let these words guide your healing. Repeating them daily helps shift your thoughts, build emotional resilience, and rewire your self-talk.

Daily Gratitude Reminder:

After completing your journal prompt each day, take a moment to write down 1 to 3 additional things you are grateful for. These could be people, moments, comforts, or anything that brought you peace or warmth today—no matter how small. Gratitude is a gentle yet powerful way to return to the present and remind yourself of what still supports you.

Remember, there is no right way to journal. Write as much or as little as you need. You can follow the prompts exactly or let them take you somewhere else. Let the prompts be a guide—not a rule. If your heart leads you elsewhere, follow it. These pages are yours. Let them carry what you're holding—no expectations, no perfection required.

DAY 1
GRATITUDE FOR THE JOURNEY

—— ··•·· ——

Quote: *"Gratitude turns what we have into enough."* - Aesop

Journal Prompt: What are three things you've gained through this heartbreak that you're grateful for today?

Activity: Write a thank-you note to the version of yourself who didn't give up.

Daily Gratitude: What small moment brought you a sense of peace or comfort today?

Let This be Enough: You showed up. You listened inward. You honored your process. That is enough. That is healing.

DAY 2
FINDING LIGHT IN THE DARKNESS

—— ··•·· ——

Quote: *"Even the darkest night will end, and the sun will rise."* – Victor Hugo

Journal Prompt: Think of one of the hardest days of your healing. What got you through it?

Activity: Make a list titled "What Got Me Through." Keep it somewhere visible.

Daily Gratitude: What support—big or small—are you grateful for today?

Let This be Enough: You remembered your strength in the dark. You honored what helped you through. That is enough. That is healing.

DAY 3
LESSONS WRAPPED IN LOSS

Quote: *"Sometimes when things are falling apart, they may actually be falling into place."*

Journal Prompt: What is one painful experience from this past year that taught you something meaningful?

Activity: Create a mantra from the lesson. ("I am stronger because I learned _____.")

Daily Gratitude: What lesson are you grateful to have learned?

Let This be Enough: You found meaning in what hurt. You turned pain into wisdom.
That is enough. That is healing.

DAY 4
CELEBRATING INNER STRENGTH

Quote: *"You never know how strong you are until being strong is your only choice."* – Bob Marley

Journal Prompt: What moment proved your strength to yourself?

Activity: Write your name in the center of a page and surround it with words or phrases that describe your growth.

Daily Gratitude: What is one thing you love about the person you are becoming?

Let This be Enough: You stood in your power. You named your growth.
That is enough. That is healing.

DAY 5
HONORING YOUR HEALING

Quote: *"Healing isn't about going back. It's about embracing who you've become."* – Katina Lee

Journal Prompt: How have you changed in the past 12 months?

Activity: Choose a photo of yourself from the beginning of this journey and write a note of gratitude to her.

Daily Gratitude: What healing win are you celebrating today?

Let This be Enough: You looked with compassion. You gave thanks to the version of you who endured. That is enough. That is healing.

DAY 6
GRATITUDE FOR THE UNEXPECTED

Quote: *"Some of the most beautiful chapters in our lives won't have a title until much later."*

Journal Prompt: What surprising thing came from this heartbreak that you're grateful for?

Activity: Write a list titled "Good Things I Didn't See Coming."

Daily Gratitude: What unexpected joy are you holding onto today?

Let This be Enough: You opened to surprise. You embraced joy where you least expected it. That is enough. That is healing.

DAY 7
WEEKLY REFLECTION – A GRATEFUL HEART

Reflection Questions:

1. What was the hardest thing to feel grateful for this week?
2. What helped shift your perspective?
3. What does it mean to carry gratitude into your future?

Activity: Write a letter titled "Thank You, Life" reflecting on how your journey has shaped you.

Daily Gratitude: What are you most thankful for as this week ends?

Somatic Exercise

"The more grateful I am, the more beauty I see." – Mary Davis

Nurture and Receive – Self-Compassion Hold

This week focused on receiving love—not just from others, but from yourself. This somatic practice is a gentle, physical reminder that you are worthy of care and softness.

Instructions

1. Find a quiet space and sit or lie down comfortably.
2. Close your eyes and take three deep breaths, slowly inhaling through your nose and exhaling through your mouth.
3. Place one hand over your heart and the other hand on your belly.
4. As you breathe, gently press your hands into your body with nurturing pressure—like you're offering yourself a loving embrace.
5. As you continue to breathe, repeat silently or aloud:
6. "I am safe to receive love."
7. "I am open to comfort and care."
8. "I am worthy of tenderness."
9. Stay in this position for 2–3 minutes, allowing your body to soften and your breath to deepen.
10. When you're ready, open your eyes and thank yourself for showing up to this practice.

Let this be a reminder: You can receive love, even from yourself.

Optional Reflection Prompt

How did it feel to offer yourself love instead of waiting for it from someone else?

Let This Be Enough:

You received. You softened. You chose gratitude.

That is enough. That is healing.

WEEK 3

INTRODUCTION
TURNING PAIN INTO PURPOSE

You've walked through heartbreak, sat in silence with your grief, and found light in places you once thought were only shadows. Now comes the question: *What will I do with what I've learned?*

This week isn't about forcing a grand life purpose or pushing yourself to turn your pain into something "productive." It's about noticing what has already shifted. Pain changes you—yes—but it also deepens you. It shapes your capacity for empathy, for presence, for honesty. It teaches you what matters. It makes room for something new to emerge—not overnight, and not in a tidy package—but slowly, quietly, with time.

You may not feel "healed" yet. That's okay. Purpose doesn't wait for perfection. Some of the most powerful wisdom comes from people who are still walking the path. Maybe your story helps someone feel less alone. Maybe it gives you clarity on what you no longer tolerate—or illuminates the kind of relationships, career, or lifestyle that truly align with your values. Maybe it reminds you that even on your hardest days, you were becoming someone who could hold space for others *and* herself.

Turning pain into purpose doesn't mean pretending it didn't hurt. It means choosing to make something meaningful out of what once felt meaningless. It could look like mentoring someone through their own grief. Starting a creative project that reflects your journey. Living more intentionally. Or simply waking up and deciding, *"Today, I will show up differently."*

Purpose isn't a destination—it's a way of living. And often, our deepest sense of purpose comes from the very wounds we've tended to with the most care. This week, you'll reflect on the lessons you've learned, the wisdom you've earned, and the power you now carry—not in spite of your pain, but because of it.

You've already been transforming. Now, let's honor that transformation and ask: *Where does this wisdom want to go next?*

Affirmation for the Month:

"I honor the journey that has brought me here. I am proud of my growth, my resilience, and the person I have become."

Affirmation for the Week:

"My pain has shaped my purpose. I am turning my journey into something meaningful."

WEEK 3

TURNING PAIN INTO PURPOSE JOURNAL ACTIVITIES

Focus: This week is about turning dreams into motion. You'll shift from vision to aligned action—one small, soul-honoring step at a time. Instead of waiting for the perfect moment, you'll begin building the life you want through daily choices, consistent effort, and quiet courage. Progress doesn't have to be loud to be life changing.

Visualization:

Close your eyes and place your hand over your heart. Imagine a glowing ember inside you the part of you that endured pain and now burns with purpose. Feel it brighten as you whisper, 'My journey matters. My story has power.' Let that warmth fill you, then gently open your eyes with intention.

Daily Practice Reminder:

At the start of each day this week, take a moment to write down and speak aloud:

Your **monthly affirmation:** *"I honor the journey that has brought me here. I am proud of my growth, my resilience, and the person I have become."*

Your **weekly affirmation:** *"My pain has shaped my purpose. I am turning my journey into something meaningful."*

Let these words guide your healing. Repeating them daily helps shift your thoughts, build emotional resilience, and rewire your self-talk.

Daily Gratitude Reminder:

After completing your journal prompt each day, take a moment to write down 1 to 3 additional things you are grateful for. These could be people, moments, comforts, or anything that brought you peace or warmth today—no matter how small. Gratitude is a gentle yet powerful way to return to the present and remind yourself of what still supports you.

Remember, there is no right way to journal. Write as much or as little as you need. You can follow the prompts exactly or let them take you somewhere else. Let the prompts be a guide—not a rule. If your heart leads you elsewhere, follow it. These pages are yours. Let them carry what you're holding—no expectations, no perfection required.

DAY 1
LESSONS YOU CARRY FORWARD

Quote: *"Your story could be someone else's survival guide."*

Journal Prompt: What are three lessons you've learned that you'd want to share with someone going through heartbreak?

Activity: Choose one and turn it into a short "note to your past self."

Daily Gratitude: Who has helped you along the way that you're grateful for today?

Let This be Enough: You named your wisdom. You gave your past self grace.
That is enough. That is healing.

DAY 2
THE POWER OF YOUR STORY

Quote: *"You don't have to share your story with the world—but don't hide it from yourself."*

Journal Prompt: What would it feel like to share your story with someone else?

Activity: Record a voice memo to yourself retelling your healing journey like a story.

Daily Gratitude: What part of your story are you most proud of?

Let This be Enough: You told your truth. You honored the path that shaped you.
That is enough. That is healing.

DAY 3
FROM SURVIVOR TO SUPPORTER

Quote: *"What once hurt now helps."*

Journal Prompt: How could your experience help someone else?

Activity: Make a list of ways you might use your growth to serve or encourage others.

Daily Gratitude: Who in your life today reminds you that love still exists?

Let This be Enough: You turned pain into compassion. You became a light for others. That is enough. That is healing.

DAY 4
LIVING WITH PURPOSE

Quote: *"Purpose is not something you find. It's something you live."*

Journal Prompt: What values guide you now? How can you build your life around them?

Activity: Write a personal mission statement.

Daily Gratitude: What decision did you make today that aligns with who you are becoming?

Let This be Enough: You aligned with your truth. You chose to live on purpose. That is enough. That is healing.

DAY 5
INSPIRATION IN THE EVERYDAY

Quote: *"Your ordinary is someone else's inspiration."*

Journal Prompt: What "ordinary" part of your journey might inspire someone else?

Activity: Reflect on one simple act of courage you've shown.

Daily Gratitude: What moment today reminded you of how far you've come?

Let This be Enough: You saw the beauty in the ordinary. You celebrated your quiet courage. That is enough. That is healing.

DAY 6
BECOMING THE PERSON YOU NEEDED

Quote: *"Be who you needed when you were hurting."* – Ayesha Siddiqi

Journal Prompt: What kind of support did you need most during your heartbreak?

Activity: Write a letter to someone who is just starting their healing journey.

Daily Gratitude: What are you grateful to be able to offer others now?

Let This be Enough: You became the support you once longed for. You chose to give what you didn't receive. That is enough. That is healing.

DAY 7
WEEKLY REFLECTION – MAKING IT MEANINGFUL

Reflection Questions:

1. What surprised you about your purpose?
2. How does it feel to know your story has meaning?
3. How do you want to keep using your journey for good?

Activity: Choose one way you'll carry your purpose forward—no matter how small—and write a commitment statement.

Daily Gratitude: What is one thing you're proud of creating from your pain?

Somatic Exercise

"Owning our story and loving ourselves through that process is the bravest thing we'll ever do." – Brené Brown

Authenticity in Motion – Expressive Movement Practice

This week was about shedding masks and reclaiming your truth. Today's somatic exercise invites you to connect with your body through movement that is entirely your own—free, intuitive, and real.

Instructions

1. Find a private space where you can move without judgment or interruption.
2. Put on music that resonates with how you feel today—something that mirrors your energy, whether it's calm, bold, reflective, or fiery.
3. Close your eyes and take a deep breath. Let go of how movement "should" look.
4. Begin to move—slowly at first. Let your body lead. This is not about dancing to impress. It's about expressing your truth through motion.
5. Let the movement grow. Maybe your arms sweep wide, maybe your shoulders sway. Maybe you stay seated and just move your fingers. Whatever it is—make it yours.
6. As you move, say quietly or internally:
7. "This is my truth."
8. "I don't have to hide anymore."
9. "I move as the real me."
10. After 3–5 minutes, come to stillness. Place your hands on your heart. Feel your heartbeat. Feel your truth.
11. Whisper to yourself: "I am free to be fully me."

Optional Reflection Prompt

What did it feel like to move without performing or pretending?

Let This Be Enough:

You moved with truth. You chose presence over perfection.

That is enough. That is healing.

WEEK 4

INTRODUCTION
STEPPING INTO YOUR NEXT CHAPTER

You've made it to the final week—and that is something to be deeply, unapologetically celebrated.

This chapter isn't just about looking back. It's about recognizing the truth of who you are *now*. You've sat in the discomfort of heartbreak. You've questioned everything, rebuilt your confidence, reclaimed your voice, and relearned how to trust yourself. You've grieved. You've grown. You've changed.

You've done the work—not to "fix" yourself, but to return home to yourself. And now, you're standing at a powerful threshold. Not because you're fully healed or because life is suddenly perfect, but because you are no longer defined by what hurt you. You're no longer just surviving. You're *choosing*. Creating. Expanding. *Becoming*.

This week marks a sacred turning point. The end of a healing chapter is not a finish line—it's a new beginning. You carry with you a deeper clarity about what matters, stronger boundaries, and a tenderness for the parts of yourself you've reclaimed. You walk forward not with naïveté, but with hard-won wisdom. You've already lived through what you once thought would break you—and now you move forward with that same courage, but with far more peace.

You'll spend this week setting intentions—not out of pressure to get everything "right," but from a place of *possibility*. What would it mean to live as the healed version of yourself? What do you want to create in this next chapter? Who do you want to be now that you're writing from *wisdom*, not from fear?

You get to choose what comes next. You get to leave behind the pain, take the lessons, and build something new. *This isn't just an ending. It's the beginning of everything you thought you had lost—and more.*

Affirmation for the Month:

"*I honor the journey that has brought me here. I am proud of my growth, my resilience, and the person I have become.*"

Affirmation for the Week:

"*I am proud of who I've become, and I am ready for all that's ahead.*"

WEEK 4

STEPPING INTO YOUR NEXT CHAPTER JOURNAL ACTIVITIES

---···•··———·

Focus: This week is a reminder that fear and faith can walk together. You'll choose to believe in your capacity to grow, to rise, and to receive. By leaning into possibility and letting go of perfection, you'll step into a future that reflects your worth. Expansion begins with belief—and you are ready.

Visualization:

Breathe deeply and picture yourself standing at the edge of a new beginning. Before you is an open field, wide and full of possibility. Behind you, the road you've walked glows with lessons and light. Step forward in your mind. Say to yourself, 'I am ready.' Then smile as your next chapter begins now.

Daily Practice Reminder:

At the start of each day this week, take a moment to write down and speak aloud:

Your **monthly affirmation:** *"I honor the journey that has brought me here. I am proud of my growth, my resilience, and the person I have become."*

Your **weekly affirmation:** *"I am proud of who I've become, and I am ready for all that's ahead."*

Let these words guide your healing. Repeating them daily helps shift your thoughts, build emotional resilience, and rewire your self-talk.

Daily Gratitude Reminder:

After completing your journal prompt each day, take a moment to write down 1 to 3 additional things you are grateful for. These could be people, moments, comforts, or anything that brought you peace or warmth today—no matter how small. Gratitude is a gentle yet powerful way to return to the present and remind yourself of what still supports you.

Remember, there is no right way to journal. Write as much or as little as you need. You can follow the prompts exactly or let them take you somewhere else. Let the prompts be a guide—not a rule. If your heart leads you elsewhere, follow it. These pages are yours. Let them carry what you're holding—no expectations, no perfection required.

DAY 1
WHO YOU'VE BECOME

——•••●••———•

Quote: *"You are not who you were a year ago. Celebrate that."*

Journal Prompt: In what ways have you changed over the past 12 months? How would your past self view who you are now?

Activity: Write a list of words that describe the current version of you—strong, grounded, joyful, etc.

Daily Gratitude: What about your own growth are you most grateful for?

Let This be Enough: You recognized your transformation. You saw yourself clearly. That is enough. That is healing.

DAY 2
DEFINING YOUR VALUES

——•••●••———•

Quote: *"When you know what matters most, everything becomes clearer."*

Journal Prompt: What values are most important to you moving forward?

Activity: Create a "Values & Vision" page in your journal that includes your top 5 values and one action step for each.

Daily Gratitude: What part of your life currently reflects your values?

Let This be Enough: You named what matters. You chose to live aligned with your truth. That is enough. That is healing.

DAY 3
CREATING YOUR FUTURE

Quote: *"You are the author of your story. What do you want the next chapter to say?"*

Journal Prompt: What kind of life do you want to create from here? Be bold, be detailed, be honest.

Activity: Write a vision letter to yourself one year from now, describing what you hope to see, feel, and experience.

Daily Gratitude: What dream are you most excited to pursue?

Let This be Enough: You dreamed forward. You wrote with hope.

That is enough. That is healing.

DAY 4
YOUR LIFE, YOUR TERMS

Quote: *"You don't have to follow the old script. You get to write a new one."* – Katina Lee

Journal Prompt: Are there any "shoulds" or expectations you're still carrying that no longer serve you?

Activity: Cross out one "should" from your mental list today and replace it with something aligned with what you genuinely want.

Daily Gratitude: What permission are you giving yourself today?

Let This be Enough: You released the script. You claimed your freedom.

That is enough. That is healing.

DAY 5
BUILDING A RITUAL OF SELF-CELEBRATION

——•••••——

Quote: *"Celebrate every step. You've earned this."*

Journal Prompt: How do you want to honor the end of this journey? What feels most meaningful to you?

Activity: Plan a celebration ritual: a solo date, a keepsake, a letter to yourself, or anything that marks this powerful transition.

Daily Gratitude: What are you celebrating about yourself today?

Let This be Enough: You honored your journey. You celebrated your strength.
That is enough. That is healing.

DAY 6
LIVING WITH INTENTION

——•••••——

Quote: *"The future isn't something you wait for—it's something you create."*

Journal Prompt: How can you begin living with more intention each day?

Activity: Choose one small, meaningful habit to carry into your next chapter.

Daily Gratitude: What moment today reminded you that life is full of possibility?

Let This be Enough: You chose purpose. You moved with awareness.
That is enough. That is healing.

DAY 7
WEEKLY REFLECTION – THE NEW BEGINNING

Reflection Questions:

1. What feels different as you finish this journey?
2. What strengths will you carry with you into the next chapter?
3. What does the phrase "beyond the break" mean to you now?

Activity: Write a final statement of intention: "I am stepping into my next chapter with _____." (Fill in the blank.)

Daily Gratitude: What are you most thankful for as this year of healing comes to a close?

Somatic Exercise

"And suddenly you know: It's time to start something new and trust the magic of beginnings." – Meister Eckhart

Wholeness Ritual – Grounding Touch + Full Body Integration

This final week focused on wholeness—reclaiming all the parts of yourself and welcoming them home. Today's somatic practice is about sealing in that sense of integration, safety, and embodiment.

Instructions

1. Find a quiet space to sit or lie down comfortably.
2. Close your eyes and take 3 deep breaths. With each exhale, let go of tension.
3. Starting at the crown of your head, gently use your hands to press or tap each area of your body in a slow, intentional rhythm. Move down your body:
4. Forehead
5. Shoulders
6. Arms
7. Chest
8. Abdomen
9. Thighs
10. Calves
11. Feet
12. As you touch each part, say (aloud or internally):
13. "This part belongs."
14. "This part is worthy."
15. "This part is me."
16. Once you've completed the full-body circuit, place your hands over your heart and say:
17. "I am whole. I am home in myself."
18. Sit in stillness for a moment. Let your body absorb this sense of peace and completeness.

Optional Reflection Prompt

Which part of yourself felt the most healing to reclaim?

Let This Be Enough:

You came home to yourself. You embraced every piece.

That is enough. That is healing.

Monthly Reflection: Month 12

What emotions were most present for me this month?

What was the hardest part of this month's journey?

What breakthrough or insight did I have?

A moment I'm proud of:

A quote, mantra, or affirmation I want to carry forward:

On a scale of 1–10, how connected do I feel to myself right now?

1 ☐ 2 ☐ 3 ☐ 4 ☐ 5 ☐ 6 ☐ 7 ☐ 8 ☐ 9 ☐ 10

What do I need more of next month?

☐ Rest

☐ Joy

☐ Connection

☐ Confidence

☐ Creativity

☐ Other: _____

One word to guide me next month:

FROM MY HEART TO YOURS: CLOSING OUT MONTH 12

Dear You,

Look at you.

You made it through an entire year of rebuilding—day by day, page by page. Whether you completed every prompt or simply showed up when you could, you showed up. And that alone is worth celebrating.

I know this healing journey wasn't something you asked for—but you walked it anyway. With courage. With honesty. With a quiet strength that I hope you now see in yourself.

You've faced heartbreak, grief, anger, and loss—and still, you kept going. You chose growth over bitterness. Healing over hiding. You chose *you*.

This isn't an ending—it's a beginning.

You are not the same person who started this journal. You're wiser, stronger, more self-aware. You've reclaimed your voice, your joy, your independence, and your worth. You've built a life beyond the break—and now, *you* get to decide where that life leads next.

So, pause. Breathe. Acknowledge how far you've come. And when you're ready, step boldly into your next chapter.

Not because everything is perfect. But because *you* are ready.

Ready to live fully.

To dream again.

To love with intention.

To protect your peace.

To keep becoming who you were always meant to be.

Carry this truth with you:

You are whole. You are worthy. You are free.

I am so proud of you.

There's no prompt today—just space. Reflect, release, or dream out loud. You've earned this moment.

With all my heart,

Katina Lee

PS: If you find yourself drawn back to a prompt, a memory, or a moment—you're allowed to return. The pages will meet you where you are, not where you were.

Sometimes, the second time you write it… you hear yourself more clearly. That is healing too.

MONTH 13

BEYOND THE BREAK – MONTH JOURNAL INTRODUCTION

Stepping Into a New Chapter

You have journeyed through a year of healing, self-discovery, and transformation. The heartbreak that once felt unbearable has become a source of strength, wisdom, and growth. You have allowed yourself to grieve, to feel, to release, and to rebuild. Now, you stand at a new threshold—not just surviving but thriving.

This final month is about integration. It's about looking back with clarity, recognizing how far you've come, and stepping forward with confidence. Beyond the break, there is no longer a focus on what was lost, but on what has been found—your resilience, your identity, and your ability to create a life that aligns with your truth.

What to Expect This Month:

- ✓ Week 1: Reflecting on the journey—how your perspective has shifted over time
- ✓ Week 2: Acknowledging the lessons learned and the growth you've experienced
- ✓ Week 3: Celebrating your progress and embracing new beginnings
- ✓ Week 4: Setting intentions for the next chapter of your life

Healing is not about erasing the past, but about transforming it into something meaningful. This month, you will honor the version of yourself who survived the heartbreak, embrace the person you've become, and step fully into your future with an open heart.

Reflection Question: What new chapter are you ready to write for yourself now that you've moved beyond the break?

Affirmation for the Month:

"I am no longer defined by my past—I am stepping fully into the life I am meant to live. My heart is open, my spirit is free, and my future is mine to create."

WEEK 1
INTRODUCTION
REFLECTING ON THE JOURNEY

———••●•• ———

There's power in looking back—not to relive the pain, but to recognize your resilience. This week marks the beginning of your final chapter in this journal, and it starts with reflection. Think about the version of yourself who began this journey. She may have felt lost, broken, afraid, or unsure of who she was without the relationship that ended. But she still picked up this journal and said yes to healing. That alone is worth honoring.

Reflection is not just about memory—it's about meaning. As you revisit the past year, you may see moments you once saw as failures, but now recognize as pivotal steps toward your growth. The breakdowns that made space for breakthroughs. The silence that taught you how to listen to yourself. The grief that cleared the way for deeper joy.

Psychologists often refer to this as "post-traumatic growth"—the way hardship can not only be endured, but transformed into strength, clarity, and purpose. That's what this week is about. You're not just remembering what you've survived—you're claiming what you've *become*.

Your healing is not about being fully "done" or "over it." It's about being present to your progress and proud of who you've become along the way. This is your time to see yourself clearly—and celebrate her.

Affirmation for the Month:

"I am no longer defined by my past—I am stepping fully into the life I am meant to live. My heart is open, my spirit is free, and my future is mine to create."

Affirmation for the Week:

"I honor my journey and celebrate my growth."

WEEK 1

REFLECTING ON THE JOURNEY JOURNAL ACTIVITIES

Focus: Looking back with compassion and clarity to recognize the strength, healing, and transformation that have unfolded throughout your journey.

Visualization:

Close your eyes and visualize the version of yourself at the beginning of this journey. Picture her clearly - what she was feeling, carrying, and hoping for. Then, visualize the version of yourself today. Notice the differences in her energy, posture, and spirit. Allow yourself to feel proud of how far you've come.

Daily Practice Reminder:

At the start of each day this week, take a moment to write down and speak aloud:

Your **monthly affirmation:** *"I am no longer defined by my past—I am stepping fully into the life I am meant to live. My heart is open, my spirit is free, and my future is mine to create."*

Your **weekly affirmation:** *"I honor my journey and celebrate my growth."*

Let these words guide your healing. Repeating them daily helps shift your thoughts, build emotional resilience, and rewire your self-talk.

Daily Gratitude Reminder:

After completing your journal prompt each day, take a moment to write down 1 to 3 additional things you are grateful for. These could be people, moments, comforts, or anything that brought you peace or warmth today—no matter how small. Gratitude is a gentle yet powerful way to return to the present and remind yourself of what still supports you.

Remember, there is no right way to journal. Write as much or as little as you need. You can follow the prompts exactly or let them take you somewhere else. Let the prompts be a guide—not a rule. If your heart leads you elsewhere, follow it. These pages are yours. Let them carry what you're holding—no expectations, no perfection required.

DAY 1
LOOKING BACK WITHOUT SHAME

Quote: *"You may not be proud of everything you've done, but you can be proud of how far you've come."*

Journal Prompt: Think back to who you were at the beginning of this journey. What did she need? What would you want to say to her now?

Activity: Write a kind letter to your past self—acknowledging her strength, grace, and grit.

Daily Gratitude: What part of your growth are you most grateful for?

Let This be Enough: You looked back with love. You offered yourself grace.

That is enough. That is healing.

DAY 2
SMALL WINS MATTER

Quote: *"Healing isn't loud. Sometimes it's just breathing through a moment you once would have drowned in."* – Katina Lee

Journal Prompt: What are three small wins you've had during this healing journey that others might not even notice—but you know were huge?

Activity: Write each one on a sticky note or small piece of paper. Put them somewhere you'll see this week.

Daily Gratitude: What quiet victory are you celebrating today?

Let This be Enough: You honored the quiet victories. You gave yourself credit.

That is enough. That is healing.

DAY 3
YOUR HEALING MILESTONES

———— ··•·· ————

Quote: *"You might not have noticed it as it happened, but one day you realized—you were lighter."*

Journal Prompt: What moments made you realize you were healing, even just a little? Describe one that surprised you.

Activity: Create a timeline of 5 moments that marked progress (even if it wasn't linear).

Daily Gratitude: What is something you can do now that felt impossible at the beginning?

Let This be Enough: You saw the signs. You recognized your progress.

That is enough. That is healing.

DAY 4
PRIDE WITHOUT PERFECTION

———— ··•·· ————

Quote: *"You don't have to be fully healed to be proud of your progress."* – Katina Lee

Journal Prompt: Are there parts of you that are still tender, still working through things? How can you honor your healing even in the middle of it?

Activity: Write down 3 things you're proud of—no qualifiers or disclaimers.

Daily Gratitude: What is one way you've shown up for yourself recently?

Let This be Enough: You stood proud—right where you are.

That is enough. That is healing.

DAY 5
CELEBRATING YOUR STRENGTH

Quote: *"You didn't get stronger because you wanted to. You got stronger because you had to. And you did."*

Journal Prompt: What inner strength have you discovered or deepened in the past year?

Activity: Name your strengths as if you were writing your own character bio. Be bold. Be honest. Brag a little.

Daily Gratitude: What are you most grateful for in your own character?

Let This be Enough: You named your strength. You claimed your power.

That is enough. That is healing.

DAY 6
WHAT YOU'VE OUTGROWN

Quote: *"Sometimes growth looks like walking away from what once felt comfortable."*

Journal Prompt: What habits, beliefs, or patterns have you outgrown in the past year?

Activity: Light a candle and sit with a list of these patterns. Fold the list and say, "Thank you for serving me. I no longer need you."

Daily Gratitude: What is something new you've made space for?

Let This be Enough: You released what no longer fits. You made space for more.

That is enough. That is healing.

DAY 7
WEEKLY REFLECTION – HONORING YOUR JOURNEY

Reflection Questions:

1. What part of your growth are you most proud of?
2. What would your past self be most amazed by?
3. How can you keep celebrating progress without needing it to be perfect?

Activity: Record a voice memo or short video to yourself saying, *"I'm proud of you."* Save it to revisit when you need it.

Daily Gratitude: What makes you feel proud today?

Somatic Exercise

"The journey isn't about becoming a new you. It's about remembering who you were before the world told you to be someone else." – Unknown

Embodied Intention – Posture + Voice Activation

As you begin this final chapter of renewal, today's practice centers on integrating your intention not just mentally—but physically and vocally.

Instructions

1. Stand tall with your feet firmly planted on the ground. Let your spine rise with dignity.
2. Place one hand over your heart and the other on your lower belly.
3. Take 3 deep, slow breaths. Feel the rise and fall beneath both hands.
4. Speak aloud this intention slowly and clearly:
5. "I am creating a life rooted in truth, peace, and possibility."
6. Repeat this 3 times—each time a little louder, with more conviction.
7. Now, walk slowly in a small circle or straight line, continuing to breathe with intention. Feel the alignment between your breath, your body, and your words.
8. End by standing still, arms relaxed, and say one final time:
9. "I am ready to begin again."

Optional Reflection Prompt

What does it feel like to let your body carry your intention?

Let This Be Enough:

You spoke. You stood tall. You began again.

That is enough. That is healing.

WEEK 2
INTRODUCTION ACKNOWLEDGING LESSONS AND GROWTH

Every heartbreak carries lessons—and this week is about uncovering them. Not from a place of blame or regret, but from the wisdom that only experience can teach. The journey you've walked has not just been about getting through the pain, but about becoming someone new on the other side of it.

If last week was about remembering your resilience, this week is about recognizing the wisdom that came from it. Every heartbreak holds teachings. Some arrive loudly, in the heat of tears and tough decisions. Others come as quiet whispers, months later, when you suddenly notice that you're reacting differently—or loving yourself better.

You'll explore what you now know about love, about yourself, about boundaries, and about what you truly deserve. You may have outgrown old beliefs that once felt like truth. You may have learned to listen to your gut, to protect your peace, to let go of what you can't control, and to walk away from anything that asks you to abandon yourself. Those aren't just coping skills—they are signs of deep inner transformation.

In psychology, this process is called meaning-making—the human ability to create insight, purpose, and growth from adversity. Studies show that people who reflect on the meaning behind their struggles are more likely to feel hope, peace, and emotional well-being moving forward. That's your invitation this week: to find the thread of meaning in your experience and carry it with you.

These lessons were hard-earned. They were won in moments no one else may have seen—moments when you chose growth over comfort, truth over denial, and self-worth over fear. Let this week be about naming what you've learned, claiming how far you've come, and honoring the wiser, stronger, more grounded version of yourself that's emerging.

This week is about looking at your story with gentle eyes and honoring the wisdom it gave you. You'll reflect on how your beliefs have evolved, how you've learned to love differently—including yourself—and how those hard-won lessons will shape your future.

Let yourself feel proud of what you now know. That knowledge was earned through tears, resilience, and unwavering self-discovery.

Affirmation for the Month:

"I am no longer defined by my past—I am stepping fully into the life I am meant to live. My heart is open, my spirit is free, and my future is mine to create."

Affirmation for the Week:

"Every experience has shaped me into someone wiser and stronger."

WEEK 2

ACKNOWLEDGING LESSONS AND GROWTH JOURNAL ACTIVITIES

—··●··—

Focus: Uncovering the insights and personal truths gained through heartbreak, and recognizing how they've shaped the person you are becoming

Visualization:

Imagine yourself standing at the top of a mountain looking back at the path you've climbed over the past year. Along the trail are markers - moments of clarity, lessons learned, boundaries set, and love reclaimed. With each marker, pause to feel the wisdom and strength you picked up along the way.

Daily Practice Reminder:

At the start of each day this week, take a moment to write down and speak aloud:

Your **monthly affirmation:** *"I am no longer defined by my past—I am stepping fully into the life I am meant to live. My heart is open, my spirit is free, and my future is mine to create."*

Your **weekly affirmation:** *"Every experience has shaped me into someone wiser and stronger."*

Let these words guide your healing. Repeating them daily helps shift your thoughts, build emotional resilience, and rewire your self-talk.

Daily Gratitude Reminder:

After completing your journal prompt each day, take a moment to write down 1 to 3 additional things you are grateful for. These could be people, moments, comforts, or anything that brought you peace or warmth today—no matter how small. Gratitude is a gentle yet powerful way to return to the present and remind yourself of what still supports you.

Remember, there is no right way to journal. Write as much or as little as you need. You can follow the prompts exactly or let them take you somewhere else. Let the prompts be a guide—not a rule. If your heart leads you elsewhere, follow it. These pages are yours. Let them carry what you're holding—no expectations, no perfection required.

DAY 1
GRATITUDE FOR THE JOURNEY

Quote: *"Gratitude turns what we have into enough."* – Melody Beattie

Journal Prompt: What are three things you've gained through this heartbreak that you're grateful for today?

Activity: Write a thank-you note to the version of yourself who didn't give up.

Daily Gratitude: What small moment brought you a sense of peace or comfort today?

Let This be Enough: You gave thanks. You honored your path.
That is enough. That is healing.

DAY 2
FINDING LIGHT IN THE DARKNESS

Quote: *"Even the darkest night will end, and the sun will rise."* – Victor Hugo

Journal Prompt: Think of one of the hardest days of your healing. What got you through it?

Activity: Make a list titled "What Got Me Through." Keep it somewhere visible.

Daily Gratitude: What support—big or small—are you grateful for today?

Let This be Enough: You remembered your strength. You named your light.
That is enough. That is healing.

DAY 3
LESSONS WRAPPED IN LOSS

—··●··—

Quote: *"Sometimes when things are falling apart, they may actually be falling into place."*

Journal Prompt: What is one painful experience from this past year that taught you something meaningful?

Activity: Create a mantra from the lesson. ("I am stronger because I learned _____.")

Daily Gratitude: What lesson are you grateful to have learned?

Let This be Enough: You found wisdom in the pain. You turned loss into learning. That is enough. That is healing.

DAY 4
CELEBRATING INNER STRENGTH

—··●··—

Quote: *"You never know how strong you are until being strong is your only choice."* – Bob Marley

Journal Prompt: What moment proved your strength to yourself?

Activity: Write your name in the center of a page and surround it with words or phrases that describe your growth.

Daily Gratitude: What is one thing you love about the person you are becoming?

Let This be Enough: You owned your resilience. You stood in your power. That is enough. That is healing.

DAY 5
HONORING YOUR HEALING

Quote: *"Healing isn't about becoming who you were before. It's about embracing who you are now."*

Journal Prompt: How have you changed in the past 12 months?

Activity: Choose a photo of yourself from the beginning of this journey and write a note of gratitude to her.

Daily Gratitude: What healing win are you celebrating today?

Let This be Enough: You saw your growth. You honored your becoming.
That is enough. That is healing.

DAY 6
GRATITUDE FOR THE UNEXPECTED

Quote: *"Some of the most beautiful chapters in our lives won't have a title until much later."*

Journal Prompt: What surprising thing came from this heartbreak that you're grateful for?

Activity: Write a list titled "Good Things I Didn't See Coming."

Daily Gratitude: What unexpected joy are you holding onto today?

Let This be Enough: You embraced the surprises. You let joy in.
That is enough. That is healing.

DAY 7
WEEKLY REFLECTION – A GRATEFUL HEART

Reflection Questions:

1. What was the hardest thing to feel grateful for this week?
2. What helped shift your perspective?
3. What does it mean to carry gratitude into your future?

Activity: Write a letter titled "Thank You, Life" reflecting on how your journey has shaped you.

Daily Gratitude: What are you most thankful for as this week ends?

Somatic Exercise

"Gratitude is the fairest blossom which springs from the soul." – Henry Ward Beecher

Release and Receive – Breath + Gesture

This practice helps your body symbolically let go of the old while opening to what's next.

Instructions

1. Stand or sit upright in a quiet space.
2. On each inhale, reach your arms out wide to the sides and then lift them overhead—as if gathering light or fresh energy.
3. On each exhale, gently lower your arms and sweep your hands down the front of your body—as if releasing anything heavy you've been carrying.
4. Repeat this movement 5–7 times, syncing your breath with the motion. Breathe deeply and intentionally.
5. On the final round, place your hands on your heart and whisper:
6. "I release what no longer serves me."
7. "I receive what I'm ready for."
8. Close your eyes and feel the spaciousness created by your breath and movement.

This simple, rhythmic gesture helps the nervous system shift from holding to opening—making space for peace, hope, and renewal.

Optional Reflection Prompt

What did you feel yourself releasing—and what are you now ready to receive?

Let This Be Enough:

You let go. You opened. You chose gratitude.

That is enough. That is healing.

WEEK 3
INTRODUCTION
CELEBRATING PROGRESS AND NEW BEGINNINGS

This week is a celebration—not just of what you've let go of, but of everything you've stepped into. A new sense of self. A quieter confidence. A vision for your life that's clearer, more aligned, and rooted in self-trust. You've done the work, and now, you get to honor the person who rose from the heartbreak.

So much of healing is invisible. It happens in the choices no one sees: the moment you chose peace over chaos, the boundary you held even when it hurt, the softness you gave yourself when you used to be so hard. Those quiet victories are sacred. And they deserve to be seen, named, and celebrated.

After all you've endured, it's easy to stay in survival mode—even when the storm has passed. But this week is your permission slip to shift out of "just getting through" and into fully recognizing the transformation that's taken place. This is a milestone moment—not because you're done healing, but because you've changed, and that change deserves to be honored.

Celebration isn't about perfection. It's about presence. It's about saying, *"Look how far I've come."* It's about letting joy and growth coexist. It's acknowledging that you can still be healing and still be happy. That you can still feel tender and still be proud. You don't have to wait until everything is perfect to be allowed to feel good.

And celebration is more than looking back—it's also a powerful declaration of what's ahead. It's the energetic shift from healing the past to creating the future. This is your soft but powerful emergence. The beginning of your next chapter. You're not erasing the past—you're carrying its wisdom as you step forward with intention and clarity.

This week is your milestone. A turning point where you no longer live defined by your pain but empowered by your growth. It's about reclaiming your joy unapologetically and allowing yourself to dream again—not in spite of what you've been through, but *because* of it.

Let yourself honor the journey. Let yourself feel the pride. Let joy live here. Let new dreams be born here. Let this be the week you start trusting happiness again—not as a distant goal, but as something you're allowed to feel, right here, right now.

You've earned every bit of this new beginning.

Affirmation for the Month:

"I am no longer defined by my past—I am stepping fully into the life I am meant to live. My heart is open, my spirit is free, and my future is mine to create."

Affirmation for the Week:

"I am proud of my progress and open to what's next."

WEEK 3
CELEBRATING PROGRESS AND NEW BEGINNINGS JOURNAL ACTIVITIES

Focus: Honoring the transformation you've undergone and welcoming the new version of yourself with joy, pride, and renewed possibility.

Visualization:

Picture yourself stepping out of a dimly lit space into sunlight. With each step, you feel lighter, freer, more whole. Surrounding you are the parts of your story - lessons, tears, breakthroughs - cheering you forward. You arrive at a celebration of your own becoming.

Daily Practice Reminder:

At the start of each day this week, take a moment to write down and speak aloud:

Your **monthly affirmation:** *"I am no longer defined by my past—I am stepping fully into the life I am meant to live. My heart is open, my spirit is free, and my future is mine to create."*

Your **weekly affirmation:** *"I am proud of my progress and open to what's next."*

Let these words guide your healing. Repeating them daily helps shift your thoughts, build emotional resilience, and rewire your self-talk.

Daily Gratitude Reminder:

After completing your journal prompt each day, take a moment to write down 1 to 3 additional things you are grateful for. These could be people, moments, comforts, or anything that brought you peace or warmth today—no matter how small. Gratitude is a gentle yet powerful way to return to the present and remind yourself of what still supports you.

Remember, there is no right way to journal. Write as much or as little as you need. You can follow the prompts exactly or let them take you somewhere else. Let the prompts be a guide—not a rule. If your heart leads you elsewhere, follow it. These pages are yours. Let them carry what you're holding—no expectations, no perfection required.

DAY 1
LESSONS YOU CARRY FORWARD

Quote: *"Your story could be someone else's survival guide."*

Journal Prompt: What are three lessons you've learned that you'd want to share with someone going through heartbreak?

Activity: Choose one and turn it into a short "note to your past self."

Daily Gratitude: Who has helped you along the way that you're grateful for today?

Let This be Enough: You shared your truth. You passed the torch.
That is enough. That is healing.

DAY 2
THE POWER OF YOUR STORY

Quote: *"You don't have to share your story with the world—but don't hide it from yourself."*

Journal Prompt: What would it feel like to share your story with someone else?

Activity: Record a voice memo to yourself retelling your healing journey like a story.

Daily Gratitude: What part of your story are you most proud of?

Let This be Enough: You honored your journey. You gave voice to your becoming.
That is enough. That is healing.

DAY 3
FROM SURVIVOR TO SUPPORTER

Quote: *"What once hurt now helps."*

Journal Prompt: How could your experience help someone else?

Activity: Make a list of ways you might use your growth to serve or encourage others.

Daily Gratitude: Who in your life today reminds you that love still exists?

Let This be Enough: You turned pain into purpose. You offered hope. That is enough. That is healing.

DAY 4
LIVING WITH PURPOSE

Quote: *"Purpose is not something you find. It's something you live."*

Journal Prompt: What values guide you now? How can you build your life around them?

Activity: Write a personal mission statement.

Daily Gratitude: What decision did you make today that aligns with who you are becoming?

Let This be Enough: You chose to live aligned. You named your truth. That is enough. That is healing.

DAY 5
INSPIRATION IN THE EVERYDAY

Quote: *"Your ordinary is someone else's inspiration."*

Journal Prompt: What "ordinary" part of your journey might inspire someone else?

Activity: Reflect on one simple act of courage you've shown.

Daily Gratitude: What moment today reminded you of how far you've come?

Let This be Enough: You saw beauty in the ordinary. You stood in your quiet power. That is enough. That is healing.

DAY 6
BECOMING THE PERSON YOU NEEDED

Quote: *"Be who you needed when you were hurting."* – Ayesha Siddiqi

Journal Prompt: What kind of support did you need most during your heartbreak?

Activity: Write a letter to someone who is just starting their healing journey.

Daily Gratitude: What are you grateful to be able to offer others now?

Let This be Enough: You became the support you once longed for. That is enough. That is healing.

DAY 7
WEEKLY REFLECTION – MAKING IT MEANINGFUL

Reflection Questions:

1. What surprised you about your purpose?
2. How does it feel to know your story has meaning?
3. How do you want to keep using your journey for good?

Activity: Choose one way you'll carry your purpose forward—no matter how small—and write a commitment statement.

Daily Gratitude: What is one thing you're proud of creating from your pain?

Somatic Exercise

"Your pain is the breaking of the shell that encloses your understanding." – Kahlil Gibran

Grounded Heart – Seated Root + Chest Opener

This practice brings together stability and openness, anchoring you in the present while inviting emotional expansion.

Instructions

1. Sit in a comfortable position on a chair or the floor with your feet firmly grounded or legs gently crossed.
2. Place one hand on your heart and the other on your lower belly.
3. Inhale slowly and feel your belly rise. Exhale slowly and feel your body settle.
4. After a few breaths, lift your chin slightly, open your chest, and imagine a soft light glowing from your heart center.
5. With each inhale, say silently or aloud:
6. "I am rooted in who I am."
7. With each exhale: "I open to what's possible."
8. Continue this for 1–2 minutes, allowing your breath and posture to create a sense of both strength and openness.
9. End by gently bowing your head and whispering:
10. "I am safe to grow."

This embodied posture helps you feel both grounded and expansive—ideal for integrating lessons and embracing new beginnings.

Optional Reflection Prompt

What is one truth you now carry forward with both strength and softness?

Let This Be Enough:

You rooted. You opened. You honored your meaning.

That is enough. That is healing.

WEEK 4
INTRODUCTION SETTING INTENTIONS FOR THE NEXT CHAPTER

You've reached the final week of this journey—not an ending, but a powerful new beginning. After a year of facing heartbreak, rediscovering your strength, and returning to yourself, you now stand at the edge of a blank page. This is where healing turns into creation. This is where you stop surviving and start envisioning what's next—not based on what you lost, but on everything you've found.

This week is an invitation to dream forward. To consciously decide who you want to be, how you want to live, and what kind of love, joy, and meaning you want to welcome into your life. It's not about fixing anything—because you were never broken. It's about choosing alignment. Alignment with your truth, your values, your boundaries, and your deepest desires.

So many of the choices we've made in the past came from a place of pain, fear, or survival. But now? You get to choose from a place of wholeness. From the self-aware, wise, and grounded version of you who knows her worth. The one who no longer chases love or approval, who trusts her intuition, and who refuses to settle for anything less than authenticity and joy.

Intention-setting is more than goal setting. It's energetic. It's sacred. Studies show that people who set and write down their intentions are more likely to follow through—but even more than action, intention brings clarity. It gives your heart and mind a direction. It says: *I am choosing this version of myself, and I am walking into this new chapter on purpose.*

This week, you'll take time to reflect on what matters most, to articulate your vision for the future, and to create practices and rituals that support the life you're building. Because you're no longer living from the wound—you're living from the wisdom.

Let yourself dream boldly. Let yourself believe again. And let this next chapter be written with your whole, healed, unapologetic heart.

And that wisdom is ready to shape your next chapter.

Affirmation for the Month:

"I am no longer defined by my past—I am stepping fully into the life I am meant to live. My heart is open, my spirit is free, and my future is mine to create."

Affirmation for the Week:

"I am ready to create a life that reflects who I truly am."

WEEK 4

SETTING INTENTIONS FOR THE NEXT CHAPTER JOURNAL ACTIVITIES

---•••---

Focus: Stepping into your future with intention, clarity, and empowerment - choosing what you want your next chapter to reflect

Visualization:

See yourself opening a new journal - the pages blank and inviting. In your mind's eye, begin to write the title of your next chapter. Feel the excitement of possibility as you write down the first sentence. What energy do you want to carry forward? What kind of life are you ready to create?

Daily Practice Reminder:

At the start of each day this week, take a moment to write down and speak aloud:

Your **monthly affirmation:** *"I am no longer defined by my past—I am stepping fully into the life I am meant to live. My heart is open, my spirit is free, and my future is mine to create."*

Your **weekly affirmation:** *"I am ready to create a life that reflects who I truly am."*

Let these words guide your healing. Repeating them daily helps shift your thoughts, build emotional resilience, and rewire your self-talk.

Daily Gratitude Reminder:

After completing your journal prompt each day, take a moment to write down 1 to 3 additional things you are grateful for. These could be people, moments, comforts, or anything that brought you peace or warmth today—no matter how small. Gratitude is a gentle yet powerful way to return to the present and remind yourself of what still supports you.

Remember, there is no right way to journal. Write as much or as little as you need. You can follow the prompts exactly or let them take you somewhere else. Let the prompts be a guide—not a rule. If your heart leads you elsewhere, follow it. These pages are yours. Let them carry what you're holding—no expectations, no perfection required.

DAY 1
WHO YOU'VE BECOME

Quote: *"You are not who you were a year ago. Celebrate that."*

Journal Prompt: In what ways have you changed over the past 12 months? How would your past self view who you are now?

Activity: Write a list of words that describe the current version of you—strong, grounded, joyful, etc.

Daily Gratitude: What about your own growth are you most grateful for?

Let This be Enough: You named your growth. You stood in your becoming.
That is enough. That is healing.

DAY 2
DEFINING YOUR VALUES

Quote: *"When you know what matters most, everything becomes clearer."* -Unknown

Journal Prompt: What values are most important to you moving forward?

Activity: Create a 'Values & Vision' page in your journal that includes your top 5 values and one action step for each.

Daily Gratitude: What part of your life currently reflects your values?

Let This be Enough: You chose what matters. You rooted in truth.
That is enough. That is healing.

DAY 3
CREATING YOUR FUTURE

Quote: *"You are the author of your story. What do you want the next chapter to say?"*

Journal Prompt: What kind of life do you want to create from here? Be bold, be detailed, be honest.

Activity: Write a vision letter to yourself one year from now, describing what you hope to see, feel, and experience.

Daily Gratitude: What dream are you most excited to pursue?

Let This be Enough: You dreamed boldly. You wrote your next chapter.

That is enough. That is healing.

DAY 4
YOUR LIFE, YOUR TERMS

Quote: *"You don't have to follow the old script. You get to write a new one."* – Katina Lee

Journal Prompt: Are there any "shoulds" or expectations you're still carrying that no longer serve you?

Activity: Cross out one "should" from your mental list today and replace it with something aligned with what you genuinely want.

Daily Gratitude: What permission are you giving yourself today?

Let This be Enough: You released the script. You reclaimed your voice.

That is enough. That is healing.

DAY 5
BUILDING A RITUAL OF SELF-CELEBRATION

——— ··●·· ———

Quote: *"Celebrate every step. You've earned this."*

Journal Prompt: How do you want to honor the end of this journey? What feels most meaningful to you?

Activity: Plan a celebration ritual: a solo date, a keepsake, a letter to yourself, or anything that marks this powerful transition.

Daily Gratitude: What are you celebrating about yourself today?

Let This be Enough: You honored your journey. You celebrated your light.

That is enough. That is healing.

DAY 6
LIVING WITH INTENTION

——— ··●·· ———

Quote: *"The future isn't something you wait for—it's something you create."*

Journal Prompt: How can you begin living with more intention each day?

Activity: Choose one small, meaningful habit to carry into your next chapter.

Daily Gratitude: What moment today reminded you that life is full of possibility?

Let This be Enough: You chose presence. You moved with purpose.

That is enough. That is healing.

DAY 7
WEEKLY REFLECTION – THE NEW BEGINNING

Reflection Questions:

1. What feels different as you finish this journey?
2. What strengths will you carry with you into the next chapter?
3. What does the phrase "beyond the break" mean to you now?

Activity: Write a final statement of intention: "I am stepping into my next chapter with _____." (Fill in the blank.)

Daily Gratitude: What are you most thankful for as this year of healing comes to a close?

Somatic Exercise

"And the day came when the risk to remain tight in a bud was more painful than the risk it took to blossom." – Anaïs Nin

Becoming – Embodied Future Self Visualization + Movement

This final somatic practice invites you to physically become the version of yourself you've been growing into for 13 months.

Instructions

1. Stand tall, feet planted firmly on the ground. Take three grounding breaths, letting each exhale soften your body.
2. Close your eyes and visualize your healed, whole future self—confident, peaceful, radiant. Imagine how she moves, breathes, speaks, and holds herself.
3. Begin to walk slowly around your space, embodying her.
4. With each step, imagine: "This is who I am now."
5. Let your posture shift to match her strength.
6. Let your breath mirror her calm.
7. Let your energy rise to meet her truth.
8. After 1–2 minutes, pause. Place both hands over your heart and whisper:
9. "I have arrived."
10. "I am proud of who I've become."
11. "This is only the beginning."
12. Smile softly. Stand in stillness. Let the moment anchor in your body.

This practice is your full-body confirmation: you're not just thinking differently—you're living differently.

Optional Reflection Prompt

How did it feel to step into the version of you you've been becoming?

Let This Be Enough:

You became her. You arrived. You are already living the beginning.

That is enough. That is healing.

An Invitation to Revisit

Is there a prompt or activity from this week, this month, or even earlier in your journey that you'd like to return to?

Maybe something you weren't quite ready to write then—but feel differently about now.

This space is still yours.

You get to move at your own pace.

Revisiting isn't going backward—it's deepening your healing with new eyes and a stronger heart.

Healing isn't linear.

Revisiting a page doesn't mean you're stuck—

It means you're brave enough to look again.

Monthly Reflection: Month 13 – Beyond the Break

What emotions were most present for me this month?

What does "beyond the break" mean to me now?

How will I carry this healing into my next chapter?

A moment I'm proud of:

A quote, mantra, or affirmation I want to carry forward:

On a scale of 1–10, how connected do I feel to myself right now?

1 ☐ 2 ☐ 3 ☐ 4 ☐ 5 ☐ 6 ☐ 7 ☐ 8 ☐ 9 ☐ 10

What do I need more of next month?

☐ Rest

☐ Joy

☐ Connection

☐ Confidence

☐ Creativity

☐ Other: _____

One word to guide me next month:

♡ FROM MY HEART TO YOURS: CLOSING OUT MONTH 13

———··•··———

Dear You,

You've made it.

A full year of reflection, release, rebuilding—and rising.

You began this journey carrying heartbreak, confusion, and pain. You weren't sure how to move forward—you just knew you didn't want to stay where you were. And yet, here you are. One page, one breath, one brave day at a time... you kept going.

You sat with hard truths. You asked the questions most people avoid. You faced anger, grief, shame, guilt—and you didn't run from any of it. That is the definition of courage.

What you've done this year matters. Every entry, every tear, every whispered prayer or shouted frustration—every moment you showed up for yourself helped shape the woman you are today.

And she is powerful.

She is wise.

She is soft and strong.

She is deeply worthy of love—her own and others.'

You are not just someone who survived a breakup.

You are someone who used that pain as a portal to deeper healing. Someone who turned heartbreak into growth, grief into wisdom, and emptiness into possibility. You didn't just change your relationship status—you changed your soul.

I want you to pause and breathe in this moment.

Let it land.

Let yourself feel proud.

Let yourself feel free.
Because your story isn't ending.

It's unfolding.

From here, you get to create whatever comes next.

You decide who has access to your heart.

You choose how you want to be loved.

You set the standard for the life you now know you deserve.

And you do it all with full confidence—because you've already done something extraordinary.

You've gone beyond the break.

And there is so much beauty ahead.

With all my heart,

Katina Lee

FINAL ACTIVITY

Letters from the Healed You

You made it.

You've walked through 13 months of grief, growth, and becoming. You've shed old stories, reclaimed your voice, and rebuilt a life rooted in truth. Now, it's time to close this chapter with reflection, love, and release.

At the very beginning, you wrote two letters—one to yourself, and one to the one who broke you. Before writing today, go back and reread those letters. Witness how far you've come.

This time, you'll write again. Not from pain—but from power.

Letter 1: To the You Who Started This Journey

Write to the version of you who was hurting, uncertain, or afraid when this journey began. Let her know:

- What you wish she had known
- How proud you are of her courage
- What changed that once felt impossible
- How you see her now—with love and reverence

This is a letter of celebration. Of compassion. Of recognition. She got you here.

Letter 2: To the One Who Broke You

Write a final letter to the one who caused your heartbreak—not for revenge, not to reopen wounds, but to speak your truth one last time.

- What truths do you now see clearly?
- What have you let go of—for good?
- What no longer belongs to you?
- How has your power returned?

This is not a letter for them. It's for you. To name your freedom. To honor your healing. To release the weight.

Optional: A Ritual of Closure

After writing your letters, choose a ritual that feels right:
- Burn the letters in a safe, sacred way—watch the past turn to ash
- Seal them in an envelope and tuck them away as a time capsule
- Read them aloud, then close the journal with your hand on your heart

You don't need closure from anyone else.

You've already given it to yourself.

You are no longer living in the story of heartbreak.

You are the author of everything that comes next.

YOUR CLOSING RITUAL

This journal may be ending—but you are just beginning again.

You've moved through 13 months of grief, healing, truth-telling, and rediscovery. Let this ritual be your line in the sand—your declaration that you are no longer living in the story of heartbreak, but in the story of becoming.

Choose one or more:

- Light a candle in honor of the version of you who made it through. Sit in silence for 3 minutes. Whisper: "Thank you. I see you. I release you."
- Tear out one page from the beginning of the journal. Let that symbolically stay in the past.
- Write a letter to your future self—the one who loves again, who lives fully, who remembers her power.
- Take a walk in nature. As you move forward, speak one new truth you've claimed for yourself.
- Close the journal with your hand on the cover. Say aloud: "I have become more than this pain. I am ready for what comes next."

There is no right way to close this chapter. Only your way.

You are not broken. You are becoming.

ABOUT THE AUTHOR

Katina Lee is a certified life coach, hypnotherapist, speaker, and author who helps people rebuild after heartbreak and rediscover their strength. After walking through her own painful journey of love, loss, and self-reclamation, she turned her healing into a mission: to guide others through the spaces no one prepares you for—when you're left to piece together your heart and your life, one moment at a time.

She is the founder of Katina Lee Life Coaching and Hypnotherapy and the co-founder of My Hippie Health, a holistic wellness company focused on natural products and natural healing.

Katina is a proud mom and grandma, currently co-writing a children's book series with her grandchildren called *Mick, Emmy, & Max: Life Lessons Through Mischief and Magic*.

She believes in the power of second chances, the sacredness of stillness, and the radical bravery it takes to start again.

You can read her blog, explore her coaching resources, and follow her journey on her website.

Continue your journey with Katina:

Scan the code or visit KatinaLee.com

More from Katina Lee

If you've found healing in these pages, you may also enjoy:

Jesus and the Woo Woo

A heartfelt, eye-opening exploration for those raised in faith who now find themselves drawn to practices like meditation, manifestation, and energy healing. This book bridges the gap between spiritual curiosity and Christian upbringing—giving you permission to explore without fear.

Available exclusively on Amazon.

Beyond the Break: Rebuilding Your Heart and Life

The companion book to this journal, *Beyond the Break* offers deeper stories, insights, and healing strategies to help you process heartbreak, reclaim your identity, and move forward with purpose.

Also available on Amazon.

Want updates on upcoming books—including Katina's children's series *Mick, Emmy, & Max: Life Lessons Through Mischief and Magic*

Visit KatinaLee.com or scan the QR code on the previous page.